THEATRE IN THE CHOCOLATE FACTORY

Providing a new way of thinking about industrialism and its history through the lens of one of Britain's most recognisable heritage brands, Catherine Hindson explores the creativity that was at the heart of Cadbury's operation in the early twentieth century. Guided by Quaker Capitalism, employees at Bournville took part in recreational and educational activities, enabling imagination to flourish. Amidst this pattern of work and play arose the vibrant phenomenon that was factory theatre, with performances and productions involving tens of thousands of employees as performers and spectators. Home-grown Bournville casts and audiences were supplemented by performers, civic leaders, playwrights, academics, town planners, and celebrities, interweaving industrialists with the city's theatrical and visual arts as well as national entertainment cultures. This interdisciplinary study uncovers the stories of Bournville's theatre and the employees who made it, considering groundbreaking approaches to mental and physical health and education.

CATHERINE HINDSON is Professor of Theatre History at the University of Bristol and Fellow of the Royal Historical Society. Her research focuses on how theatre helps us understand societies past and incorporates topics including celebrity, heritage, ghosts, and wellbeing. She has previously published two books: *Female Performance Practices on the Fin-de-Siècle Stages of London and Paris* (2007) and *London's West End Actresses and the Origins of Celebrity Culture, 1880–1920* (2016); the latter was shortlisted for the Society for Theatre Research's Book Prize.

THEATRE IN THE CHOCOLATE FACTORY

Performance at Cadbury's Bournville, 1900–1935

CATHERINE HINDSON
University of Bristol

Shaftesbury Road, Cambridge CB2 8EA, United Kingdom

One Liberty Plaza, 20th Floor, New York, NY 10006, USA

477 Williamstown Road, Port Melbourne, VIC 3207, Australia

314–321, 3rd Floor, Plot 3, Splendor Forum, Jasola District Centre, New Delhi – 110025, India

103 Penang Road, #05–06/07, Visioncrest Commercial, Singapore 238467

Cambridge University Press is part of Cambridge University Press & Assessment, a department of the University of Cambridge.

We share the University's mission to contribute to society through the pursuit of education, learning and research at the highest international levels of excellence.

www.cambridge.org
Information on this title: www.cambridge.org/9781009271882

DOI: 10.1017/9781009271837

© Catherine Hindson 2023

This publication is in copyright. Subject to statutory exception and to the provisions of relevant collective licensing agreements, no reproduction of any part may take place without the written permission of Cambridge University Press & Assessment.

First published 2023

Printed in the United Kingdom by CPI Group Ltd, Croydon CR0 4YY

A catalogue record for this publication is available from the British Library.

Library of Congress Cataloging-in-Publication Data
NAMES: Hindson, Catherine, author.
TITLE: Theatre in the chocolate factory : performance at Cadbury's Bournville, 1900–1935 / Catherine Hindson.
DESCRIPTION: Cambridge ; New York, NY : Cambridge University Press, 2023. | Includes bibliographical references and index.
IDENTIFIERS: LCCN 2022059694 (print) | LCCN 2022059695 (ebook) | ISBN 9781009271882 (hardback) | ISBN 9781009271837 (ebook)
SUBJECTS: LCSH: Theater – England – Bournville – History – 20th century. | Theater and society – England – History – 20th century. | Chocolate industry – England – History. | Cadbury (Firm) – History.
CLASSIFICATION: LCC PN2596.B58 H56 2023 (print) | LCC PN2596.B58 (ebook) | DDC 792.09424/96–dc23/eng/20230322
LC record available at https://lccn.loc.gov/2022059694
LC ebook record available at https://lccn.loc.gov/2022059695

ISBN 978-1-009-27188-2 Hardback

Cambridge University Press & Assessment has no responsibility for the persistence or accuracy of URLs for external or third-party internet websites referred to in this publication and does not guarantee that any content on such websites is, or will remain, accurate or appropriate.

As far as industrial life today is concerned, Work and Play are not closely related subjects, but one subject
                    Bournville 1926: *Work and Play*

Contents

List of Illustrations	*page* ix
Acknowledgements	x
Note on the Text	xii
List of Abbreviations	xiii
Introduction: Playing at Work/Working at Play	1

PART I FACTORY THEATRE

1 Staging Bournville's Spirit: Cadbury's Industrial Performances — 21

2 Theatre in the Bournville Factory: Performance at Work — 59

PART II THEATRE IN THE FACTORY GARDEN

3 Marketing Fresh Air: Outdoor Performance at Bournville's Factory in the Garden — 95

4 Serious Play: John Drinkwater's Masques at Bournville — 125

PART III THEATRE, EDUCATION, AND WORKER WELL-BEING

5 Keeping It on the Right Lines: Making Theatre in Bournville's Recreational Societies — 165

6 Dramatic Methods of Teaching: Theatre and Education at Bournville 200

Conclusion 231

Bibliography 236
Index 245

Illustrations

1	'Orinoco Assorted', *tableau vivant*	*page* 2
2	'Our Visitors'	53
3	'Daisy Will Find It'	60
4	'Daisy Will Find It'	60
5	Programme for the 1928 New Year Party at Bournville	64
6	'Sylvia Chocolates', *tableau vivant*	70
7	'Esmond Assorted', *tableau vivant*	70
8	'The Cadbury Concert Hall'	73
9	'The Hall, from the Stage' in the New Dining Hall	76
10	'The Entertainment Hall in the Girls' Baths'	83
11	'Modern Advertising'	90
12	'An Empire Selection'	114
13	'The Burlesque Cricket Match'	117
14	'Purity and Strength', *tableau vivant*	119
15	'The Burlesque Man-agerie'	122
16	'A View of the Audience at *May Day*'	127
17	'Sherwood's Queen, A Tableau in the Pastoral Play'	130
18	'The Coming of the Romans', from John Drinkwater's *An English Medley*	138
19	'A Picture Map of Bournville', 1923. Bernard Sleigh and Ivy A. Ellis	140
20	'The Pied Piper', John Drinkwater's *The Only Legend: A Masque of the Scarlet Pierrot*.	150
21	'The Dancers in the Interlude of the Night'	157
22	'Cophetua'	173
23	'No Song, No Supper!'	189
24	'The Pageant of Plays and Playgoers'	203
25	'A Scene from Alcestis'	213

Acknowledgements

The combination of a global pandemic and several leadership roles has made this book a slow burn, but I have loved writing it. A good part of that pleasure is down to the many people I want to thank for aiding and supporting the process. The first thanks must go to Sarah Foden, Jackie Jones, and Sarah Welch at Cadbury Archives and Heritage Services (Mondalez International) for their help in locating the material I needed, their enthusiasm for the project, and their kindness during my visits. It is rare that my work does not owe a debt to the staff of the University of Bristol Theatre Collection. This book is another example of how they enable and enrich my research; in this case, the background research on events and individuals who appear in the following pages has been strengthened by my 'home' collections and their staff. A British Academy Small Research Grant (SG150545) enabled research at Bournville, Port Sunlight, and New Earswick, making it possible for me to uncover and contextualise the stories I sought to tell about industrial communities and theatre. I am grateful, also, to the University of Bristol Institute for Advanced Studies for a Research Fellowship that gave me the time and space to reflect, draw my thoughts together, make connections, and draft the first version of this book. The University also funded a wonderful student intern – Imogen Senter – who helped gather material related to this project from collections connected with Fry's chocolate factory held at Bristol Records Office, and from digital newspapers. Staff at Unilever archives, Port Sunlight Village archives, and the Borthwick Institute, University of York, helped with my enquiries and research visits. Thanks are due to them and to the volunteers at 'Saltaire Stories' who generously responded to my questions. Kate Brett from Cambridge University Press was a supportive advocate for this project from early on, and I have to thank her for the wonderful title. I would also like to thank Emily Hockley and George Laver for their editing and support through to production, Sunantha Ramamoorthy for her expertise and care throughout the production process, and the two readers, whose support for the book and pertinent questions were very much appreciated – particularly at a time when pandemic workloads remained very high.

I am grateful to have been surrounded by friends, family, and colleagues during the writing of this book. Colleagues at the Theatre and Performance Research Association and in my home department at the University of Bristol have listened to many iterations of this work, and their attention and questions have strengthened it. Presenting work at several events organised by the International Sport and Leisure History Cluster helped me develop the project, particularly its intersections with sports and wider recreational histories. Thanks are due to Dave Day and Margaret Roberts for these opportunities, and for their kindness and hospitality. The Theatre and Visual Culture in the Long Nineteenth Century research team, led by Jim Davis, Kate Newey, Pat Smyth, and Kate Holmes, has offered another vital space to share and develop my research. Conversations with Jayne Gold have benefitted my thinking around early twentieth-century education and theatre. My backstop writing this book has been, as always, Phil, Gracie, and Martha. Always in my corner. I couldn't – or wouldn't – do it without them.

Note on the Text

I have used Cadbury's to refer to the Bournville cocoa and chocolate firm throughout this study. The name the firm operated under changed during the period I cover here, but Cadbury's was used consistently on products for the greater part of it.

Abbreviations

BI	Borthwick Institute, University of York
BWM	*Bournville Works Magazine*
BWWCM	Bournville Works Women's Committee Minutes
CAHS	Cadbury Archives and Heritage Services
CMM	*Bournville Works Committee of Management Minutes*
CWM	Cocoa Works Magazine
GWCM	Girls' Works Council Committee Minutes (Bournville)
MWCM	Men's Works Council Committee Minutes (Bournville)
NEVCM	New Earswick Village Council Minutes
PSVC	Port Sunlight Village Council Minutes

Introduction
Playing at Work/Working at Play

To the great relief of Cadbury's organising committee, the sun shone down brightly on the 8,000 employees and their families who crowded on Bournville's recreation grounds for 1914's summer works party (*B.W.M.*, August 1914: 239). Against the backdrop of the temporarily silenced red-brick cocoa and chocolate factory, workers had gathered to celebrate midsummer and another year of Cadbury's industrial success. The party's entertainment programme was eclectic, and long. Running from three o'clock in the afternoon until ten o'clock at night, the attractions on offer were part village fete, part school sports and celebration day, and part variety hall. Across the large open-air grounds, a series of outdoor performance spaces had been constructed, from small temporary wooden platform stages to a large, earthwork amphitheatre designed to accommodate a cast of over one hundred, and audiences of thousands. Revues were staged alongside burlesques, and sports matches and swimming demonstrations were framed and played out within theatrical narratives. Folk dances, brass bands, orchestral and choir performances, and may-pole dancing were also on offer, along with refreshments and fairground sideshows.

Amidst the many diversions laid on for 1914's partygoers was a tableaux-vivants competition; an event that pitted staff teams from the factory's departments against each other to design and stage living pictures created from their bodies, costumes, and props. The winners were B Block top, triumphing with their tableau 'Orinoco Assorted' – an embodied representation of a popular Cadbury's chocolate selection box that won the judges over with its 'prettiness' and its 'originality' (240; Figure 1). 'Orinoco Assorted' was performed by thirty-five Cadbury's employees, all of whom were women. For most of the performance, their bodies were concealed within a custom-made, huge wooden chocolate box. Crouched down and motionless, all that was visible to the audience were parallel rows of swim-hat style headdresses, each designed to look like a chocolate from the popular Orinoco selection line. Together the workers' bodies created

Introduction

A TABLEAU by "B" BLOCK TOP.

The "chocolates" are the headgear of the girls taking part, who at a given signal turned and revealed themselves. The originality of the idea and pretty effect gained for the tab'eau the first place.

Figure 1 'Orinoco Assorted', *tableau vivant*
Bournville Works Magazine, August 1914

an illusion of one of the products that was made in the factory behind them. Then – in a moment of synchronised movement that marked the end of the tableau – the thirty-five women rose to standing, revealing their identities as members of the factory's workforce, dressed as chocolates. The image was fleeting, yet complex. It simultaneously fused and advertised a well-known Cadbury's product, the firm's well-crafted company image, the identities of staff members, and the familiarity of performance as a means to model and promote the Bournville factory, its people, and its brands. As one event within one works party entertainment programme, 'Orinoco Assorted' is, in many ways, a tiny and momentary flicker in the rich, varied history of the three and a half decades of performance culture at Cadbury's that I explore in this book. There were many examples that I could have selected to open with, but this one tableau vivant – this one moment – neatly captured the combination of people, place, and objective that defined performance at Bournville in the early decades of the twentieth century. Embodied within accounts of this group of female employees contained within a chocolate box are lingering traces of factory performance's business potential and the significance of performance to Cadbury's industrial operation. 'Orinoco Assorted' offers a recipe for early twentieth-century performance at Bournville.

Staging Bournville

The prominence of theatre and performance at Bournville was made possible by Cadbury's out-of-town factory estate. In 1879, under the leadership of George (1839–1922) and Richard (1835–1899) Cadbury, the firm had relocated their relatively small cocoa production and sales operation from Birmingham's city centre Quaker business district to a marshy greenfield space north of the city boundary. It was a risky move, but one that paid off. Over the next fifty years, the firm crafted a bespoke industrial estate at the place they named Bournville, developing an iconic modern headquarters that was meticulously designed to materialise and facilitate Cadbury's business, social reform, and aesthetic ambitions. It was during these first decades at Bournville that Cadbury's was transformed from a small operation into a globally recognised household name. Theatre was an important part of that story, and an astonishing amount of it was staged at the site between 1900 and 1935. As 1914's summer works party has already indicated, Cadbury's factory buildings and grounds were used as venues and backdrops for entertainments in which thousands of employees participated. Smaller theatrical performances were a popular feature of factory parties and other in-house and external events. Readings, skits, and semi- and fully staged productions of plays were key elements of the content and pedagogy of the firm's adult education programmes and common activities for many of the factory's recreational societies. A wide range of factory staff were involved in these entertainments. Adults and children, clerks, chocolate box-makers, engineers, handymen, typists, the firm's resident dentist, gymnastics instructors, chemists, in-house artists, journalists and designers, forewomen and foremen worked alongside each other to make Cadbury's theatre. Occasionally, these home-grown casts were supplemented by professional performers, playwrights, and producers, a practice that interwove the Birmingham-based Quaker cocoa and chocolate makers with the birth of the city's first repertory theatre company, local visual artists, and wider, national entertainment cultures, celebrities, and trends.

Bournville's theatrical repertoire was similarly expansive. In addition to tableaux vivants, outdoor plays and masques, pantomimes, folk dancing, revues, burlesques, Punch and Judy shows, operettas, comic sketches, avant-garde new writing, concert parties, maypole dancing, ventriloquism, magic shows, and musical comedies were all familiar fare for Bournville's audiences. Factory entertainments included pieces specifically written for local performers and spectators that were dependent on factory knowledge, in jokes, and representations of familiar Cadbury's personalities, alongside examples that are familiar from contemporary amateur theatre and educational drama repertoires, music hall acts, fairground entertainments, emerging regional repertory theatre programming, and experimental theatrical groups focused on staging new writing. The factory's performance culture was made possible by the creation of a series of inside and outside, temporary and permanent, licensed, and unlicensed performance spaces at Bournville. Between 1900 and 1935, these included an outdoor auditorium on the Girls' Recreation Grounds, proscenium arch stages in the Girls' and Men's Dining Rooms, temporary platform stages in the Lecture Room, the Clerks' Club, the Sports Pavilion, and the Girls' Swimming Baths and the construction of a Concert Hall seating around 1,050 within the factory buildings. The need for these spaces is evidenced by records of the audiences that attended factory entertainments. Even the most conservative of calculations based on *Bournville Works Magazine* accounts of sell-out performances considered alongside the capacities of factory performance spaces indicates that tens of thousands of employees and others watched theatre staged at the factory. The size and demographic of these audiences varied: some entertainments were restricted to factory staff, while others were open, and advertised, to the wider public. Some were free admission, while others required the purchase of a ticket. Audience sizes ranged from 30 to more than 3,500 and represented both quiet, seated auditoriums of spectators and peripatetic, multi-generational, outdoor crowds. To try and capture a sense of those who watched theatre at Bournville it is worth noting that – depending on the event – these audiences could include Cadbury's employees, local residents, journalists, local dignitaries, political representatives, and international specialists in industrial communities, education, human relations, science, technology, town planning, and social reform. In addition to the live reception of these events, several of the factory's entertainments were filmed by the firm and screened to cinema goers in the Birmingham area, and countrywide. Accounts of both the size of Bournville's audiences and the different groups of individuals factory performances entertained indicate the scale, reach and multiple functions of Cadbury's theatrical activity during the first decades of the twentieth century: activity that was deliberately enabled and encouraged by the firm's key business principles, organisational structure, and people and estate management.

Today, Bournville continues to connote a 'golden era' of British industrial heritage – the heyday of British manufacturing. An image that has been sustained despite its merger with Schweppes in 1969 and the hostile takeover by the American company Kraft Foods/Mondelez International that significantly reshaped the brand's story in the early twenty-first century. Early twentieth-century architecture, landscapes, and features continue to prevail in Bournville's factory buildings, green spaces and adjacent village with their now familiar, utopian-inflected Arts and Crafts aesthetic. Lampposts in the distinctive shade of purple that has typified Cadbury's packaging and company image since 1914 demarcate the area. On the surface, Bournville is chocolate box Britain. It oozes a nostalgic charm. A visit is unlikely to prompt an immediate sense that you are occupying spaces that ruptured and redefined thinking around work, life, industry, and social reform in the early twentieth century. But beneath that surface lies an architecturally and socially engineered landscape connected with lingering ideals of a new industrial culture and progressive, employee-focused management, one that has moulded many of our ideas about British industrial heritage and social reform. In this book, I propose that making sense of Cadbury's history – and the wider industrial history it shaped – depends on recovering the intangible culture that Bournville's factory spaces were designed to enable. That creativity, play, and theatre shaped and defined the firm's identity, securing its continuing industrial success and enduring legacy. Factory performances actively contributed to the creation of Bournville as a powerful site that sat at the core of Cadbury's company image, advertised chocolate and cocoa products, and showcased the firm's progressive employee welfare schemes through the active performing bodies of its staff. Theatre shaped and represented Cadbury's. Every Bournville performance was simultaneously work and play.

Playing at Work and Working at Play

Theatre formed part of the extensive range of out-of-work hours recreational and educational activities that Cadbury's provided for its employees. Between 1900 and 1935, Bournville workers could choose from a range of free or heavily subsidised pastimes delivered by the firm that included gardening, cycling, ballroom dancing, literature, gymnastics, motoring, athletics, model yachting, photography, radio, chess, swimming, hockey, netball, cricket, folk dancing, music, and theatre. While a key impetus behind this provision was the Cadbury family's Quaker-led commitment to 'social duty', ethical business practices, and the reinvestment of excess capital into good working conditions, engaging staff in recreational pastimes was also understood to make good business sense (Cadbury, 1912: xii). The success and familiar public image of Bournville's factory community owed much to the dominant image and practices of Quaker businesses that had emerged in the early eighteenth century and been strengthened during the nineteenth. By the time the founder of Cadbury Bros, John Cadbury (1801–1889), started selling cocoa at his shop in Birmingham's Bull street, Quakerism and ethical, honest, productive business practices were aligned. Deborah Cadbury's *Chocolate Wars,* a history of cocoa and chocolate production, firmly locates Cadbury's within the movement of Quaker Capitalism; a distinctive commercial sector characterised by a network of high-profile family businesses and a strong reputation for ethical business practice (2010: 43–44; see also King, 2014; Turnbull, 2014; Mees, 2016). Beginning with a group of seventy-four family banks that accrued a strong, collective, enduring reputation for honesty and integrity and careful, rigorous day-to-day financial accounting and management, Quaker industrialists came to shape turn-of-the-century British industry with market-leading companies including Bryant and May, Clarks, Frys, Carrs, Rowntrees, and Allen and Hanbury sharing Quaker origins and business practices. To put this in context, Richard Turnbull has noted that in 1850 Quakers represented just over 0.5 per cent of the British population; a striking statistic that further emphasises the extent of their leadership of manufacturing and banking (9–10). Two reasons are regularly offered for this phenomenon. First, that the longstanding prohibition of the Friends (and other non-conformists) from British teaching universities and selected professions that remained in place for most of the nineteenth century drove Quakers towards banking and manufacturing. Second, that the qualities fostered through Quaker practice and the ways in which the faith's central tenets aligned with effective business practice and people management proved a sound formula for commercial success. In his 1912 early business studies manual, *Experiments in Industrial Organisation,* Edward Cadbury (1873–1948) – George Cadbury's son, Managing Director of the firm from 1899 to 1937, Chairman from 1937 to 1943, and devout Quaker – devoted a full chapter to the 'recreative and social institutions' that the firm established and supported at Bournville, opening with the statement that recognising the 'value of the development of the employees socially' was critical to Cadbury's innovative people management, creative product design, and marketing and commercial success (221). Rather than staid and static, the Quaker business model proved adaptive and responsive through generations of Cadbury leadership.

Factory recreational activities took place at lunchtime or after work, in indoor and outdoor spaces, and were delivered through various models. Some were run by specialist members of part-time permanent staff – the firm had gymnastics instructors and musical directors on the payroll. Others were managed by societies and committees comprised of employees, or by factory departments or management. All were facilitated, funded, and monitored to some extent by the firm's senior management teams and executive board through a complex structure of welfare and recreation committees. The logistics and demands on resources that delivering such a large-scale programme of recreational activity required should not be underestimated. Staff numbers at Bournville increased from around 300 on the firm's move to the greenfield site in 1879 to 3,600 in 1902. By 1911, Cadbury's employees numbered 5,700, and further growth took that number to more than 8,000 in 1936. Some of these staff members worked away at satellite sites in Britain or around the world, or were employed as travelling sales representatives, but the majority were based at Bournville and had regular access to the recreational and educational schemes it offered. Edward Cadbury's *Experiments in Industrial Organisation* documented the interest that Cadbury's focus on employee physical, emotional, mental, and spiritual health attracted and cemented the firm's reputation as a world leader in innovative industrial approaches. By 1901, the American economist and social welfare specialist Dr William Howe Tolman (1861–1928) had identified Bournville as 'the most comprehensive' international prototype of industrial betterment: a slow-grown model, grounded in trust between employer and employee; an 'application station' where experimental ideas had been established and delivered (928). Industrial betterment was accepted as business as usual at Cadbury's by the time of Bournville's first performances.

Experiments in Industrial Organisation was followed by other texts, published in-house or externally, that offered detailed information about the recreational opportunities Cadbury's provided, and the positive impacts that these were understood to have on business and employee wellbeing. Brandon Head's 1903 *Food of the Gods: A Popular Account of Cocoa* took Bournville as a key case study. Head dedicated ten pages to images and descriptions of the sports and hobbies on offer at the factory, presenting these activities as an 'aggressive sign of the firm's belief in the motto 'mens sano in corpore sano' (a healthy mind in a healthy body) and of the 'thoughtful care abundantly evident in the general air of health and comfort which pervades the whole factory' (54). Interest in the Cadbury's business model continued to grow as the twentieth century progressed, with business leaders and thinkers paying increasing attention to the firm's ability to ride out periods of economic uncertainty and depression, while their competitors floundered. As Charles Dellheim has since noted, 'the success of Cadbury's is all the more impressive because the company prospered as Britain declined economically' (1987: 14). The firm continued to position recreation at the core of their operation and its ongoing success throughout such challenging periods. In his 1931 business history of Cadbury's, Iola Williams also dedicated a chapter to coverage of the firm's welfare and recreational schemes, celebrating the 'opportunities for a fuller understanding and enjoyment of life [that are] open to those who work there' (190). 1936's *Bournville Works and its Institutions,* published a year after the end date for this study of theatre at Bournville (and produced in-house on Cadbury's printing presses) reiterated, and celebrated, the range of sports, theatre, dance, music, and art activities that were delivered at the factory, alongside information about the firm's education programmes and the material resources and spaces that were freely supplied to facilitate both. In this publication the language framing Cadbury's recreational activities as a business strategy is particularly authoritative and confident. The opening statement records that the publication was prompted by 'frequently expressed demands for information in a concise form regarding the various schemes and institutions connected' with the factory. *Bournville Works and Its Institutions* offered readers no explanation, justification, or discussion of the firm's practices. Its language and contents represent both assured acceptance of the rationale behind offering recreation to employees and the value of recreation to the firm, and a realisation of the firm as *the* model for industrial betterment working practices and structures (3).

The shared consensus of these publications had been clearly articulated in 1926's short book *Work and Play,* also printed in-house and designed to be circulated to factory visitors and journalists. 'Work and Play are two distinct subjects', it opens:

> We think of them, indeed, as things quite opposite. But oppositeness implies a relation, and the nature of the relation on closer consideration is seen to be complementary rather than antithetical. To reach our point in a stride, the main purpose of these pages is to show that, as far as industrial life today is concerned, Work and Play are not only closely related subjects, but *one* subject (1).

At Cadbury's, play was an element of business. Theatre and performance then – as key areas of factory play and playing in the factory – were also a recognised part of Bournville's business, and one that was understood to offer significant public-facing and community-building potential.

Through the examples I introduce and discuss in this book, I will argue that theatre and performance activity at Cadbury's headquarters needs to be understood on its own terms. As its own category. It is tempting to turn to definitions and understanding of amateur performance in relation to activity at Bournville. However, while factory events and activities can be productively aligned with Nadine Holdsworth, Jane Milling, and Helen Nicholson's definition of amateur work as 'an ecology of practices' that 'recognises shared knowledge', creates 'friendships and informal networks', 'shapes lives, defines communities and contributes to place-making', the role of Bournville's theatre in *and as* business simultaneously locates it as part of, and distinct from, this world (2018: 6). Cadbury's theatre and performance did all these things, but it cannot be neatly defined as amateur. Most of the performers may have been amateur actresses, actors, stage managers, designers, or producers (some were not, as this suggests), but they performed those roles as part of their professional work identities and their performances were recognised as beneficial to the business operation. Performers were employees – appearing as themselves and as embodiments of Cadbury's cultural and social values and business strategies. Part amateur, part professional, these performances sat at the intersection of work and play: or, following Cadbury's definition, modelled their fusion as subjects that were not 'closely related', but 'one subject'.

Bodies at Work: Theatre, Sport, and Recreation

If familiar at all, the ideas introduced in the section above are most likely to be recognisable from knowledge of organised company sports. While theatre at Bournville has attracted a small amount of interest in works on performance history, amateur theatre, visual culture, and individuals connected with the firm (Hoffman, 1993; Nicholson, 2004; Holdsworth, Milling and Nicholson, 2018), there has been a recent surge of scholarly interest in recreational sport at factory estates, with publications in a range of disciplinary areas including social history, urban geography, and town planning focusing on Bournville and other industrial communities (McCrone, 1991; Bromhead, 2000; Chance, 2007, 2012, 2017; Crewe, 2014; Vamplew, 2015, 2016). The traces of Bournville's historic sporting culture are easier to detect than any material remains of the factory's performances: sports pitches, pavilions and pools still mark the estate's landscape. Yet, during the first decades of the twentieth century, there was far less separation of these two core areas of recreational activity than we have tended to assume from our present-day perspectives, experiences, and disciplinary foci. Bournville's sporting and theatrical events were invariably viewed through similar lenses, and they were regularly described in a shared language that concentrated on the display and embodied spectacles they offered. Football and cricket matches, plays, burlesques, costumed dance, and swimming and diving displays were regularly scheduled on the same entertainment programmes, and described as 'acts' within them. Sporting matches and displays framed by theatrical narratives and featuring costumed characters were drawn on to entertain Bournville's spectators, with football and cricket burlesques proving popular attractions at the firm's summer works parties. Faced with the challenge of piecing together remaining evidence to capture past live events, it is all too easy to lose sight of the bodies that created them; but these bodies were critical to Cadbury's. The plays, sporting matches, tableaux vivants, and other entertainments that constituted a significant part of Cadbury's culture of spectacle presented the healthy bodies of the firm's employees in a space designed for, and dedicated to, their physical and mental health and wellbeing. Sport and theatre shared and exhibited visual and verbal languages of display that underpinned and promoted Cadbury's recreational schemes. The firm's belief in the health and community benefits of competitive spirit further entwined theatrical and sporting activity at the factory site. Elements of Bournville's theatre were clearly framed as competitive events. For one clear example of this dynamic, we can return to the inter-factory tableaux vivants competitions, including the 1914 occasion that saw 'Orinocco Assorted' claim first prize. Eisteddfods were also organised for the Bournville community and staged on the recreation grounds. Categories included best departmental production of a set scene, and monologue and duologue competitions. Prizes and Dramatic Arts Scholarships were awarded for playwriting and for acting; a process that involved external industry professionals.

Competition and performance, sport and theatre were familiar playmates at the factory. As late as 1923, theatrical productions were referred to as 'fixtures' in the Cadbury's season (*B.W.M.*, May 1923: 148). Nonetheless, consideration of sport has been notably absent from the brief explorations of the factory's theatre and performance that have appeared to date, and vice versa. Kathleen McCrone's assertion in an article focused on Bournville that 'during the nineteenth century the complicated processes of industrialization and urbanization produced a revolution in leisure and recreation of which sport was the most spectacular' characterises this pattern (1991: 159). Cadbury's sport was indeed spectacular, but it took place within, and as part of, a wider culture of carefully crafted industrial spectacle that was co-created with performance events. Music and the visual arts were other key components of this activity, and while theatre is foregrounded, they will also feature regularly throughout the book. Read through a site-specific – or perhaps more accurately in this case place-specific – lens, the benefits of recreational provision and attention to good physical and mental health were clearly foregrounded in theatre and performance activity at Cadbury's factory. Sport and theatre licensed and required sustained scrutiny of the human bodies on display, with both activities proudly showcasing the bodies of Cadbury's staff. Both were integral to the creation and sustention of the visual culture at the core of the Bournville-based business; a 'visual environment' that – Joel Hoffman argues – 'functioned as both an agent and expression of community values' (1993: 9–10). There are many cases in which disciplinary separation has impeded considerations of theatre's history: at Cadbury's, it makes little sense to separate out sporting from other recreational acts and events. Bournville's performances were staged within this wider, culture of creative and sporting participation and recognised as part of it. The repeated points of connection and intersection between them will be evident throughout this book.

The location of recreation at the axis of working life at Cadbury's, coupled with the management and promotion of Bournville's 'leisure at work' activities, supplied an outer frame for the production and reception of theatre and performance at the factory, and it is solely performances staged at the factory, or created at the factory and staged (or screened) elsewhere, that I focus on in this study. Helen Nicholson has noted that 'amateur theatre has a long history of being allied to place-making and was regarded as particularly socially beneficial to residents in newly imagined communities' (Holdsworth et al, 2018: 164). This was certainly the case at Cadbury's Bournville and the function of factory performance as a place- and community-making agent is an important foundation for this project, but the imagined community I uncover here is that of the factory, and of the firm's employees. I do not follow Nicholson (and many others) down the path to the industrial – or model – village constructed adjacent to the factory and analogise the two spaces. For over a century, misunderstandings of the distinct purposes and operational independence of the Cadbury's factory and Bournville village have characterised non-academic and academic writings. Bournville village was a social experiment founded in 1900 that ceased to be connected to the Cadbury's business in any way in 1901 when George Cadbury signed over the management, capital, and revenue to the newly formed Bournville Village Trust (the same body that continues to manage the community and its resources today) (Groves et al, 2003: 6). The most commonly encountered misconception is that the village housing was designed to offer residential provision for Cadbury's workers. This was never the case. In the words of Reverend Canon Hicks, writing for *The Manchester Guardian* in 1903, 'the common impression about Bournville is that it was founded to house the Cadbury work people. This is a complete mistake' (18 July: 6). In 1901, less than 40 per cent of Bournville village residents were workers at the factory. Indeed, the number of workers employed at the factory – 2,865 at the beginning of 1901 – already far exceeded the living space that was available in the village by this date (*B.W.M.*, April 1931: 100). Even if all Cadbury's workforce had desired to live in Bournville, it would not have been possible to accommodate them at any point in its history.

The lingering misunderstanding of Bournville's function was, at least in part, nourished by the firm. Alongside the emphatic insistence on division between the two spaces was a tendency to depend on the village as a materialisation of ideas about fresh air, wellbeing, and purity of production that sat at the heart of Cadbury's marketing. The mixed messages did not go unnoticed. 1910's 'Bourneville Bunkum' – a critique of Cadbury's recent publication *The Factory in a Garden* that appeared in the Liberal magazine *John Bull* – took to task the implicit claim by Cadbury's that 'all their employees both work and live under ideal garden city conditions' when only around 20 per cent resided in Bournville Village and argued that the village should not feature in their advertising strategies. Acknowledging the *John Bull* article, the *Penny Illustrated Paper* responded in defence of Birmingham's cocoa and chocolate maker, noting, 'were we in the position of Messrs Cadbury we should take every possible means to let the public know that they were buying articles of food made in clean and healthy surroundings' (31 December 1910: 841). In the brief printed controversy evidenced by this exchange of views insights into the effectiveness and widespread awareness of Cadbury's use of Bournville as both production site and dominant marketing image are offered. By 1912, the in-house author of the company publication *Bournville Housing: A Description of the Housing Schemes of Cadbury Bros Ltd* felt a need to clearly articulate the purpose of Bournville Village:

> THE VILLAGE AND THE WORKS. It will perhaps be as well to clear up any misapprehension which may still exist as to the relation of Bournville Village to Bournville Works, to say here that the development of the housing estate surrounding the Bournville factory was entirely a private undertaking on the part of Mr George Cadbury […] when it was founded, and as it exists today, was, and is, not intended for Messrs Cadbury's only. (Bournville Publications: 10)

The works magazine, published in the factory for factory staff, carries very few articles about the village. Key capital investments including new schools or public buildings, annual events that often took place on the factory grounds, and the buildings used to deliver the factory's staff education programmes are covered, but the village is not a regular feature in the content offered to employees. Visitors taken on tours around Bournville began with the factory, were entertained at the factory and on occasion were taken on a village tour after this section of their guided visit (a practice that declined as the twentieth century progressed). Grounded in this distinction within the Cadbury's operation, my focus here is on the world of the factory, with the village featuring as a material and ideological backdrop to, and occasional element of, its theatre and performance activity. Regardless of a play's fictional setting, it was the factory environment – its physical buildings and guiding principles – that constituted an omnipresent outer frame around each Bournville performance event. Theatrical activity consistently took the form of a play within a play, with the factory site and the firm's cultural values supplying a permanent backdrop against which theatre was created and appeared. Yet, this did not stifle the range of performances that occurred, or the creativity of the people who staged them. It is these stories – of the productions, places, and people that made theatre at Bournville – and the complexities of industrial theatre at Cadbury's factory they reveal that guide the following chapters.

Uncovering the Stories of Theatre in the Chocolate Factory

By 1935 – the year with which this study closes – ghostly imprints of performances past permeated the Bournville factory site. The performances I explore across the following chapters reveal a theatre history that was interwoven with the firm's business history, Birmingham's theatrical companies, and recreational and educational schemes at Cadbury's. Cadbury's shows were not charged with bringing an immediate financial return through ticket sales or any other takings, but they were factored into the wider economics of the business, positioned as a site of considerable investment and resource, and held recognised commercial value for the firm through the promotional potential they held and the staff recreational opportunities they represented. Committee minutes, in-house publications, memorandums, press articles, interviews, and promotional materials indicate that Cadbury's senior managers understood the potential of theatre to offer a complex, inter-connected set of returns across several areas of the business, including productivity, team working, worker health, and advertising.

The comprehensive, rich, diverse Cadbury's company archives held by Mondalez International at the Bournville site have made this study possible, enabling me to research across theatre and business records. Records of Lever Bros held at Unilever's headquarters at Port Sunlight and the University of York's Borthwick Institute Rowntree archives have further developed the project. I am not the first theatre historian to consider business and economic archives. Several scholars have trodden the path before me (Charnow, 2005; Davis; 2007). To date, however, these studies have predominantly focused on the economics of the theatre industry and cognate areas, including literature, print culture, fine art, celebrity culture, and fashion, and most of the key evidence has been drawn from theatrical archives. The research for this book has predominantly taken place in archives collected and, in the case of Cadbury's and Lever Bros, held by commercial organisations that built theatre spaces and fostered theatre in the service of productivity and that hold those records as part of extensive, wider operational business archives. Encounters with on-site collections and other material remains – archival, architectural, and landscaped – are at the core of this project.

Cadbury's business and theatre histories are intricately interwoven. This study is focused on their points of intersection, on how performance operated within the factory's innovative industrial community, the social, economic, and religious forces that were at play in the wide range of theatrical activity that was produced, and the location and agency of theatre within the commercial agendas and structures that drove the firm within the rapidly changing business and production cultures of the early twentieth century. Theatre's functions at Bournville are reflected in the archival material this study is grounded in. The costs of the factory's theatre were subsidiary expenses within larger budgets, as a result collecting practices differed from those that have shaped most performing arts collections. Evidence of Bournville's theatre is typically found embedded within records of larger, wider discussions. As a part of this wider factory life and business, theatre was approached and documented in particular ways. The harnessing of performance as recreational activity and advertisement – as promotion for company strategies, brands, and approaches – produced different types of documentation that resulted from the distinctive function of performance in the factory space. Theatrical activity at the Cadbury's factory represented a distinctive, complex, and historically specific type of non-commercial/commercial theatre that is materially reflected in the organisation of the archive, and in the records themselves. The integration of multiple forms of theatre and performance into factory life means there has been no excision of certain forms of performance from the archive, all are accorded similar levels of status. There is no cultural hierarchisation in the records. Photographic documentation of events for the company record was of a good standard, and most events were photographed. Programmes produced for company entertainments have been routinely collected and well preserved. Employee records are comprehensive and offer details about participants' ages and their roles within the firm that have been supplemented by accounts, retirement and marriage notices and obituaries published in the *Bournville Works Magazine*. The works magazines have also offered a rich resource of information about recreation, theatre, and factory life. While the publication's function as a company mouthpiece necessitates careful evaluation of the evidence it supplies through recognition of its routine use as a soft propaganda tool for the firm, it is important to note that the magazine was simultaneously designed to serve as a community-building tool. The tone that emerges from these two interconnected objectives is helpful, together they capture a holistic sense of how theatre was located within the firm's wider ambitions and company identity, and a window onto how the experience of theatre as a performer or spectator was 'sold' in house, as part of the firm's wider recreational schemes.

Outside of the archives and their holdings, access to factory spaces has provided important information for this project, enhancing my understanding of their use for performance and display and their relationship with other factory spaces and the outside world. The recreation grounds are accessible and in some cases the factory performance spaces I discuss are extant. Research trips saw me stay in the factory environs, and the village. At the Old Farm Inn, Woodbrooke College, and the Beeches I lived in buildings I would write about, albeit for short periods of time. Thanks to the archivists and site management team at Mondalez; I have also been able to access off-limit spaces, including the Concert Hall and the Girls' Baths. Experiencing these spaces, particularly their scale, acoustics, and location in the wider factory complex, has been crucial to this project and the ways in which I have approached the material and understood, interpreted, and analysed performance events.

Theatre in the Chocolate Factory is divided into six chapters covering the range of indoor and outdoor theatre made at Bournville. In the first chapter, I open with an exploration of the Bournville Spirit, an energy created inhouse that manifested Cadbury's core values and ambitions as both employer and manufacturer, and move on to trace synergies and differences between the firm's factory site and other earlier and contemporaneous industrial communities, with a specific focus on the sites' leisure provision and wider cultural offers. Brief considerations of earlier models – including New Lanark, Saltaire, and Bromborough Pool – are followed by more detailed explorations of Lever Bros's Wirral-based Port Sunlight factory, and Cadbury's fellow cocoa and confectionery manufacturer and Quaker business operation, Rowntree's of York. Through these comparative industrial communities, the chapter acknowledges the wider contexts and industrial networks Bournville was located within and presents a case for the distinctiveness of Cadbury's enterprise. In Chapter 2, we move inside the Bournville factory. As Cadbury's staff numbers grew over the first three decades of the twentieth century, several indoor performance spaces were created across the estate to accommodate the increasing number of entertainments created and staged in-house. These spaces varied enormously, from purpose-built parts of major factory expansions and developments, to found spaces that were temporarily re-appropriated for performance. Framed by a range of performance case studies, the chapter identifies the complexity of Cadbury's indoor performance and explores the entwined recreational, promotional, and business functions theatrical activity served at the firm's Bournville headquarters.

Bournville's garden theatre forms the subject of both Chapters 3 and 4. Fresh air and green spaces were key to the development of Cadbury's company image, and to the marketing of their cocoa and chocolate products. The creation of Bournville's industrial pastoral landscape – widely marketed as the Factory in the Garden – was grounded in the firm's recreational activities and theatrical performances. Outdoor performance was a key ingredient in this imagery, and a significant amount of theatrical activity was staged on the factory's recreation grounds, including masques, Shakespeare and Robin Hood plays and Ancient Greek tragedies. Focusing on Cadbury's summer works party performances, Chapter 3 considers performances that attracted audiences of between 5,000 and 6,000, who were offered rich, lengthy entertainment programmes that lasted up to eight hours, and brought together fairground side-shows, burlesques, sports, tableaux vivants, dances, song, brass bands, appearances from well-known professional performers, plays, maypole dancing, and aquatic spectacles. From 1908 to 1914 each summer party included a large-scale outdoor play, and these productions are considered in Chapter 4. Performed by casts of between 80 and 150 employees, between 1911 and 1914 these plays were written and produced by local theatrical personality John Drinkwater (1882–1937). Alongside other parties, charity occasions, and wartime entertainments that took place in the grounds, these performances demanded huge investments of time and money. What is clear is that they also offered

Introduction

a return, and these two chapters explore how outdoor theatrical events worked for and at Bournville and the ways in which they told stories about Cadbury's and the Cadbury's factory to in-house and external audiences.

Having explored the extensive amount of high-profile, large-scale theatrical activity at Bournville that took place before the factory's first dramatic society was established in 1912, Chapter 5's focus is the emergence of this group, its key players, and the connections between the society, the Birmingham Repertory Theatre, Birmingham Children's Theatre, and the city's wider cultural networks. Cadbury's first recreational theatrical society proved a useful resource for the firm, and its repertoire, personnel, and programmed appearances at Bournville functions are explored alongside the challenges faced by leaders and members. The closing section of this chapter considers theatrical performances and entertainments that were produced by other recreational societies and groups of employees at the works. These approved leisure activities operated within strong, discursive frameworks of self-development and wellbeing, and in this way, the chapter's focus on the uses of theatre in recreational societies at Cadbury's prepares the ground for, and intersects with, the book's final chapter on education at the firm. In many ways, the entire Cadbury's enterprise was rooted in a commitment to the ongoing education and development of all staff. When (Louis) Barrow Cadbury (1862–1958; Chairman of the firm, from 1918 until his death) reflected on the first century of the firm in 1931 – in a speech that focused almost entirely on the five decades it had been located at Bournville – he placed considerable emphasis on the role that the Adult School Movement had played within its creation and its principles, and the ways in which the movement could be seen to represent Cadbury's central values. Both, he stated, have 'much to do with the creation of what we call the Bournville spirit' (*B.W.M.*, April 1931: 106). Bournville's spirit is a key focus of attention in Chapter 1. What it is important to highlight here is that the education programmes created and sponsored by the firm sought to do more than secure accrual of knowledge, and that recreational activities that foregrounded learning new skills were understood to be as important as the content of more formal educational curricula. Both were viewed as self-development opportunities. As 1926's *Work and Play* asserted, 'the worker acquires in himself sharpened faculty and fuller capacities derived from his experience [in participating] in those activities, and a larger knowledge of men and affairs' (4). Chapter 6 details the range of educational opportunities on offer to employees, alongside those that the firm supported that were not exclusively for their own staff – including the Day Continuation Schools and Fircroft and Woodbrooke

Colleges, and considers the use of drama as an innovative pedagogic tool at Bournville and performances staged for, *and as*, learning.

Bournville's theatre served multiple, simultaneous functions and through the examples selected for this book, I have sought to capture the complexities of performance contexts, genres, styles, and audiences at Cadbury's headquarters. Theatrical activity at the chocolate factory formed part of an intricate – and invariably inseparable – web of ideas and practices that encompassed business, recreation, and health and became an important area of opportunity and advertising for the firm. The closely interwoven histories of theatre, company identity, and community-making that follow begin with consideration of the factory world within which theatre-making at Bournville flourished, amidst a wider exploration of other industrial sites and factory communities that influenced and coexisted with Cadbury's carefully crafted headquarters.

PART I

Factory Theatre

CHAPTER I

Staging Bournville's Spirit
Cadbury's Industrial Performances

The inaugural issue of *Bournville Works Magazine* appeared in November 1902. Distributed to all factory staff, this monthly publication was designed to connect and engage Cadbury's rapidly growing number of employees with the firm's ethos, offer up-to-date information about the recreational activities and opportunities that were on offer to them, and create a record of life at the factory. The first copy opened with an editorial devoted to the 'binding force' that represented the firm and created and sustained the factory's community, a force identified as the 'Bournville Spirit' – 'for lack of a better word'. At the heart of this force was a guiding ethos of 'fellowship' and 'mutual service' shared by management and the firm's rapidly increasing number of factory production and office workers (1). The year 1902 signalled Cadbury's first attempt to define and share this spirit, the energy at the centre of the growing firm, with staff, but the focus on people and community that it foregrounded can be traced back to the very early days of the family business, when John Cadbury moved his small-scale cocoa production operation to a shop and small factory in Bridge Street, Birmingham, in 1847. Quaker morning meetings were a regular part of the expanded staff's working day at this new site, and these religious gatherings continued after the firm's move out of the city, with weekly meetings including readings and hymns taking place at Bournville up until the First World War. Early twentieth-century shifts in the business operation, coupled with the rapid expansion of the factory site and workforce, required a set of new community-building strategies, and while Quaker business principles remained embedded in the firm's priorities and policies, during the first decades of the 1900s, the overt presence of the Cadburys' faith became less immediately visible to employees during the working day.

As an experiment in industrial community building, the Bournville Spirit was to prove a useful innovation that endured throughout the period covered by this book and formed the nucleus from which the firm's support of theatre emerged. Created to drive employee engagement and activity, it represented an intangible, skilfully crafted essence of industrial betterment through which the firm sought to mould, nourish, and sustain their factory community and secure a robust position in an increasingly competitive and complex global market. At the opening of the twentieth century, Cadbury's was entering new territory with its recreational and welfare provision. As a 1931 souvenir retrospective issue of the works magazine noted, this was a moment at which Cadbury's established 'the beginnings of the application of the new principle which underlie the building of a large-scale modern business'. 'Those principles were not found readymade', the article continued 'for it was a little before the day when the science of business administration might be learned from a handbook!' (49). That lack of a better word for the Bournville Spirit can be explained, at least in part, by the absence of precedents for what the firm desired to achieve: this was a point at which Quaker business strategies and values intersected with the firm's more secularly framed engagements with the worlds of academia, social reform, politics, policymaking, and the press. This dynamic moment was modelled, captured, and responded to through factory recreation – an area of provision and participation that morphed and adapted as the twentieth century progressed. Simultaneously Bournville's Spirit served as criteria by which recreational activities were assessed, supported, and valued, with theatre and performance at the factory estate modelling and showcasing its core values. In this chapter, I contextualise Cadbury's within the industrial communities and experiments that preceded and coexisted with its Birmingham factory estate and explore the organisational structures through which the Bournville Spirit was created and sustained at the firm's headquarters.

Industrial communities sit at the heart of Britain's manufacturing history, peppering its story from the Industrial Revolution to the turn of the twentieth century, and sitting at the core of the nostalgic image of an industrial golden age. Their carefully crafted sites and organisational structures marked a new era of industrial life, production, and people management that foregrounded cultural – as well as sporting – activities. Cadbury's Bournville was by no means the first of such experiments, although it was to be one of the last. As the ground was broken at the firm's new greenfield site, a set of other earlier and concurrent industrial communities offered available, useful case studies. There were regular opportunities for industry's leaders to share and reflect on their approaches to workers, work, and play in spaces offered by their professional and personal networks, publications, and conferences that focused on areas of industry and industrial life. For Quaker industrialists, these networks were larger and richer, as their faith-driven focus increased the amount of social reform–directed activity in the proportionally large number of businesses they led. From the housing, recreational provision, and educational activities offered by the shoemakers (and fellow Quaker industrialists), Clarks to their relatively small staff numbers in the Somerset village of Street, to the extensive residential areas constructed by William Lever at Port Sunlight, Chivers Jam at Histon near Cambridge, Metropolitan Vickers at Trafford Park near Manchester, and Vickerstown built by Vickers Shipbuilding and Engineering, on Walney Island opposite Barrow, activities at other factory estates are key to understanding what happened at Bournville.

There is a temptation to group these places, categorising them as multiple outcomes of the same social and industrial drivers and reflecting their centrality to the nostalgic vision of British manufacturing's golden age. Straightforward comparisons can be drawn between their geographies, architecture, urban planning, industrial management, and their founders' political, nonconformist religious, and financial practices with relative ease. Yet, each example of these carefully planned environments was distinct and distinctive. Jacqueline Yallop records over 400 purpose-built industrial communities in Britain, making a strong case for each as a materialised 'personal fantasy' (2015: x). Cautioning against falsely homogenising such places into one overarching blueprint, John Minnery stresses the range and complexity of motivations that lay behind their creation, from 'utopian idealism to religious fervour to business acumen to paternalism and to mixtures of all four' (2012: 309). Across the following pages, I look closely at five other key examples of industrial communities that span a century of experiment and development and the network of industrialists behind them. New Lanark, Saltaire, Bromborough Pool, New Earswick, and Port Sunlight were innovatory environments in their times, the scenes of creative, educational, cultural, and theatrical activities, but each was different. Together they materialise the emergence and development of 'patterns of labour' and the 'jobs-for-life' economy that Helen Nicholson has identified as critical to amateur theatre' (Holdsworth et al, 2018: 170). Like Bournville, some remain familiar names, thriving and surviving as heritage attractions. Others amongst them are not so widely known today. Considered together these spaces offer a backdrop against which synergies and differences with Cadbury's Bournville factory community and its theatre can be considered and better understood.

Healthy Fun: New Lanark, Saltaire, and Bromborough Pool

About 104 years before Cadbury Brothers relocated their factory to Bournville, the planning and construction of a new industrial mill community began on a greenfield site just under thirty miles south-east of Glasgow. The build was financed by the son of a Glasgow shopkeeper, weaving apprentice, trader in yarn, nonconformist preacher, banker, entrepreneur, and philanthropist David Dale (1739–1806) and the industrial inventor Richard Arkwright (1732–1792) to support and develop their new business. New Lanark's status today as an UNESCO World Heritage Site affirms the innovatory social-industrial model the site represented. Nonetheless – and this is a narrative shared by the developments covered in this chapter – a main impetus behind the creation of New Lanark was pragmatic; a response, as John Minnery notes, to the remoteness of the site and the subsequent challenges of getting the workforce to work (311). Richard Arkwright was an experienced pair of hands when the construction of New Lanark began in 1785, bringing his recent knowledge of setting up a mill with connected worker housing at Cromford, Derbyshire, in 1771 (now also a World Heritage site). Dale and Arkwright's business partnership was not long-lasting; it was dissolved after just a year, with Dale continuing to manage the business and site alone, using its worker housing, amenities, and the better standard of living conditions they offered, as successful incentives to attract the large number of workers the firm required.

Public displays and performances of New Lanark life were an early feature of the industrial site, serving as a means to entertain, create community, and define and exhibit identities of both place and people. The New Year holiday of 1797 was celebrated with a parade through the village, in which 420 'young folk' processed through its streets dressed in matching uniforms provided by their employer (*Caledonian Mercury*, 1 December 1797: 3). Two years later, about 2,000 workers were employed at Dale's New Lanark factory, prompting a need for further provision of residential and community space that was guided by the new leadership of Dale's son-in-law Robert Owen (1739–1806) (Historic Scotland). While housing conditions in the village were superior to those experienced by factory workers more generally, Owen was unimpressed by the behaviour of New Lanark'a needs workers and villagers. He took immediate, social reform-targeted action, putting in place a suite of regulations and behaviour management schemes that governed their work, home, and social lives – a process that

Richard Foulkes (and others) have labelled as a 'practical experiment in paternalistic socialism' (1997: 99). Personal and domestic cleanliness was prioritised, with villagers invited to lectures on orderliness and tidiness, and fines were imposed for drunkenness. In return, the size of the accommodation offered to workers was increased, the cooperative village stores improved, and whisky kept on sale. With the New Lanark community and its governance re-established, new employees at the firm were carefully sought and vetted: an advertisement for staff in the *Aberdeen Press and Journal* on 29 April 1807 sought 'cleanly, industrious and well-behaved families' with three or more children of ten years and over who were native to the Scottish Highlands or Lowlands and who could 'procure properly authenticated testimonials of their good character' (2). Together Dale and Owen created a space in which reduced rent, good quality housing, and an increasing amount of recreational provision encouraged workers to travel to the out-of-town mill location, improved the firm's staff retention rate, and secured sufficient interest in jobs at the mill for the owners to be able to selectively recruit (Bell and Bell, cited in Minnery: 311). New Lanark's new community generated much public interest. Dale and Owen's site became a tourist attraction, with 'some 15,000 visitors' flocking to the village while Owen was in charge, attracted 'not ... by an ideal community, but an efficient enterprise' (Bell and Bell, cited in Minnery: 311).

Central to Robert Owen's ambitions and environmentally determinist social improvement plans for the New Lanark community was the development of a dedicated recreational venue for its residents – a proposal that prompted dissent from his financial backers. Owen sought to create a 'New Institute' – a refit of an unused village space to be used 'exclusively for school classes, church, lectures, concerts and general recreation', an early iteration of the mechanics institutes that would begin to flourish around the 1820s. Committed to the importance of education for all and convinced of the potential benefits such a building would bring for workers and for the business's profit margins, Owen drew up plans for the institute and sent them off to his business partners in 1809. Their response was one of alarm at the costs involved, and they refused to fund the social venture, prompting Owen to buy them out and seek other investors. The issue rumbled on, and history repeated itself as Owen's new partners also refused to support his plans for increased and innovative education and leisure provision at New Lanark. In 1813, Owen resigned as Managing Director and headed back to London to seek support for the model of working life and recreation he was proposing. The mill, its lands, and the village were put up for sale at the end of the same year. The sale publicity offers some detail of Owen's recreational scheme and its fit within plans for the village. The listing includes a lengthy description of a currently unused building, 145 × 40 feet in size, that was 'planned' to serve as a public kitchen, eating and exercise room, lecture room, and church for New Lanark's current population of 2,200, and that could be 'fitted up' to fulfil this multi-use function for 'a sum not exceeding' 2,500 pounds (*Manchester Mercury*, 5 October 1813: 1). The online currency converter and purchasing power index created by the National Archives in London calculates 2,500 pounds to represent just over 100,000 pounds in 2017 (the latest year that conversions are offered for), or the equivalent of 16,666 days of pay for skilled labourers. Owen's was a significant proposed investment. In the same advertisement, we can see the beginning of an understanding and language of onsite recreational and educational provision as sources of industrial and economic benefits. It states: 'this arrangement [of the currently unused space], may be formed so as to create permanent and substantial benefits to the inhabitants of the village and the proprietors of the mills'. Owen returned from London with new backers from amongst the Quaker community and bought the mill. The planned building – named the 'Institute for the Formation of Character' – opened on New Years' Day 1816, followed by the School for Children in 1817. Chapel-like in its exterior design, the institute's spaces were predominantly dedicated to educational provision, including pioneering classes for preschool and infant school-age children, but the main room was used for concerts and dancing lessons, with galleries for seating, with the around 600 children who lived in the community 'instructed in singing and dancing' (McLintock and Strong, 1877: 497; Siméon, 2017: 53). At New Lanark, performance and creativity – although not drama at this point – were recognised as elements in the formation of character, marking the beginning of an association that was shared at all the industrial experiments considered in this chapter.

Echoing the early parade of young workers through New Lanark, day-to-day village life became an important part of the spectacle and performance offered to visitors. Drawing on Robert Owen's own record that nearly 20,000 visitors came to New Lanark between 1815 and 1825, William Wilson concluded that 'the schoolroom became a theatre, the pupils performers, and Robert Owen the publicity agent for the show' (1984: 101). Cornelia Lambert notes that 'as many as two hundred children at a time performed in a ninety-by-forty-foot room specially designed with galleries for spectators. Many if not most of the twenty thousand visitors who came to New Lanark in the period from 1815 to 1825 were shown a performance by the children of dancing, singing, and military drill' (2011: 419).

This presence of a public gaze, the dynamic of spectatorship it created, and the focus on social life, recreation, and education through the image of industrial workers, in and out of work, as a site of performance position New Lanark as an innovatory, incipient example of a new performance phenomenon. Schooling in the village was 'child centred', 'kind', and designed to 'instil self-confidence': public performances of its presence and outcomes can be read as social and political statements, as well as community celebrations (Davidson, 2010: 235). As Lambert has persuasively argued, schoolchildren's performances at Owen's village 'exposed middle-class English travellers to "regenerated" paupers whose bodies and movements defied the expectations of those whose ideas about pauper children had been defined by less gracious experiences. What education could do, Owen demonstrated, was create a unified social body made of "living machines" which could act rationally and perform culturally significant activities on a national stage' (420). The industrial worker's body becomes a kinetic, ideological motif in this reading, choreographed and governed by movement and rhythm and watched by influential external, as well as internal, audiences.

While recreational dance and music were available to villagers throughout the nineteenth century, there is little discernible history of theatre until the turn of the twentieth century, putting this early model community on a similar timeline of theatrical activity as much later developments. What is significant about the New Lanark model is that Robert Owen's innovative centring of recreation, albeit a model that seems, with hindsight, heavily governed and framed by industrial paternalism, was received as groundbreaking, prompting tension, disagreement, and funding challenges (it is of note, and of interest to later histories of Bournville, that it was Quaker financial backers who came forward to support the scheme). Later narratives celebrated the way that New Lanark's community 'prospered both materially and morally', but the entwined model of work, education, and leisure these reports responded to had evolved and grown with industrial communities (Mclintock and Strong: 497). Jacqueline Yallop argues that New Lanark was a blueprint for development and that most well-known examples of model villages grew out of 'Owen's influential approach', as 'confident, if ultimately paradoxical, expressions of socialism and community, of utilitarian approaches and capitalist politics' (32). Owen's influence is clear, but the increasing presence of Quakerism, New Liberalism, Non-Conformism, Freemasonry, and academic and policymaking debate in later industrial village developments were to become equally influential forces in their creation, management, and differences. New Lanark offers an important early model: as newer industrial communities emerged, the dynamics between governance and recreation, and thus theatre, shifted.

Moving 175 miles south and travelling forward nearly 7 decades in time to the mid-nineteenth century, we reach the outskirts of Shipley in West Yorkshire and the mill and industrial village built by industrialist and investor Sir Titus Salt (1803–1876). Following a similar model to New Lanark, the industrial village of Saltaire was established in 1854 to house the community of around 400 workers needed to resource the new, out-of-town manufacturing site, who were currently transported to work by trains out of Bradford station. Saltaire also holds UNESCO World Heritage Site status, cementing the site's significance to Britain's first industrial revolution. Salt's residential industrial community grew rapidly. By 1871 census records reveal that Saltaire was home to 4,389 residents, who were living in 775 houses and the village's alms houses (Holroyd, 1873: 81). Villagers' needs were met by girls' and boys' schools, churches, a covered swimming pool, chapels, washhouses, recreation grounds, an infirmary, and a large public park (81–82). Free time was also provided for and structured. Recreational societies established in the village by 1873, when Abraham Holroyd wrote his early history of Saltaire, included horticultural and cricket clubs, a brass band, a string and reed band, and a glee and madrigal society (87). The most relevant of Salt's provision for my interests in this book was the large village club and institute building, which were opened in 1871. Salt had been impressed by the educational activities and programming delivered by mechanics institutes around the country but was also alerted to the model's constraints, particularly the 'limited extent of means of social intercourse and healthy relaxation' they offered (Balgarnie, 1877: 230). He became increasingly convinced that his workforce needed a similar space to fill their social lives, but one that offered greater 'healthy relaxation' and 'innocent and intelligent recreation' (Salt cited in Holroyd, 1873: 51). The outcome of this conviction was the Saltaire Institute (now known as the Victoria Hall), a multipurpose building that contained a range of social, educational, and performance spaces, some designed to serve multiple needs, with others purpose built for specific recreational activities. Its grand façade, with central parapeted tower, led the way to a reading room. A separate library sat alongside a scientific laboratory, chess and draughts rooms, a smoking room, a billiard room, a bagatelle room, a school of art that was affiliated with South Kensington, classrooms, a curator's house, a gymnasium, and a rifle drill room (Towle, 1872: 831). Two lecture theatres were also housed within the hall, one of which had a capacity of at least 800, and a platform stage that was thirty-five feet wide by seventeen feet deep and that also served as a performance space. A useful comparison is offered by the Leeds Theatre Royal, opened in 1878 with a stage width of twenty-five feet and stage depth of fifty-five feet. While it is clear that anything staged at the Victoria Hall would not offer the same depth of spectacle that spectators would be accustomed to in a large commercial theatre, this was nonetheless a large performance area that was used for theatrical production.

Over the course of the nineteenth century, recreation in industrial communities slowly shifted to increasingly self-governed models, but Saltaire's Institute remained a top-down, governed space during the 1870s, reflecting the intentions behind the build that were set out in a pamphlet distributed during the hall's construction period in May 1870 in which Salt stated that the building was designed for 'lectures, concerts, and other events of an approved description' (cited in Holroyd, 1873: 58). The venue was managed by a committee, which included Salt family members, and any activities that took place in the building required their endorsement. Membership fees were kept low to allow as many as possible to attend and benefit from authorised recreational activities. Theatre was an early feature of these events, with organised, staged drama becoming a part of Saltaire's social life within the first decade of the Institute's history. In March 1878, the Shipley and Saltaire Elocution and Dramatic Society staged three performances of Charles Wells's dramatic poem, *Joseph and His Brethren* at the venue. Sell-out audiences were recorded, and a re-staging took place in May. Records make it clear that this event exceeded a reading, the costumes worn by the cast of thirty were praised, as was the 'placing' of the groups of performers throughout the twenty-four scenes (*Shipley Times and Express*, 30 March 1878: 4). This was a theatrical production. Its success was followed by an advertisement for an elocution tutor to lead the group's future activities (*Yorkshire Post*, 8 August 1878: 2). The society's name framed its activity as primarily elocution based, closely aligning their dramatic performances with the intelligent, relaxing recreation Salt sought to deliver through the Institute, but *Joseph and his Brethren*, and other productions, strongly suggest that fully produced, stage spectacles that far exceeded elocutionary benefits, were welcomed and encouraged at Saltaire by the late 1870s. Following the successful staging of Wells's dramatic poem, the autumn of 1878 saw the installation of a new proscenium, act drop, and scenery at the Victoria Hall, funded by the Salts at a significant cost of 230 pounds (*Shipley Times and Express*, 24 May 1879: 4). Economic investment in theatre was combined with social and moral approval, symbolised by the Salt family's attendance at dramatic society events: following the well-received production of Tom Robertson's cup-and-saucer comedy *Society* by a 'large and fashionable audience' a year later, Titus Salt presided over the presentation of an engraved gold watch to Ernest Schutt (1847–1916), yarn merchant, and the society's stage manager (*Leeds Mercury*, 15 April 1879: 8; *Shipley Times and Express*, 24 May 1879: 4). Following the short ceremony, fellow group member, Arthur B. Catty (1854–1920) took to the platform to deliver a speech that made the case for 'the stage as an educational force which should be cultivated' in order to 'raise the moral and social condition of the people under its influence' (*Shipley Times and Express*, 24 May 1879: 4). As an assistant headteacher of the Salt Boys School, Catty's words carried significant weight in this community and – coupled with Salt's active role in the ceremony – affirmed staged drama as a valued activity and part of the 'rational relaxation' the venue had been designed to deliver (Salt, cited in Holroyd, 1873: 53). Saltaire's Institute was celebrated as 'a rare tribute to learning and letters, designed to afford recreative instruction to the operatives after their day's work; of interest to the story of theatre in industrial communities is the positioning of staged performance as a recognised part of this approved, governed activity by the end of the 1870s (Towle, 1872: 831).

Throughout the 1880s, fully staged theatrical productions and shorter plays became regular fare at Saltaire's social events, including Spenser Theyre-Smith's (1834–1911) fashionable, one-act comedietta *Cut off with a Shilling* that was performed at the fashionable Victoria Hall conversazione in 1882 (*Saltaire Journal*, 1:2, 2009). Spectacle remained an important feature: costumes, in particular, were an area where much of the production budget was spent; leading to routine praise in local newspaper reviews. On at least one occasion, costumes were sourced from major London-based designers, with the opening production of autumn 1881's season – Tom Robertson's *The Ladies' Battle* – dressed by well-known London-based costumier Messrs Simmons. The visual spectacle this offered was well received, while the play was judged to be 'tolerably well represented', it was 'beautifully dressed' (*Leeds Times*, 12 November 1881: 5). By the mid-1880s, Saltaire had a minstrel troupe, alongside its ongoing elocution and dramatic society, and continued to attract fashionable, regional audiences and reviewers to productions staged at the hall. School plays were a feature of village life, visiting companies were booked to appear at the Victoria Hall, including one of D'Oyly Carte's touring companies with a production of *Iolanthe* in July 1884, and Saltaire's resident performers were used to entertain guests at company functions with dramatic sketches and recitations.

Theatrical activity continued, and increased, during the early decades of the twentieth century, with charity performances by local dramatic, operatic, and school groups, and the existence of a standalone dramatic society – with no reference to the art of elocution in their name – by 1925 (*Drama: The Quarterly Theatre Review*, 1925: 192).

In 1877, an extended essay on 'The English Workingman's Home' published in *Scribner's Monthly* magazine argued that if Saltaire had been founded on business objectives, it was an undeniable success. 'In the opinion of a member of the firm, as given to the writer, Saltaire has paid abundant interest', the author recorded, for 'it has attracted to the works a superior class of workers and has kept them there for years' (356). Like New Lanark, Saltaire was identified as a site of paternalistic socialism in which recreation – and theatre and performance – were harnessed as instrumental parts of wider cultural strategies aimed at local, and national social reform. By the 1870s, such places brought acknowledged recruitment, retention, and behaviour-management benefits, as the *Scribner's* article makes clear. In the case of Saltaire, the same decade also brought opportunities for theatrical entertainment, as either a participant or a spectator. The story of theatre's presence in industrial communities was to develop in later builds, including those that remain well known today and less well-known creations, including Bromborough Pool in North West England.

In the same year the ground was broken at Saltaire, the Wirral landscape on the North-West coast of Britain saw the raising of a model village built to house workers employed at Price's Patent Candle Works new factory. William Price (1772–1860) and his two sons George (1822–1902) and James (1818–1890) had expanded their candle-making operation based in Vauxhall, London, creating a production site that offered easier and cheaper import and export potential and a greater amount of space to purpose build and expand. The result was Bromborough Pool. Described as a 'pretty landing place for the Mersey steamer' with a stately home, parkland and a 'charming flowery dell' near the mill, Bromborough offered the same backdrop of natural beauty that characterised New Lanark and Saltaire (Sharpe, 1855: 67). Indeed, William Price had been born in Lanarkshire, and John Nelson Tarn identified an affinity between the Price's management and that of Robert Owen, suggesting that while the Prices were 'neither so idealistic or so radical', 'they appeared to share many of [Owen's] fundamental convictions' (Tarn, 1965: 331). Driven by their deep evangelical Christian faith, and the acceptance of their responsibility for staff welfare, moral instruction, and quality of life it prompted, the Prices were committed to providing for their employees.

For the most part, Bromborough Pool adhered to the organisation of earlier planned industrial village communities, offering good quality housing, gardens, allotments, works schools, and sports facilities. A resident chaplain was also employed to offer daily services in the factory and tend to the villager-employees' spiritual needs. There was precedent within the firm for some of this provision, the Wirral site drew on and extended the Vauxhall factory's educational activities at night and day schools, countryside excursions and Mutual Improvement Society (Tarn, 1965: 331; Brack, 1980: 165). Dedicated to education and recreation, mutual improvement societies offered diversion that the *South London Chronicle*'s report of an entertainment at Price's Vauxhall factory society labelled 'healthy fun' (9 November 1878: 7). Christopher Radcliffe has noted their democratic nature and connection with radical groups – including the Owenites, concluding that such societies 'were of the people not for the people' (1997: 141). In each of the three villages considered to this point, recreation was entwined with capitalism, social reform, and radical politics. Bromborough Pool's entertainment history begins with the village's history: a branch of the Belmont Mutual Improvement Society (named after the Vauxhall factory) was established during the village's first year and used as the village school and library, for reading and writing lessons, musical concerts, magic lantern talks, penny readings, and lectures (Tarn, 1965: 332–334; Brack, 1980: 168). Gillian Darley identifies the society and its 'instruction and intellectual recreation' as the centre of village life from 1854 onwards, and as the major innovation of the Wrights' industrial community (2007: 65). When the new school was built in the 1890s, a village hall was provided by repurposing the original school building into a multi-use community space with a stage. By this time, the village consisted of 142 houses and was home to a population of 728. Dramatic classes were in place by 1901, run by the village Reverend, Edward Trevitt (1857–1915), under the aegis of the Mutual Improvement Society. Trevitt's classes led to staged performances in the village hall; these were practical lessons, not dramatic reading sessions (*Birkenhead News*, 4 January 1902: 7). By the following year, the village's dramatic society were performing at other local venues, drawing attention to the Bromborough Pool community and its cultural recreation (*Birkenhead News*, 12 February 1902: 2). Building plans from November 1899 and theatrical licences dating from 1903 and 1910 further reveal that public dramatic performances were regularly staged in the village hall from at least the early twentieth century, offering some competition for Port Sunlight's Dramatic Society who were performing just a short distance away (Wirral Archive Services, ZP/38/11/1-4; Unilever Archives, GB1752.PRU/412/1/7-8).

In his 1965 article on the planning of Bromborough Pool, John Tarn noted the village's relative absence from scholarship on model villages and made a case for its location as the first of the garden villages that was grounded in the focus on green and open spaces that characterised its planning (332). The occlusion of Bromborough Pool can be traced back to at least the turn of the twentieth century. In his 1909 guidebook, *A Perambulation through the Hundred of Wirral,* Harold Young had encouraged tourists to take a 'detour' to the 'not greatly visited' Bromborough Pool, describing it as a 'well worthwhile' excursion (40). Ewart Gladstone Culpin's 1913 *The Garden City Movement Up-To-Date* makes no reference to the village, while Port Sunlight receives an extensive entry (41). Throughout history Price's works and housing have been consistently eclipsed by their more renowned neighbour, Port Sunlight, creating an absence that impedes histories of theatre and recreation in British industrial communities.

New Lanark, Saltaire, and Bromborough Pool supply three key examples of purpose-built industrial communities sited outside of polluted urban spaces. Together they originated visual and verbal images of a pastoral industrial world and practical, working case studies that were available to later developers, including Lever Bros at Port Sunlight, Rowntree's of York at New Earswick, and Cadbury's at Bournville. Recreational provision was at the core of all three, but as the German economist Gerhart Schulze-Gaevernitz noted in 1900, in some cases it came at a cost: writing of Saltaire he argued that while 'externally' the village 'is a most magnificent example of care for the workman', this first impression means that its 'drawbacks are not such as to be observed by the hasty observer'. However, he continued, 'inquiries amongst its inhabitants will show that their wellbeing is purchased at the price of liberty' (58). The recreation inhabitants (and employees) could access under paternalistic industrialism were governed and managed to varying degrees. As was daily life. In the three examples introduced above, a clear, two-phase pattern is evident. First came the organisation of recreational sports, education, and music, followed by a second phase that focused on the provision of wider cultural or creative recreational activities, including drama. The reasons behind this were, in part, practical. Sports pitches were relatively quick and cheap to lay out, education was an increasingly recognised need with growing legal requirements. Across the nineteenth century, and into the twentieth, and across places and under different leaderships this pattern began to shift, as did the presence of theatre. Stable models of fully governed, controlled recreation were modified as the new century saw key drivers change from 'paternalism' to 'pragmatism' (Chance, 2017: 16). Two final case study communities – Port Sunlight and New Earswick – form the subject of the next section, modelling these changes. With their roots in the final years of the eighteen hundreds, these two spaces marked a step-change in recreational provision and tell different stories of residential provision, employee welfare, and dramatic activity. Social reform action, the acceleration of industrial production and global markets, and growth of sociological and urban planning studies and literature brought renewed energy to the industrial communities of the fin de siècle, entwining manufacturing, beauty, and leisure in images that were a far cry from the smog bound, pollution filled imagery of city-based production. Amidst these shifting discourses around theatre, education, recreation, and people management, theatrical activity increased, with performance supporting and harnessing these new dynamics, feeding into, shaping, and changing them, and playing a part in the gradual process that transmuted solid, delivered models of rational recreation into more interlocutory sets of exchanges between employer and employee, worker, and player.

Port Sunlight

Just over three and a half decades after the creation of Bromborough Pool, work began on Port Sunlight's factory and village spaces, less than five-minute's walk away. Today Port Sunlight remains the home of Unilever's headquarters and the site of two separate archives – one covering the factory and the other the village. Like Saltaire and New Lanark, the village continues to attract significant tourist numbers; visitors keen to explore its history, streets, and art gallery, following in the steps of late nineteenth- and early twentieth-century sightseers, academics, and professionals drawn by its architecture and Lever's innovative approach to work, wellbeing, and play. In 1909, the factory magazine *Progress* reported 53,471 visitors up to the end of November (January 1910: 96). Five years later, *The Music Herald* devoted an article to the village's musical activities, noting that the village had attracted 50,000 village visitors in the past year (1 March 1914: 72). Like other industrial villages, Port Sunlight had internal and external, professional, and residential audiences. Railway posters and guidebooks make its status as a visitor attraction – a destination – clear. The reach of Port Sunlight is further signalled by the Gaiety Theatre's 1912 production of *The Sunshine Girl* by Paul Rubens (1876–1917) and Cecil Raleigh (1856–1914); a musical comedy telling the story of Port Sunshine's soap-works owner who disguises himself as a factory employee (in characteristically convoluted burlesque style) and falls in love with the eponymous heroine, played by star actress and Gaiety Girl Phyllis Dare (1890–1974). Reflecting the acceleration of new advertising cultures and global brand marketing, Port Sunlight was a household word and a romanticised location by the early decades of the twentieth century.

Work began on William Hesketh Lever's (1851–1925) new Port Sunlight factory headquarters for his soap bar production business in the autumn of 1887. Having outgrown its existing location, Lever had invested in fifty-six acres of swampy land in a 'rural district' near Bebington, on the Wirral. Twenty-four acres was assigned to production, the remaining thirty-two allocated to fulfil Lever's plans for an industrial village, with housing restricted to factory workers and their families. Rapid expansion over the next fifteen years resulted in a 230-acre industrial site by 1902, of which just over 60 per cent was devoted to housing and religious, educational, and recreational buildings (*The British Architect*, 4 April 1902: 247). Port Sunlight's housing design was diverse. Lever played out his own architectural aspirations on the Wirral site, commissioning domestic and community buildings from a range of designers that were quickly recognised for their entwined beauty and functionality – a reflection of the Arts and Crafts ethos that also shaped Cadbury's Bournville, and one that led author Thomas Davison to conclude that the 'combination of the practical and the artistic has been achieved [at Port Sunlight] with outstanding success' (1916: viii). Alongside its architecture, recreational provision became an early defining feature of the site, with the scale of the cultural and sporting pastimes on offer regularly featuring in external and internal reports. In November 1900, the Lever Bros company magazine *Progress* noted that while 'it may not be generally known', it is 'nevertheless fact, that in Port Sunlight there are more societies and clubs for social work and mutual benefit etc, than in any other "village" in the world' (593). *Bow Bells* listed these in 1896, identifying their existence as a response to 'relieving the tedium of existence spent in monotonous mechanical work' that 'has evidently been especially studied by the paternal government of the Sunlight community' (27 November: 545). Activities included science and art classes, literary and debating societies, chess, cricket, billiards, football, gymnastics, quoits, cycling and bowling clubs, a band (with instruments and uniforms supplied by the company), minstrel troupe, choral society, dramatic society, dancing school and a musical comedy/light opera group.

Recreational activity was organised and delivered by the village council in a series of community spaces created by the firm that included several publicly licensed entertainment venues with permanent stages. George

Benoit-Levy, founder of the French Garden City movement, lauded the number of buildings that offered flexible space for 'public festivities' in his 1904 account of his visit to Port Sunlight; a report so positive it was subsequently translated and published in *Progress* for the factory readership (October 1904: 18). As this suggests, the village offered flexible community spaces that served multiple purposes, enabled recreational activities for villagers and staff, offered occasional space for company events, and were deliberately showcased by Lever Bros. Writing for *The British Architect* in 1902, Lever identified 'the first public building at Port Sunlight [as] the Gladstone Hall, opened in November 1891'; a 'simple, unpretentious' space, 'admirably adapted for the purpose for which it was designed' (4 April: 247). Simple, unpretentious, flexible, and very well-used: on weekday lunchtimes, the Gladstone Hall served as a dining room for factory workers, while in the evenings recreational activities took over. Dramatic society rehearsals were on Monday evening, the minstrel troupe on Tuesdays. The choir had a regular booking on Wednesdays, with Thursday evenings left free for weekly entertainments by outside companies or performers, programmed and administered by the village council. On Fridays, the chemistry class took place in the hall and, at the end of the week, it was the turn of the Sunday service, a weekly occasion that was more akin to a public lecture than a religious event. A second community venue, Hulme Hall, opened in 1901, with a proscenium stage and theatrical licence. The village schools were also equipped for dramatic performances. Theatrical activity was a factor in the planning of community buildings at Port Sunlight, and present from the earliest stages of the village's recreational activity.

Port Sunlight's Dramatic Society arrived early in the site's recreational activities; established in 1894, eighteen years before the formation of Cadbury's equivalent group at Bournville. From 1895, all societies were governed by the newly formed Port Sunlight Village Council, and most adopted a subscription model to cover their day-to-day costs. In the case of the dramatic society, budgets were supplemented by larger one-off production expenses – including the hiring of lights or of playscripts – being met by the council, and by default by the firm, who funded the council. The first years of their activity saw the society stage regular performances at the Gladstone Hall, perform at other local charity events, and attract billings and reviews from the local press and national publications, including *The Sketch* (13 May 1896: 101). The backbone of their early repertoire was made up of musical comedies and operettas, particularly those of Gilbert and Sullivan, with the dramatic and choral societies regularly working closely together to stage productions. 1897 saw *The Sketch* report on the group's work again, in a commentary that praised the quality of theatrical production in the village. Quality – of production, performances, and elocution – was repeatedly stressed as an important part of the society's outputs, evoking the idea of the professional amateur, an amateur performer who sought to equal the performance of a professional performer within a production context that was high quality. Port Sunlight's dramatic society appear to have met this threshold, at least in the view of newspaper reviewers. Echoing *The Sketch*'s praise of the quality of their performances that had appeared six years previously, *The Birkenhead News*'s review of a 1903 production concluded that, 'if all local amateur dramatic societies were of the merit of Port Sunlight's, there would not be so much justifiable complaint about amateurism' (19 December 1903: 6). Press reviews made Port Sunlight's theatre and performance visible to external local and national audiences, widely advertising Lever's community and its recreation.

Taking into account the acclaim that the society's productions appear to have received, it is interesting to discover that other records indicate that while drama appeared to be thriving in Port Sunlight's early years, the society struggled during the 1890s, nearly folding on two separate occasions due to a 'lack of enthusiasm' (Boumphrey and Hunter, 2002: 10; 12). Two separate occasions that align with *The Sketch*'s positive attention. There are several possible reasons for this. Without wishing to verge on conjecture, the first may have been connected to local competition. The dramatic society did not hold the monopoly on Port Sunlight's entertainment. In addition to visiting companies appearing in the village, other village entertainment groups existed, and were popular enough to perform outside of Port Sunlight's spaces, in Bootle, at local Liberal clubs, and at charity appearances at workhouses and hospitals. The most popular of these groups was the minstrel troupe. Appearing in blackface, the use of burnt cork or theatrical make up to change skin colour that was common practice in music hall song and comedy from the 1840s and played a significant role in Britain's racist ideologies and visual iconographies on stage and in print culture, 'The Sunlight Darkies' had fifty members by 1895, including a band of eight musicians (Pickering, 2008). The group was managed by eight elected members, was well resourced, with 'all the outfit, music, instruments [...] necessary for modern high-class minstrelsy', and had administrators charged with booking appearances and managing their fees (*Progress,* February 1895: 2). In this village-originated racist grotesquery intersections between theatrical production in the industrial village, local urban centres, and national entertainment trends are revealed. Children's performances were also staged outside of the dramatic society's activity.

Other groups and activities continued as the twentieth century turned. The year 1910 saw the opening of the social club hall and the connected formation of the Shakespearean Reading Circle. 'Privately formed' to read the trial scene from *The Merchant of Venice* at the end of a lecture by Reverend T. H. Martin, the group went on to offer a production of the play in the new social club in May. On this occasion, the quality acting of the dramatic society was not met: 'the golden mean between acting too much and not acting enough is hard to find, even by professionals. Everyone agreed that our beginners were diligently on its tracks' recorded the works magazine (*Progress,* April 1910: 91).

The dramatic society's 1890s struggles appear to have passed by the early twentieth century, and 1903's production of Arthur Wing Pinero's (1855–1934) farce *The Magistrate* (1885) offers a useful example of the function and operation of staff-performed theatre at this point. The first performance was at the Gladstone Hall in mid-February, with the reviewer from *The Birkenhead News* recording it was well attended and well received, and that any profits would be donated to the Village Nurse Fund (14 February 1903: 5). During the following week the play was re-staged at the Joyville Theatre, Thornton Hough – a private space in the Lever home that will be discussed later in this section – in front of an invited audience of Lower Bebington District Council members (*Birkenhead News*, 21 February 1903: 7). Mid-December saw a second revival feature as part of a fundraising event for The Hot Pot Fund – which offered Christmas dinner to thousands – at Birkenhead Town Hall (*Birkenhead News,* 12 December 1903: 4). Through *The Magistrate* we can begin to understand the multiple functions of theatre at Port Sunlight, and its increasing connections with publicity, wider community, charity, recreation, and education. Theatre was part of Port Sunlight's meaning and place-making. Stage backdrops used in the Gladstone and Hulme halls featured images of the village streets that hung at the rear of the platforms during some of their entertainments, and other uses. In this way, Port Sunlight's stages were imprinted as Port Sunlight spaces. The outside was brought inside and acted as an outer frame for theatre, entertainment, and recreation.

In 1903, Lever opened the most ambitious of his public space-building projects at Port Sunlight – an open-air theatre with a capacity of around 2500 (George, 1907: 110). The inaugural performance featured the dramatic and musical societies and attracted national and international press coverage, much of which was accompanied by illustrations or photographs. Located in the Dell, an area of land now known for its famous vista of the village's bridge, the Auditorium was the site of a wide range of events including roller-skating competitions, boxing matches, dances, the village flower show, film screenings, and cycling events. Theatre infused many of them: 1917's horticulture show, offers a strong example, as an event that featured not only plants, but also a public appearance from the actress Olga Nethersole (1866–1917) and a speech from the dramatist Hall Caine (1853–1931) in a complex occasion fusing patriotism, war work, industrialism, and performance. It also served as a key public site for William Hesketh Lever's playing out of his own interwoven professional, social, and political public identity, offering space for large workforce meetings and when – after five failed attempts – Lever was returned as Liberal MP for the Wirral in 1906, a bunting-covered venue to house his victory celebrations (*Observer*, 26 January 1906: 7). Lever's auditorium was identified and celebrated as the first open-air theatre in Britain and a pioneering new experiment in employee wellbeing and recreation. 'The intellectual wellbeing of the adults [at Port Sunlight] has not been forgotten', reported Walter George in his 1907 study *Engines of Social Progress*, 'the most interesting attempt in that direction is the Auditorium', which offers' unlimited possibilities of intellectual development' (120). Aligning intellectual development with the Auditorium's entertainments is a strong indicator of the extent to which performance's role as approved recreation had expanded by this point, for theatre came to be at the heart of the venue's 'unlimited possibilities'.

Despite the Auditorium's range of uses, it had been particularly well equipped for theatre, with a raised stage, good lighting and sightlines, a sunken orchestra pit, a green room, prop and scene stores, and dressing rooms for actors and actresses. Alongside home-produced theatre, appearances from a range of touring companies and performers were booked. The first of these was the Avenue Pierrot Company (including ventriloquists and comedians) who were programmed to appear twice a week for a short season in 1903. Frank Benson's (Francis, 1858–1939) touring company appeared later in the same year, with a charity performance of *The Merchant of Venice*, staged under the patronage of local aristocracy and civic dignitaries. Benson's company was known for al fresco Shakespeare; nationally touring outdoor performances staged in gardens and parks. The production was a perfect fit with the company's ambitions for the auditorium and reflected that centrality of the outside, the countryside, to Port Sunlight's wider imagery. The auditorium's scene store was stocked with backdrops representing village streets that were used for home-produced events and by travelling companies (George: 112). Most of those that feature in surviving images appear to have been representations of Port

Sunlight village, landscapes with meaning that also hung at Gladstone Hall (where images of Gladstone's properties were interchanged with those of the village), and at Hulme hall. When these drops were hung, the stage action was framed at least in part as local, no matter what the play, no matter what the performance. Place and play fused creativity, crafting, storytelling, and performance with Port Sunlight's village and factory, workers, and residents. In 1937, the outdoor theatre at Port Sunlight was demolished. All that remains today are earthworks that offer an outline of the site. Yet the green space – with its views of factory and village – offers important traces of theatre's history at Port Sunlight and clues to the way its imagery and activity shaped and underpinned Lever's industrial project.

The Manor Mummers

The Lever family's home was Thornton Manor, three miles from Port Sunlight in the village of Thornton Hough. It was at home that the Lever family amateur dramatic company 'The Manor Mummers' rehearsed and performed from 1904 to 1914, with a brief reappearance in 1921. Aside from 'a few exceptions' the 'small, but efficient band of actors' was made up of Lever family members, with (William) Hulme Lever – W. H. Lever's eldest son, and incoming chairman of the company – at the helm (*Liverpool Echo*, 18 January 1921: 5; *Whitby Gazette*, 2 April 1909: 6). Hulme's published memories of his father make it clear that he supported his dramatic interests, choosing the name of the company, and financing the creation of the 'Joyville Theatre' in the manor house's ballroom (Lever, 1927: 272). While occasional performances took place at social events for local estate owners and society personalities, the most familiar Manor Mummers' performances were the Christmas entertainments they produced for factory and village audiences. From 1904, Port Sunlight's staff and villagers were transported by carriage to Thornton Manor for an evening of entertainment that was repeated on successive days to allow all to attend. A programme for 1904's play, Charles Dicken's *A Cricket on the Hearth,* makes it clear that these were fully staged productions, with a focus on theatrical spectacle – individuals responsible for wigs, scenery, stage management, costume, dressing, and electric lighting are listed (Port Sunlight Village Archive). The entertainment marked a clear step up from that offered in the previous year, when a scene from *The School for Scandal* starring the village vicar Samuel Gamble-Walker (1866–1936) in the role of Sir Peter Teazle was the main feature. This second example of a 'growing sympathy between Church and Stage' in industrial village communities – following

Reverend Edward Trevitt's running of neighbouring Bromborough Pool's Dramatic and Elocution two years earlier – tracks the history of theatre as an increasingly approved activity (*Progress*, February 1903: 51). Watching a performance in an employer's home, with members of the employer's family and the village vicar amongst the cast, affirmed the recreational value of theatre, and cemented its status.

Alongside these Christmas events, the Manor Mummers gave regular performances at Port Sunlight's Gladstone Hall, a space where village and factory life intersected. Manor Mummers' performances appear to have been popular. In January 1913, the group staged a third performance of John Davidson's tragic farce *Smith*, for 'residents' and 'workpeople' who had been 'unable to gain admission' to the previous two (*Birkenhead News*, 25 January 1913: 11). Some audience members are likely to have attended out of a sense of duty, but accounts indicate that these entertainments sought to create a sense of fun. Short farces and comedies were standard fare: *Smith* followed *Mr Hopkinson*, a farce by Richard Claude Carton (1853–1928), staged in 1912. The focus on spectacle clear from records of Thornton Manor productions is also present in reviews of these Gladstone Hall productions: *Mr Hopkinson* was praised for its 'admirably arranged' 'big open stage' and scene stagings that would 'do credit to a professional stage craftsman' (*Birkenhead News*, 6 January 1912: 5). Hulme Lever remained influential and active in Port Sunlight's theatre throughout the period covered in this book, as president of Birkenhead Dramatic Society in the early nineteen twenties, and creator of plays for early nineteen thirties productions at the Gladstone Hall, including *Cinderella* (1931), and *Dick Whittington* (1932). The second of these is particularly interesting, as he co-wrote the piece with Sophie Somers (1891–1950), an advertising department manager at the firm who lived in Port Sunlight village, had previous plays produced professionally under her pseudonym George Hewitt, and was to co-author with Lever again (*Progress*, January 1921: 23; *Crewe Chronicle*, 16 January 1932: 2). Over the first three and a half decades of the twentieth century, a considerable number of Port Sunlight's staff watched senior managers at the firm play. Theatre was entangled with the village and factory communities, and the firm's innovative models of employee communications and relations.

While the Manor Mummers' performances were deliberately not educational, other strands of Port Sunlight's theatrical activity were designed to focus on drama's educational potential. Port Sunlight's Staff Training College – a day continuation school for younger employees founded in 1918 – staged regular dramatic productions during the 1920s, with a strong focus on William Shakespeare's plays. Various venues and sites were used for these events. At Port Sunlight the Lyceum, the village's early school buildings, which had been used as a military hospital during the First World War before being repurposed for the college, offered an indoor stage and grounds used for outdoor plays. Thornton Manor also welcomed the college's performers. In 1922, a production of *Persephone* was staged at an entertainment hosted by William Lever, featuring a cast of around fifty factory employees currently in college education and produced by their teachers (*The Sphere*, 26 August 1922: 36). That this occasion attracted the attention of fashionable journal *The Sphere*, which featured both a report and a photograph, is testament to the reach of industrial theatre on the Wirral. Further educational dimensions to theatre at Port Sunlight are clear in a wartime series of open lectures programmed for the Lyceum in 1916–1917, including 'Dramatic Recitals' by elocutionist John Duxbury (1871–1953), a well-known figure on touring national and international lecture circuits who had started his career as a paid scripture reciter and remained well known for his recitation performances of Charles Dickens and Robert Louis Stevenson (1911 census), 'The Theatre in these Days' delivered by Annie Horniman (1860–1937), manager of the Gaiety Theatre repertory company in Manchester, and 'Shakespeare's Hamlet, from a Woman's Point of View' by Morden Grey (Mary King Griffen, 1871–1931), actress, well-known touring lecturer and Professor of Elocution at Royal Manchester College of Music (*Progress*, January 1917: 15; April 1917: 62). All three were trained entertainers with public identities and strong affiliations with local educational and cultural landscapes that offered endorsed authoritative identities and presence. Well suited to the wartime moment, the lectures presented theatre as a valued cultural, and wider social, activity in Lever's village.

Theatrical culture was embedded in Lever's industrial project at Port Sunlight. Accounts convey his skills as a performer and crafted, honed public persona. His professional and political speeches regularly included citations from William Shakespeare's plays, with his investment in a replica of Shakespeare's birthplace – built in the village on Poets' Corner and housing four worker cottages (now demolished) – further cementing his self-alignment with theatre and performance. Unsurprisingly perhaps this filtered through to his crafted community. Performance permeated village life. Thousands of factory workers, their families and guests were entertained by or participated in school plays, fancy dress parades, Punch and Judy shows, conjurors, dramatic society performances, and the Lever family's amateur company over the first fifty years of the site's development. National entertainment trends were staged in spaces where backdrops of the village's streets framed the performance space, and where theatrical activity was presented as part of wider recreation and wellbeing agendas. A model for this thinking about performance and recreation can be discovered in an 1899 speech Lever delivered at a Girls' Institute Conversazione that had included songs, recitations, and a cinematograph entertainment screening views of Port Sunlight, accompanied by music. Rising at the end of the programme, Lever celebrated the work of the Institute, identifying participation in such activities as a key part of 'direct self preservation' and drawing clear connections between wellbeing, engaging with social and cultural activities, and the spaces that enabled them (*Progress*, November 1899: 90–91). There are multiple synergies between Port Sunlight and Bournville. Both industrial communities were crafted through purpose-built spaces that prioritised recreational and leisure provision, both attracted attention from academic, social, and political audiences – evidenced by literature and regular site visits from town planning and social reform groups, including the International Housing Conference in 1907 and 1910's Royal Institute of British Architects Town Planning Conference. Railway posters and guide books positioned Bournville and Port Sunlight as destinations and they also shared a theatricality that sat at the core of their operations and advertising. There is, however, one more influential model it is important to consider in the history of theatre at Cadbury's, and for this final part of the story we move to another cocoa and chocolate factory.

Rowntree's of New Earswick

In November 1911, the cocoa and chocolate producers H. I. Rowntree and Company hired Brynhild Lucy Benson (1888–1974) as a gymnastics instructor based in the factory's social department (Parratt, 2001). With responsibility for girls' employment, welfare, and recreation, the firm's Social Department was firmly established, well financed, and supplied with its own administration, staff, offices, and letterhead by this point (BI/BSR93/VII/Memorandum/2 June 1917). Employing Miss Benson as part of the team was presented as a coup. Having the daughter of leading Shakespearean actor-manager Frank R. Benson (who had performed at Port Sunlight's auditorium seven years earlier) and direct descendent of Quaker philanthropist, merchant, and civic leader William Rathbone (1819–1902) on the payroll was welcomed as an assertion of the firm's cultural, educational, and recreational provision (*C.W.M.*, March 1911: 1184). A position that was further cemented by a visit from her celebrity father to the factory boys' school during the following year (*C.W.M.*, April 1912, 1289). On her arrival at Rowntree's Brynhild Benson quickly involved herself in the theatre being produced by the factory's dramatic society, prompting both praise and what appears to have been a degree of jealousy from her new audiences. Her performance as Minnie Gilifillian in August Wing Pinero's *Sweet Lavender* (1893) received strong praise from the factory works magazine. The role, the reviewer noted, 'demands a degree of abandon rarely found in an amateur', but Miss Benson 'revelled in the part'. That this revelling also brought disquiet and criticism from others is clear, for 'we have heard it murmured that the part was overdone [and] at times too much attention was drawn away from the other actors'. Such complaints were met with scant patience. 'If that was so', the reviewer concluded, 'then other actors should have infused their parts with a relatively greater intensity' (*C.W.M.* March 1912: 1251–2). By 1912, theatre was entangled in Rowntree's social and cultural politics, as well as factoring in its business strategies and governance structures. While Port Sunlight's extensive recreational provision might appear to offer the closest comparison to Cadbury's Bournville factory activity, the York-based industrial community founded by fellow Quaker, friend, and chocolate and cocoa manufacturer Joseph Rowntree (1837–1925) offers an equally significant model.

Rowntree's new factory had opened in 1890, followed by the planning and construction of New Earswick village – a mile down the Haxby Road – between 1902 and 1904. Now absorbed into the city of York, the boundaries and shape of Rowntree's village are less discernible than those of the previous examples I have discussed, and the site does not have a 'heritage presence' in the way of New Lanark, Saltaire, Port Sunlight, and Bournville. In many ways, New Earswick has disappeared, but its connections with Cadbury's make it an important site for consideration here. New Earswick was created after Bournville, and shared George Cadbury's objective to supply good quality housing for a wider population of workers. As Trevor Rowley notes, Joseph Rowntree was prompted by more general concerns about housing and designed the space to offer a 'practical contribution'; a 'balanced village community' for his own staff and others (Culpin, 1913: 39; Rowley, 2006: 176). Its population evidences the success of his aim. By 1910, the village was home to 119 cottages, 45 of which were let to factory staff (Rowntree Society, 2016: 16). At this point, less than 40 per cent of New Earswick residents worked for the firm, and this proportion was to decrease over the next two decades. In comparison to the 'workers' village' myth that has perpetuated in relation to Bournville, the function of Rowntree's community has been more accurately told, possibly because the space is less visible, less well known, and less subject to forces of romanticism and nostalgia. It certainly does not lack the hallmarks of industrial community design, its location as an early build by Raymond Unwin (1863–1940) and Barry Parker (1867–1947) who were to become guiding figures in the development of the Garden City Movement cements its identity as a key urban planning experiment. Benjamin Seebohm Rowntree (1871–1954), Joseph Rowntree's son and author of the paradigm shifting, early sociological study *Poverty: A Study of Town Life* (1901) had met Unwin and Parker at 1901's Garden Cities Association Conference. The New Earswick commission gave the partners an opportunity to explore their urban planning in practice – materialising an ethos largely grounded in the aesthetics and politics of William Morris's socialist movement (Rowntree Society, 2016: 13). Of interest to this study is the way in which Rowntree's foregrounding of innovative applications of architectural design to facilitate and better society, industry, community, and quality of life in both industrial and residential spaces created separate theatre-making histories in the factory and the village.

New Earswick village was governed through a similar model to Port Sunlight, with all village recreation delivered by a village council and its sub-committees. The year 1904 had seen the formation of the self-financing Joseph Rowntree Trust, a body charged with managing the ongoing development of the village, rentals of its cottage-style homes, and recreational activity for its residents. The trust held unequivocal power over the village community; providing 'such facilities for the enjoyment of full and healthy lives as the Trustees shall consider desirable, and by such other means as the Trustees shall, in their uncontrolled discretion, think fit' (Culpin: 39). Around ten per cent of the village area was dedicated to leisure by this time, and administering and resourcing villagers' spare time was the source of a significant part of the trust's responsibility and workload, and a key site of their financial investment (*Agricultural Economist and Horticultural Review*, February 1913: 31). In October 1905, the first village community space opened. New Earswick's Assembly Rooms sounded rather grander than two houses, given, rent free, for village use, but six nights a week they offered space for newspaper reading, or playing card and board games, and dominoes. While there was no provision for theatre in this space, the rooms' governance and self-financing, subscription model set the scene for future village drama. The Assembly Rooms were managed by a village council sub-committee whose members were responsible for cleaning, lighting, supervising, and renting out the rooms, fundraising, and all membership applications and approvals (BI/NEVCM/9 September 1904).

Entertainment was on their agenda early on, with a Concert Committee formed in January 1905 to organise fundraising events throughout 1905 and 1906 (BI/NEVCM, 12 March 1906). By 1907, the Assembly Rooms was recognised as not fit for purpose, particularly – it was noted – as a space for public worship. It was replaced by the Folk Hall, a second, much improved multiuse village space, which was resourced for theatre, as well as sewing clubs, gymnastics, and village functions. Suitability for wide recreational usage had been a key design principle, with Joseph Rowntree's Personal Secretary, New Earswick property manager, and self-defined 'Jack of all Trades' Gulielma Harlock (1863–1941) charged with researching similar venues (1911 Census entry, Harlock). As part of this process Harlock made contact with her equivalent at Clarks of Street, where the Quaker shoemakers had created an early example of a community hall – the Crispin Hall – in 1885. In a lengthy, four-page reply to her enquiry, the challenges, and considerations of designing, supplying, and running such industrial community venues were laid out in detail; the author envied Rowntree 'being able to plan things afresh', 'for there are many things I would do differently if we had them to do over again' (BI/NE/21/2a). There was a growing body of experience and expertise amidst this industrialist network that far exceeded well-known industrial leaders, and spanned female and male employees.

Considerable investment was made in the Folk Hall. *New Earswick Estate Annual Statistics, 1905–1917* records that the construction of the building and provision of recreational equipment cost 3888 pounds. A useful comparative figure is provided by the cost of fourteen cottages built in the same year the hall opened, at 5061 (BI/NE21/1). One clear difference between the Clark's model Harlock had researched and the final Folk Hall design could be found in its theatrical set-up. At Clark's 'theatricals are not allowed', at New Earswick's new venue they were planned for, provided for, and showcased to journalists (BI/NE21/2a). Press accounts drew attention to the stage in the main hall, equipped with curtain, trap, and dressing room (*Sheffield Evening Telegraph,* 28 March 1907: 4). The resulting design is reminiscent of Gladstone Hall at Port Sunlight. 'Dramatic Entertainments' feature as a regular item in New Earswick Village Council Minutes from 1910, records that offer insight into the day-to-day concerns and logistics of village life and provide an interesting social history of both quotidian existence and exceptional events. Records of meetings from the early twentieth century identify theatre as one of a range of recreational activities offered to ensure villagers' 'enjoyment of full and healthy lives'. As with the fellow Quaker-driven business operation at Cadbury's, there is no sense captured in writing that theatre prompted greater anxiety than gardening or cricket: the minutes heading column from a March 1911 meeting reads 'Lawn Mower', followed directly by 'Fairy Play' (BI/NEVCM/March 20 1911). Theatre was as an accepted part of regular village life as the upkeep of communal lawns; indeed it is safe to say that during the first two decades of the twentieth century, billiards and the cricket team prompted far greater discussion, consternation, and disagreement than the village's dramatic activity.

The first references to theatre in the council minutes position it as part of the social and educational sub-committee remit, clearly locating the 'two short dramatic pieces in preparation under the direction of Mrs Sorensen' within the village's wider recreational management (BI/NEVCM/11 October 1910). Bee (Beatrice Drew, nee Arundel, 1872–1968) and Carl (Wilfred, 1872–1948) Sorensen lived at White Rose Farm (now The Garth), the farm that supplied milk for the Cocoa Works. Their daughter, Beatrice Anne, born in 1913 (–1937), married Julian Rowntree, one of Benjamin Seebohm Rowntree's four sons. The Sorensens were prominent figures in village life and York's Quaker community. They were comfortably off. The 1911 census entry sees them both in their late thirties, two years into their marriage, with a domestic servant and two dairy maids. Carl Sorensen was also Chair of New Earswick Village Council at the same time Bee was staging theatre at the Folk Hall. Theatre was at the core of the lives of senior village representatives. Bee Sorensen's production of two short pieces was followed by a children's fairy play over the Christmas period of 1910 (BI/NEVCM/19 December 1910). These must have been well received, as from 1912 a dramatic sub-committee was put in place, comprised of seven members, four women and three men, including the village vicar, to manage Folk Hall theatrical productions (BI/NEVCM/8 November 1912; 5 June 1914). A series of performances followed, each making a financial contribution to the Folk Hall's running costs, with the balance sheet and accounts of the 1912/1913 season recording net income of four pounds and sixteen shillings (JRF/4/1/9/8/8/5; BI/NEVCM/15 December 1913). Unlike other recreational pursuits, village theatre was not a subsidised activity, it was a net contributor to the community's finances.

Following a failed attempt to form a village dramatic society in the autumn of 1912, in the summer of 1914, New Earswick's village council were presented with a letter signed by over thirty residents re-petitioning for a theatrical group to be formed (BI/NEVCM/8 December 1912; 20 July 1914). It is clear that recreational management in industrial communities favoured a bureaucracy-heavy approach, with the nature of this request suggesting a desire for greater, more representative control over the community's theatre by the community. To some extent, this was achieved through the trust agreeing and suspending the council sub-group, but it would be naïve to assume that theatre was any less monitored and governed in this new model (BI/NEVCM/20 July 1914). Recreational provision was a space for practical applications of Joseph Rowntree's primary intentions, articulated in his 1904 *Founder's Memorandum* that, 'I should regret if there were anything in the organisation of these village communities that should interfere with the growth of the right spirit of citizenship [...] I do not want to establish communities bearing the stamp of charity but rather of rightly ordered and self-governing communities – self-governing, that is, within the broad limits laid down by the Trust. (BI/NEVCM, 5 September 1904; BI/RFAM/JR/8/1/1). Connections with the factory community are also clear in this phase of village drama. Irene Mockett (1895–1979) was secretary to the dramatic society and a manager at Rowntree's in a role that appears to have been equivalent of a Cadbury's Forewoman (1939 register; Borthwick 1922–1930 records). By the late 1920s, theatre in the village flourished, with the dramatic society producing seasons of work and running a fortnight summer school at the Folk Hall, with actor, pageant director, male impersonator, and playwright Gwen Lally (1882–1963) as lead tutor, offering classes in elocution, prop-making, costume, play-design, and casting (*Yorkshire Post*, 10 August 1927: 12).

New Earswick village theatre remained a site of increasing development and investment. The souvenir programme produced for the opening of a Folk Hall extension in 1935 celebrated the size of the new facility, with its capacity of over 400 spectators and 'stage of generous size having full lighting equipment of the most up-to-date type, proper stage-curtain equipment, an orchestra well, dressing rooms on either side of the stage, and under the stage a large basement providing ample storage for scenery etc'. Again, it is clear that staging theatre had been at the core of the design. The programme goes on to note that 'provision for dramatic performances in a hall of this size creates a difficulty and the present compromise was only decided upon after consultation with theatrical experts' (BI/NE2/1f). As this activity continued in Rowntree's village, dramatic recreational provision was also in place in the factory further up the Haxby Road.

Drama at the Cocoa Works

As the celebrated appointment of Brynhild Benson might suggest, the socially progressive thinking that lay behind the creation of New Earswick village also drove management and day-to-day operations at Rowntree's factory. Like the Cadburys, the Rowntree family came from long, established Quaker heritage, and social responsibility, business ethics, and a disapproval of accumulating excess capital guided the firm's operations. Employee welfare was a key business concern embedded in the running of the factory, not activity that ran in parallel alongside it. Staff numbers rose rapidly at the York manufactory during the fin de siècle, from less than 100 in 1880, to over 4,000 in 1910 and over 6,000 by 1920 (Haxby Road Historic Building Report). Under the leadership of Benjamin Seebohm Rowntree, an eight-hour day was introduced in 1896, a full-time factory doctor employed from 1904, a pension scheme started in 1906, and a five-day working week introduced in 1919 (Rowntree Society, 2016: 17–18). The first edition of the in-house *Cocoa Works Magazine* appeared in 1902, with the publication serving similar community creation and people management functions to *Progress* and *Bournville Works Magazine* (which it predated by several months). The factory's dramatic society history predates the village's. From 1912, the theatre group identified interchangeably as the Cocoa Works Dramatic Society and the Rowntree Players, performed onsite in the factory, supported by the firm's recreational schemes, and included in its annual report on education. By 1926 its use in the factory was the subject of national commentary, with the year's government report on *The Drama in Adult Education* recording that 'the welfare scheme of Messrs Rowntree and Co. has a dramatic section' (117). A listing in *The Amateur Dramatic Year Book and Community Theatre Handbook* records that society membership was restricted to Rowntree employees, with the factory's lecture theatre doubling as a performance space and referred to as the 'factory theatre' (Bishop, 1928: 154). As the years passed, their productions became increasingly outward facing, with a repertoire familiar from other industrial amateur repertoires (including Port Sunlight and Bournville), but distinguished by annual, large-scale Christmas pantomimes.

The 1920s marked the heyday of dramatic activity at Rowntree's factory. In 1925, the society joined forces with York Amateur Operatic and Dramatic Society, the York Everyman Theatre, and the York Settlement Community Players to revive the pageant *Drake,* a piece originally created by pageant master Louis Napoleon Parker (who we will meet properly in Chapter 4). Seven performances were staged in the city's museum gardens: this was high profile showcasing of the firm's theatre that attracted the attention of the fashionable, national press (*Westminster Gazette*, 14 July 1925: 4). During the following year, the factory players took part in the National Festival of Community Drama, organised by the British Drama League, making it through to the regional final at Leeds Little Theatre in

December (Ridge: 165). When drama at Rowntree's is thought-through as part of the firm's careful brand management and recreational governance, it is clear that it was positioned as an approved activity. Factory theatre was not just tolerated, it was considered an appropriate mechanism for showcasing the company and promoting its commitment to education, recreation, and wellbeing, dynamics materialised in the building and opening of the Joseph Rowntree Hall (later known as the Joseph Rowntree Theatre) in 1935. At a cost of 12,000 pounds, the build realised the ongoing aim to provide 'a hall which may be a fitting centre for those recreational and educational activities which make for a full and happy life' (Rowntree Trust Website). Rowntree's new theatre featured simple architecture, a warm colour scheme, and hidden lighting, designed to give an intimate and welcoming atmosphere to the 450 seat auditorium and to focus the audience's attention on the stage. Equipped with up-to-date acoustics, lighting and heating systems, space for a sixteen-piece orchestra, and a magnificent, curved cyclorama, this production space was created to stage a business and its people and was used for meetings, conferences, and theatre. It became the home of the Rowntree Players productions. In three decades, across factory and village, Rowntree's had constructed two venues bespoke designed and created for performance.

By 1935, Seebohm Rowntree's investment in theatre exceeded the confines of the factory and village estates. In the previous year, he had co-led a group of prominent citizens who took a lease on York's Theatre Royal to prevent its closure. Together they established a Citizens' Theatre – a business model designed to offer performances by the 'best touring companies available' – and a resident repertory company; an early model of the producing and receiving house. Publicity surrounding the initiative made it clear that the leaseholders were not interested in the theatre as a profit-making opportunity, they saw their involvement and financial contributions as 'important public service'. 'Mr Seebohm Rowntree [...] particularly feels that his employees should not be without a theatre' recorded one newspaper article (*The Observer*, 19 August 1934: 11). Then and now, Rowntree's industrial and social experiment attracted less press, popular and academic attention than either Port Sunlight or Bournville. New Earswick is absent from, or a footnote in, many studies of model villages and the later garden city movement that spend considerable time discussing Lever and the Cadburys, Port Sunlight and Bournville (see Fishman, 1982 and Beevers, 1988 for examples of this). At the York factory and village models of theatre as healthy recreation, public service, and education were carved out, models that intersected with, contributed to, and influenced the making and funding of theatre in other industrial spaces. They are an important part of these histories.

The Cadburys and Rowntrees were national colleagues and competitors, professionally and personally networked through organisations, the Society of Friends, and family connections (including marriages). Several members of the Cadbury family attended the well-known Quaker school The Mount, in York, and personal correspondence indicates social and business contact between the two prominent families at the time (BI). George Cadbury had served his apprenticeship under Joseph Rowntree senior (1801–1859), when the business was still located in central York. Multiple, often intersecting, religious, political, masonic, and professional networks connected Britain's leading industrialists, with the industrial communities they created revealing shared motivations and experiments, distinct aims and objectives, and their parallel careers in the fields of politics, education, and sociology. The story of British industrial communities told through these five case study sites is one of shift and change, with the cultural offer to workers and residents moving from second-phase of developments to planning priorities. Tracing the story of theatrical provision in these spaces tells a story of the role of culture in British industrial history and industrial relations, reflecting W. L. George's 1909 statement that 'we have at last begun to look upon the worker as something more than a dividend-earning machine' (1). In these spaces, staff work and play were sites of investment, and while governance and restrictions around culture were firmly in place, there was a gradual shift from late eighteenth and early nineteenth-century models of paternalistic industrialism towards increasingly reciprocal models rooted in an understanding that welfare, productivity, and profit were interconnected. Fuelled by the social reform agenda of New Liberalism, and progressive Quaker reform, Cadbury's activity at Bournville can be located within this wider group of business thinkers who shared core convictions that recreational, educational, and health provision was not a philanthropic act but a fundamental part of complex, religiously informed commercial strategy (Packer, 2003; Chance, 2017: 16). The significance of balancing of work and play for the sake of business, the role of delivered recreation as part of that balancing, and the promotional potential of recreational activity are clear in Lever, Rowntree, and Cadbury's business records and in the publications and events they produced for internal and external audiences. For all three, play was work, work was play, and recreation was serious business that required investment in material and human resources. The range of extant and lost performance spaces in these industrial communities capture a sense of the scale, spectacle, and significance of performance and the role of theatre in the business dynamics industrialists created and were economically dependent on. Returning to Cadbury's Birmingham headquarters, the final section of this chapter explores how theatre was fostered, resourced, and delivered at Bournville, and its significance in the creation and promotion of the firm's key people management construct, the Bournville Spirit.

Bournville's Spirit: Industrial Community and Theatre at Cadbury

The 'Bournville Spirit' editorial in *Bournville Works Magazine*'s 1902 inaugural issue was co-authored by in-house journalists, and joint editors, John Henry Whitehouse (1873–1955) and Clarkson Booth (1846–1915). Whitehouse left Cadbury in 1903, having juggled three separate professional roles that signal his position at the very heart of the firm: magazine editor; boys' club manager; and confidential clerk. That the remaining editor, Clarkson Booth, was to become central to theatre and performance at Bournville is no coincidence. Like Whitehouse, Booth held more than one role at the firm. He was also responsible for the Visitors' Department – a site of strategic investment that was entangled with the firm's innovative use of performance and spectacle. The significance of visitors to the factory was understood at Cadbury's headquarters, and a large proportion of the journalists who produced accounts of Bournville had been hosted by the factory at one of their regular press days that brought reporters to the estate by train, where they were fed, greeted by senior members of staff, and taken on organised tours that focused primarily on the factory but often included areas of the village (see Graham, 1915; *The Sphere*, 6 October 1906: 8, for examples). Illustrated guides to the factory containing key facts and figures about production, employees and villagers were published in-house and distributed to journalists and other visitors to ensure – as far as possible – the circulation of accurate information and a focus on areas the firm favoured. Representatives from the press were not the only professional visitors entertained in this way. During the first decades of the twentieth-century, Bournville's factory buildings, grounds, and village were the sites of visits by key figures involved in town planning, policy-making, and health. Individual researchers, groups of delegates from academic and professional conferences that numbered into the thousands, politicians, civic leaders, and specialist groups visited the Cadbury's estate. Meticulous planning was in place around these events, work that was also the remit of Booth's Visitors' Department.

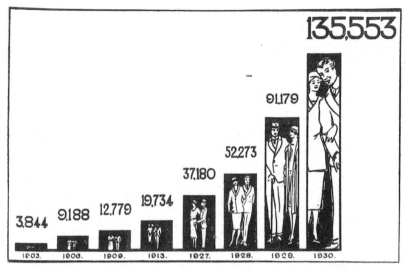

Figure 2 'Our Visitors'
Bournville Works Magazine, April 1931. Cadbury Archives and Heritage Services.

The first decade of the twentieth century saw a huge and welcomed increase in the numbers of visitors to the Bournville factory, visualised in a striking early infographic created by the firm in 1931 (Figure 2). Further detail of this growth is offered by Iola Williams's history of Cadbury's, where he records that Bournville's first visitors' book includes around 40 pages of signatures for the twenty years between 1881 and 1901, and 130 for the following six years (1931: 90). The Visitors' Department had an immediate impact: in just the first year of existence its staff organised site tours for 4,000 people (1931: 89–90). This remit of showcasing Bournville to guests linked Booth and his team with theatre and performance, staff were trained in the art of the guided tour, and theatrical events were often included at the larger occasions they managed. Investment in the Visitors' Department continued throughout economic downturns, the legacies of the First World War, and changes in factory production; this was a recognised and significant area of organisational activity that positions Bournville as a space that was watched, and watching was not only encouraged, but placed at the heart of the operation. Cadbury's was a business model that hinged on audiences. A firm that deliberately staged materialisations, and embodiments of the Bournville Spirit through its workers working and playing against the backdrop of the factory site. All its theatre took place within this wider context. At the turn of the twentieth century, Bournville's Spirit was a complex essence that blended the industrial with the pastoral, work with play, and business objectives with factory community needs. While Cadbury's robust spiritual and ethical core continued to propel and steer business activity, this was gradually entwined with a more marketable and inclusive suite of physical and material systems and resources: a manifestation of George Cadbury Junior's statement that 'only those industries can be recognized as legitimate which perform some public service' (Cadbury, 1926: 3). Over the first decades of the twentieth century, regular staff gatherings were organised that sat alongside religious meetings and they often included theatre; positioning performance at the heart of the company's community-building activities. In the Bournville Spirit Cadbury's ethical business ethos and practical frameworks for the firm's organisational structure and people management can be discovered and key to these were recreational provision, an emphatic focus on the importance of creativity, education, and play in day-to-day working life, and the fostering and rewarding of the mode of participation bred by and through a Bournville Spirit that was closely entwined with, and historically specific to, recreation during the early decades of Bournville.

Managing Recreation and Theatre at Bournville

Entertainments at the Bournville factory were the end results of a complex, well-funded set of systems and organisational structures that were continually adapted and expanded to increase recreational provision. Business structures impacted the ways theatre, and other recreational and educational activities intersected, and how they were prioritised, managed, and funded. Cadbury's theatre was facilitated by committees, and without understanding this wide industrial context we can reach only a partial history of the factory's performance. From 1902, recreation was governed by separate Girls' and Men's Works Committees, supported by a set of sub-committees. These bodies were responsible for day-to-day management of employee health and welfare, professional behaviours, and disciplinary procedures, working conditions, wages, catering, and recreation (CAHS/MWCM/1902). Each was chaired by forewomen and foremen, and included representatives from the wider staff body. All members were appointed by the Cadbury Board. In 1905, the status of the two works committees was raised to management level, indicating the growing organisational importance of the areas they represented. The year 1918 saw these structures shift, in part to accommodate the outcomes of the 1917 Whitley Report, which recommended joint industrial councils as standard practice in a new era of industrial relations that was increasingly trade unionised. Women's and Men's Works Councils were formed, new groups that adapted and extended the earlier model and formed part of a structure of shop and group committees agreed upon through a year-long consultation period between staff and management (Rogers, 1931: 67). Membership of these groups was more representative. Of the sixteen members of each, eight were elected representatives from across departments. The two new councils continued to co-ordinate and recommend on matters around discipline, health, and recreation, within a new structure that positioned their activity as part of a four-layered administrative process: a Recreation and Welfare Sub Committee was formed that reported to the Women's and Men's Works Councils, which in turn reported and recommended to a joint Works Council that was charged with making recommendations to Cadbury's Board, the Committee of Management; a body that retained all final decision-making power (CAHS/BWWCM/5 May 1919).

Minutes from all four of these factory councils document the extensive amount of time and resources committed to Cadbury's recreational provision; revealing that discussions about recreation were the key content of most meetings, and detailing the rigorous systems of checks and recommendations around the budgeting and form of factory extra-work activities. Looking solely at these records, it would be feasible to conclude that Bournville's recreational activity was delivered through a top-down model, with strict controls over access and activity. But closer reading of them, in line with other documents and minutes on other areas, indicates that that was not the case. Employee thinking about, and engagement with, recreation was allowed, indeed encouraged. Independent thought was understood to be a vital element of wellbeing and recreational activities were identified as ways to foster creative, independent ways of thinking that aligned with those at the heart of Quaker practice. Theatrical activity took place in a space between rules and creativity, governed recreation and encouraged play. This space was not stable, and I have drawn no false lines in this study to 'tidy' the diverse events and activities I have discovered. Instead, I have both accepted and embraced the complexity of how and where theatrical activity occurred and functioned, and positioned it as largely separate from the construct of rational recreation which has been widely discussed as a driver of nineteenth-century social reformation through leisure (see Bailey, 2006; Cunningham, 2016; Holt, 1990). Cadbury's provision started from the same question: 'the problem of giving the worker in industry a larger share of leisure is being succeeded by the problem of the utilisation of that leisure', opened *The Factory and Recreation* published by the firm in 1925, as a follow-up to the 1924 International Labour Conference focus on how to 'ensure profitable utilisation of leisure' across secondary and tertiary sector employers (3). The agency that individuals and groups held against such rationalising agendas is a question that has been raised by Brad Beaven, amongst others. Beaven argues that although the mid- to late-Victorian period can be characterised as one in which 'from the socialists to the Salvationists, a common strand of thinking materialised which believed that only through aggressive forms of rational recreation, taken to the heart of working-class communities, could the modern citizen be fostered', working men 'showed a remarkable propensity to manipulate the entertainment offered to coincide with their own cultural preferences' (2005: 39–40). By the early decades of the twentieth century at Bournville less of this style of manipulation was required by the women and men who worked for the company; participation in the shaping of their recreational activity was encouraged and their own needs and preferences were factored in, albeit with limitations. Residual elements of rational recreation are identifiable at Cadbury in the early 1900s, and these will be discussed throughout this study, but in general, the experience of re-creativity at Bournville, and the distinctive set of political, industrial and religious ideas and ideals it emerged from, were a significant modification of earlier approaches and practices.

Between 1900 and 1935 Cadbury's was home to a large, influential senior staff sub-group – drawn from Staff A, Staff B, Forewomen A, and Forewomen B – who were closely involved with Bournville's theatrical production and included an increasing number of women. Lists published in the works magazines record that in 1904 all twenty-seven Staff A and Staff B members were men. A further ninety-two members of staff were employed as Foremen, alongside sixty-seven Forewomen (*Bournville Works Magazine*, February 1904: 112–113). By 1921, sixteen women employees had been appointed or promoted to Staff A and Staff B positions, and a further seventy-seven were Forewomen. Their male counterparts numbered eighty-four at Staff A and B level, and one hundred and forty-four Foremen (*B.W.M.*, January 1921: 4–5). Reflecting the changing demands of early twentieth-century industry, and the prioritisation of visual culture, advertising, and staff education and wellbeing at the factory, many of these senior figures had been deliberately hired for their creative skill sets in the visual arts, marketing and journalism, or backgrounds in education. Others were rewarded with promotion in recognition of their strong commitment to Cadbury's recreational values and work ethic. These senior employees were key to the day-to-day running of Cadbury's and the creation and delivery of its ethos around health and wellbeing, and there are numerous crossovers between the lists of senior staff published annually in the works magazine and those of Bournville's entertainment casts. Senior and mid-management roles at Cadbury's came with high expectations. It was anticipated that senior employees would participate in the recreational activities the firm facilitated, as well as adhering to the clear regulations that were set out around professional behaviour and appearance. The printed codes of conduct issued to new senior staff delineated the day-to-day professional performance required of them and made it clear that their roles positioned them as embodiments of Cadbury's approaches to work and play. The centrality of this group of employees to Cadbury's performance means that representatives from it will feature regularly throughout the following chapters. Those who will make the most regular appearances are: Lottie (Charlotte) Allen (1870–1946), an accountant and forewoman who worked in the company's finance and wages department and sat on the Girls' Works Committee; Clarkson Booth, editor of the works magazine and a Foreman based in the Visitors' Department, whose name was 'well remembered by many visitors as the name of the Firm' (*B.W.M.*, December 1913: 397); Harry Northway Bradbear (1882–1917), an in-house artist and draughtsman based in Cadbury's advertising department; Arthur Knapp (1881–1939), Cadbury's leading research chemist and a well-known scientific author; Walter Pedley Hunt (1874–1957), a foreman in the engineering department; Sophia Pumphrey (1866–1923), forewoman, professional artist and long-term chair of the Girls' Works Committee and Florence Mary Showell (1877–1961), a Birmingham Council school teacher turned factory forewoman, member of many of Bournville's entertainment committees and long-term Chair of the company's dramatic society.

By the mid-1920s, the first and second generations of staff appointed to senior roles at Bournville had been iconised as embodiments of the firm's Golden Age. Amidst the fulsome programme of activities that marked the factory's 1927 bi-centenary a series of articles – 'In the Beginning' – was published throughout the year in the works magazine. Much of the content was given over to staff profiles from these senior groups (including some from amongst the employees listed above), a focus that echoed the regular publication of sets of head and shoulder silhouettes of Bournville's managers in the works magazine. In this way Staffs A and B, Forewomen and Foremen, became key players in the creation of Bournville's image and of the community spirit that came to define it, both in-house and externally. Yet, histories of early twentieth-century Cadbury have been dominated by the family: the figures of George, Richard, George Jr (1878–1954), Edward, William (1867–1957), Louis Barrow and, to a lesser extent, Elizabeth (1858–1951) and Dorothy (1892–1987) Cadbury. Since Iola Williams's 1931 study relatively little attention has been paid to the influential group of female and male in-factory personalities who were positioned at the operational and reputational heart of the company at the time. Those women and men who ran the day-to-day operations and contributed heavily to commercial strategy. With no intention of belittling the Cadbury family's labour and management – their progressive thinking and practical action is a subject that has rightly been an object of study – the examples of performance considered over the following chapters increase the narratives through which Cadbury's history circulates, and dilute the image of Bournville as a site of paternalistic capitalism governed and delivered by a very small group of public-facing individuals, one that has to some extent obscured the carefully designed, multi-layered company management structure put in place as the firm expanded. Employees were the creators, performers, and promoters of both Cadbury's theatre and the Bournville cocoa and chocolate business, and it is with one such powerful image of a factory employee at work and at play that Chapter 2's exploration of theatre in the factory begins.

CHAPTER 2

Theatre in the Bournville Factory
Performance at Work

In 1938, Cadbury's in-house staff writers published *Bournville Personalities* – a book targeted at a wide public readership that celebrated the firm's model employees. The short (forty-seven page), heavily illustrated paper-back pamphlet was designed to act as an introduction to the factory, its staff, and the company's ethos, and offered an open invitation to the reader to join the '150,000 visitors who tour the village and factory every year' (Cadbury Bros: i). Most of the first page is taken up by a photograph of Cadbury's employees arriving for their working days. With the factory buildings as their backdrop, the figures of workers blur into a mass of forms. There is little to distinguish one employee from another. A small amount of text accompanies the image. It reads: 'every day nearly ten thousand people pour in and out of Bournville. Who are they? What do they do at work – and how do they spend their leisure time?' 'Turn over the page, step in and meet some of these 'interesting people with interesting jobs' (1). The following pages are filled with photographic montages and descriptions of individual workers at the factory that spotlight individuals from the anonymous collective presented in the opening image, a series of representative 'Bournville Personalities' at work and at play.

Four pages of *Bournville Personalities* are dedicated to the typist Daisy Smart (Figures 3 and 4: 32–35). The reader is told that Daisy is a relatively new factory employee, and one who has thrown herself into the opportunities for work and play offered by Cadbury's life. Six photographs of Daisy are collaged across the two, two-page spreads. One shows her playing tennis, in another she is taking part in a gym class, and one captures her learning to bake during her day-a-week lessons at the company-run Girls' Day Continuation School, where she also 'learns a lot about citizenship and economics'. The remaining three photographs are of Daisy doing her job. There is one close-up of her hands typing, one of her working in a factory typing room, and one of her searching through company files. Evenly balanced, the images are split between three of Daisy at work and

Figure 3 'Daisy Will Find It'
Bournville Personalities (1938). Cadbury Archives and Heritage Services.

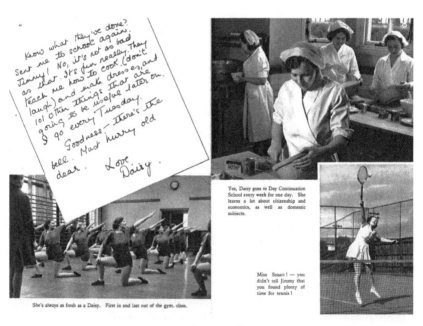

Figure 4 'Daisy Will Find It'
Bournville Personalities (1938). Cadbury Archives and Heritage Services.

three of Daisy at play. Printed alongside the photographs is a facsimile of a 'hand-written letter' from Daisy to Jimmy, in which she apologises for her recent silence, explaining that she is a 'busy young woman these days' (33). In addition to the activities captured in the photographs, the letter tells us she is also making time for the factory Dramatic Society.

Cadbury's employee records are comprehensive and – for the most part – extant. There is no trace of Daisy Smart working for the company in the archives, or through genealogical searches. Daisy was – this unusual absence of evidence suggests – a construct; a model female employee created by Cadbury's publicity team to embody and promote both the archetypal Bournville personality and model how participation in recreational activity was central to working at Cadbury's. The section's headline 'Daisy Will Find It' neatly entwined her professional skills (we are shown her locating those files) and her engagement with 'out-of-work' activities. This was an 'employee' equally adept at finding the information you needed and positive ways to fill her spare time: an ideal model that dates from three years after the end of the period covered in this study, and that had been created and nurtured by Cadbury's recreational agendas throughout the early twentieth century. On the pages of *Bournville Personalities*, Daisy performed Cadbury's values through the use and development of her healthy body and mind, signalling how recreational activity was routinely harnessed as publicity material by the firm. Guiding Quaker business principles forbade false or exaggerated marketing tactics, but imagery and evidenced claims that aligned cocoa and chocolate consumption with good health were acceptable and they had been at the core of the firm's sales strategies since the 1860s. Cocoa was widely recognised as a positive alternative to alcohol, and consumption of cocoa (and by extension the cocoa industry) had been linked with social reform and the temperance movement from the mid-nineteenth century (Fitzgerald, 2005; Surdam, 2020). More particular to Cadbury's was the image of product purity. Since the 1860s, the firm had prided themselves on the production of 'Cocoa Essence', a more expensive, non-blended cocoa powder made by pressing out a significant amount of the fat levels that made unprocessed cocoa mixture indigestible, rather than depending on the standard industry solution of adding cheap fillers, or additives, to absorb the excess fat (Bradley, 2008: 9–10). This state-of-the-art method imported from the continent required a new, costly cocoa press. To recoup the expenditure, the firm turned to a sustained marketing campaign that targeted medical professionals with samples of 'Cocoa Essence' and accompanying literature that detailed its purity. The resulting testimonials from doctors and health organisations proved to be key advertising for Cadbury's, and health, purity and wellbeing continued to sit at the core of the firm's marketing materials for many decades (12). Extending the moral, social reform, and health tenets of Cadbury's company identity to encompass employee welfare is increasingly evident in activities from the first decades of the twentieth century when a clear, overarching key message came to define both the firm, and the individual lines it produced – healthy, happy employees working in the fresh air with access to regular mental and physical exercise made for healthy, pure products. Pin-pointing these two areas – healthy products and healthy staff – as the fulcrum of their promotional activities evaded any risk of false claim or exaggeration, for both could be evidenced through quantitative and qualitative data. In this context, Bournville became a culture preoccupied with displaying its core values, rendering the staging of spectacle, narratives, and costumed bodies in factory-based theatrical activity as a site of potential and power. In this chapter, I consider a range of theatre and performance events that were staged in indoor factory spaces, and the ways in which these activities contributed to and promoted the model life of work and play captured by these advertising strategies and represented through the blueprint employee Daisy Smart.

Theatrical Performance Inside Cadbury's Chocolate Factory

As staff numbers increased and Bournville's theatrical activity gained momentum, indoor performance spaces were created across Cadbury's factory estate. Most were hidden within the buildings, off-limits to non-employees. Some were licensed and public. Over the first three decades of the twentieth-century, theatrical events with spectators took place in the earliest Girls' Dining Room, the Clerks' Dining Room which had a temporary stage installed, and the Men's Dining Room, which had a permanent 'elaborate' stage fixed at one end, as well as the Girls' Pavilion, the Girl's Baths, the Large Dining Room created as part of the 1920s factory development, and the Concert Hall (Williams: 181). Audience numbers accelerated at a greater speed than site development at various points during the period, and external spaces were used to supplement the firm's ability to stage entertainments and events, including the Assembly Rooms in the neighbouring districts of Edgbaston and Stirchley. In-factory productions took a surprising number of forms – from small-scale to large-scale productions, from silent tableaux to comic opera, from musical comedy to cabaret, from problem plays to farces and burlesques and from performances that staged Cadbury's brands to pantomime, avant-garde writing, and suffrage drama. As this range might suggest, the factory's performance spaces varied enormously in their scale, technical set-up, and backstage areas. Some were planned elements of major site expansions and re-developments, offering purpose-built spaces specifically designed to accommodate the factory's increasing number of theatrical events, and enabling a sophisticated level of theatrical production for large audiences that culminated in the 1,050 seat Concert Hall (opened in 1927). Others were found spaces within the estate that were temporarily re-appropriated for performance, presenting performers with challenges related to acoustics, space, lighting, and costume changes, and leaving traces of performance memories in the spaces when they were returned to their other, primary functions such as dining halls, small social spaces, or swimming baths.

The more of these performance spaces I discovered and explored, through the archives and in person in the cases where they still exist, the more I realised that performance was pervasive at Cadbury's Bournville – built into the industrial site, and central to the firm's carefully crafted company story and history. The spaces not only indicate that performance formed an important part of Bournville's recreational activities, but that it was considered within the firm's strategic planning, and heavily resourced. Examples of theatrical occasions, across a wide range of production scale, length, and cast and audience sizes indicate that this activity represented an innovative, responsive creation of performance models continually adapted for the communities and contexts they served. Fostered by Cadbury's recreational agenda, participation in, and spectatorship of performance were understood as pathways to wellbeing and productivity, key elements of the construction and sustention of industrial community, and strong promotional opportunities. Performances staged to mark events in Cadbury's business cycle, key anniversaries, or one-off significant developments formed a key part of this story, and it is with one such occasion – the firm's 1928 New Year Party – that this chapter continues (Figure 5).

Staff parties were central to Cadbury's factory community building and people management. Organised social occasions had been part of life at the firm since December 1866 at the Bridge Street Factory (CAHS/350/002610). The first of the Bournville events was a small New Year Gathering in 1879, followed by a series of annual celebrations with restricted guest lists made up of the company's senior management team, and their wives. Deliberately identified as 'gatherings', rather than parties, these teetotal, afternoon events offered Cadbury's senior staff an opportunity to mingle, network, and celebrate the year's business. Programmes from the last decade of the nineteenth century reveal a mixture of music, prayer, hymns,

PROGRAMME

p.m.
5.45 RECEPTION in the Girls' Dining Hall.
       Mr. & Mrs. WALTER BARROW.

6-15 LONG SERVICE
     PRESENTATIONS · · Concert Hall
       to be made by Mr. BARROW CADBURY.

MISS M. ASHMORE	T. B. BOTTOM
,, J. ELKINGTON	CARD BOX
,, A. HUSKISSON	FOREWOMAN "A"
,, F. C. ORTON	CARD BOX
,, A. WINTER	FOREWOMAN "A"
MR. H. FOWLER	MILK CHOC.
,, J. HORTON	INTRODUCER
,, J. JONES	RETIRED
,, C. KEAY	CASE SHOP
,, G. W. NEALE	WAREHOUSE
,, W. PERKINS	SHEET METAL
,, F. W. PICKARD	GENERAL OFFICE
,, W. PLUMB	STAFF "B"
,, A. H. WHEATLEY	DEPART'L MANAGER
,, J. WHEATLEY	FOREMAN "B"
,, J. WILKINS	MOULDING 4

6-30 CHAIRMAN'S ADDRESS

7-0 REFRESHMENTS
       will be served in the Terrace Restaurant.
       Musical Selections on the "Panatrope."

p.m.
8-0   ENTERTAINMENT
       in the Concert Hall.

1. OPENING CHORUS
       By Members of the Operatic Society.

2. SORCERY

3.   "VISIONS"
       A REVELATION IN 3 PEEPS

Monte Limart (of the B.Y.C.)
Theo. Broms (of the B.G.A.C.)
Puck   Bunny
Elsie   Betty
Sylvia   Foreman "A"
A Lady   A Gentleman
A Traveller   A Transport Man
A Trolley Man   A Typist
       A Factory Worker
Fairies   Pages   Gnomes
       Scene: Vague
       Time: Various
Written by Mr. W. E. Cossons.
Dances arr. by Miss A. Forbes.

4. CLOSING CHORUS
       By Members of the Operatic Society.

5. DANCING IN THE EAST DINING ROOM
                                (See over)

Figure 5 Programme for the 1928 New Year Party at Bournville
Cadbury Archives and Heritage Services.

and speeches. The words were included, indicating that participation in songs and hymns was encouraged. 1897 marked the first instance of wider entertainment, including a dramatic sketch and cinematograph exhibition (CAHS/350/002164). Later Bournville new year party activity built on these foundations of small-scale, religiously framed meetings and developed a format that remained stable for just over two decades. Lengthy speeches by Board representatives (often a member of the Cadbury family) were followed by tea, cake, and a short entertainment programme of music and song. Religious content was a common feature; hymns and prayers scaffolded the afternoon's activities, reflecting the ongoing importance of the firm's Quaker-guided practices in the increasingly secularised, wider industrial world. As the twentieth century arrived, and the scale of the Bournville factory and workforce rapidly grew, the format of Cadbury's company parties was adapted – guest lists were increased, a greater range of entertainments were offered, and the occasions became increasingly important to the company's organisational structure and operation. Even while the New Year parties remained relatively exclusive occasions, with a guest list restricted to Cadbury's senior management team, local community leaders and employees who were receiving long service awards, Committee of Management minutes make it clear that capacity was becoming an issue.

On one occasion, invitations issued to the group of managers identified as Staff B – the second tier of forewomen and foremen who oversaw the factory, employee welfare, and recreational provision – had to be retracted, as it transpired that the space was simply too small to accommodate them (CAHS/CMM/7 and 14 November 1911: 858; 868).

An invitation to the New Year Party was presented as a perk of the job, or one that rewarded staff loyalty. By the 1920s, Bournville's annual celebration continued to follow the, by now, well-established format outlined above, minus the religious content. The party started with an early evening reception, followed by a lengthy speech delivered by one of the firm's directors that detailed the previous year's business performance, recalled the highlights of Bournville's out-of-work activities during the same period, and concluded with a short film or a series of magic lantern slides. This was followed by refreshments, prize-givings, entertainments, and dancing. Records of the factory's parties signal that the entertainments they included were an anticipated and important part of the annual occasions for organisers and guests. 1928's New Year Party guests were offered three different styles of performance, in a four-act entertainment programme (See Figure 5. Programme/ CAHS/353/001919). Songs were performed by the work's Operatic Society. 'Sorcery', a magic act, was performed by William Gollings (1905–1962), who had begun his career at Cadbury's in the men's wages office in 1920 but was better known throughout the factory community for his legerdemain, or sleight of hand tricks. Magic was a popular entertainment form at Bournville, and Gollings's skills were regularly drawn on. As a small-scale and low-resource performance form, magic was a practical choice of entertainment for the factory, suited to its full range of performance spaces. It simultaneously displayed carefully studied learnt skill and reflected the interests in education, science, and spectacle that characterised Bournville's recreational activities. The firm had a number of employees who mastered the art of conjuring in their spare time, and performed at the factory's events.

The final part of 1928's entertainment was *Visions*, a three-act burlesque written by leading dramatic society member William Ernest Cossons (1890–1972). This was a familiar form for its audience, with the works magazine reviewer noting that it was a 'skit', 'as we have come to call them' at Bournville (*B.W.M.*, March 1928: 72). The format clearly held no surprises. It was house style. Cossons was an in-house journalist, editor of the *Bournville Works Magazine*, and manager of Cadbury's publications department. Promoting the firm was his day-to-day business and it is likely he was the author, or one of the authors behind *Bournville Personalities*. Together with his position as a leading member of Bournville Dramatic

Society, who had performed, written, and produced for the group since the early twenties, Cossons's skills, knowledge, professional expertise, and close familiarity with the firm's public image located him as a very 'on message' writer for this skit – one who knew exactly what he was doing when he created *Visions*' themes, form, characters, and settings.

Visions

Visions was a short play constructed from a series of staged dream sequences. The cast list published in the programme tells us there were twelve identified character parts, supplemented by groups of pages, fairies, and gnomes. The action flits between time periods. The two lead roles – Monte Limart, a member of the Bournville Youth Club and Theo. Broma, a member of the Bournville Girls' Athletics Club – were played by Arthur Whittaker (1889–1969) and Hilda Greaves (1904–1989). Like Cossons, both were well-known Bournville performers, and leading members of the firm's dramatic society. Hilda Greaves had joined Cadbury's in December 1920, taken on to join the chocolate boxing team at what was the firm's busiest time of the industrial year. By 1923, she had moved to clerical and typing work in the firm's office, and she remained at Bournville until 1937, when she married. Arthur Whittaker was appointed to head up Cadbury's newly established legal department in 1923. A qualified solicitor, he stayed at Bournville for the remainder of his professional career, directing the firm's pension schemes, becoming an expert in commercial law, and serving as a member of external professional organisation senior committees. In 1948, he became Managing Director of Cadbury's. A lengthy retirement notice published in the works magazine noted Whittaker's 'long and happy association with the Bournville stage' that dated from shortly after his arrival at the factory. But he was also an all-rounder, he would undoubtedly be remembered as an 'actor', the article reported, but also as a 'soldier and a cricketer' (October 1959: 7). Four and a half years into his long career at Cadbury, Whittaker already embodied company values and – in *Visions* – alongside Hilda Greaves, he played them out. Onstage in *Visions* Whittaker and Greaves embodied Cadbury's recreational agendas, both as themselves onstage as society performers, and as the characters they played with their connections to the Youth Club and the Girls' Athletic Club. The employees who played these roles, and their reputations and factory statuses, were significant, particularly in a play about the Bournville world that was being staged at an event held to celebrate the firm, their employees, and commercial success.

Visions opened with a scene in which Monte/Arthur Whittaker and Theodora/Hilda Greaves went on a walking trip in Somerset, a staging of the style of day trip and activity that was sanctioned, organised, and financially supported as part of Cadbury's recreational schemes. After a long walk, the two reached Cadbury Camp, an iron age fort in Somerset, located amidst the Cadbury family's ancestral landscape. Tired out from their healthy, outdoor exercise, Monte and Theodora sat down with their backs against the ancient earthwork and fell asleep. As they slumbered onstage, a group of fairies and gnomes entered, danced around, and cast a transportation spell over the pair that saw them wake up in the pre-historic period. In this conjured 'pre-time' the two performing representatives of Cadbury's current industrial model encountered ancient members of the Cadbury family who, in this pre-historical world were – of course – already mastering the art of producing cocoa. For partygoers, this theme would have echoed part of the lengthy lecture given earlier in the evening by Walter Barrow (1867–1954), one of the firm's directors. Having talked about the worlds of work and play at Bournville, Barrow used the final section of his speech to deliver a short, magic-lantern slide illustrated lecture on the origins of the Cadbury name and the family's historic connections with Somerset. Whether the reappearance of this theme in *Visions* was happenstance or carefully planned, it signals the importance of Cadbury's his-story telling to Bournville as a place, and to the company's identity (a theme that will feature in greater detail in the following chapter). The works magazine also regularly carried features on local and Cadbury family histories, geographies, geologies, and places. Cossons was tapping into a network of ideas in *Visions,* many of which (as editor of the firm's key publication) he directly created and controlled.

Swift on the heels of the ancestral Cadburys, the second act of *Visions* saw the arrival of a new character – the 'Bunnyorus' – a hybrid creature formed from the advertising device the Bournville Bunny (an image that remains familiar from today's Cadbury's marketing) and a dragon. Bunnyorus was accompanied by a young girl, 'Elsie', played by Nettie (Elsie) Waters (1906–?). After this eclectic scene, Puck arrived – fresh from William Shakespeare's *A Midsummer Night's Dream* – and cast a final spell that returned the two lead characters to the 'present' day. Tantalisingly no image of the *Visions* bunny-dragon character remains in the Cadbury's archives, but Elsie and the Bunny were core elements of Cadbury's 1920s advertising schemes and would have been very familiar to both in-house and external audience members. More recently resuscitated as the Cadbury Caramel Bunny, this earlier version of the Bournville Bunny channelled and fused the white rabbit from Alice in Wonderland and Beatrix Potter's Peter Rabbit with the firm's company values and image. He was friends with Elsie – a young girl enthralled by the wonders of Bournville who was well known from the pages of five promotional illustrated children's books published by Cadbury's – *A Visit to Bournville* (1911), *A Visit to Sunny Cocoa Land* (1913), *Bournville Bunny* (1913), *Elsie and the Bunny* (1924) and *Another Adventure of Elsie and the Bunny* (1926) – and also from an eight-minute-long advertising film – *Elsie and the Brown Bunny* (The London Press Exchange Ltd) – commissioned by the firm in 1921 to showcase both their factory site and their careful treatment of their workforce. The children's books were full colour and contained an illustration on each page, with a painting book also produced. The first showed Elsie being taken around the factory. Eight of the pages were perforated and printed with two copies of each picture that could be used as postcards, one was coloured, and one was left to be coloured in by the book's owner. The fold-out, centre spread was four pages in size and depicted a full view of the factory estate. This was Beatrix Potter style pastoral vision that meets creative promotional literature, slightly revised and reissued as *Bournville Bunny* and *Elsie and the Bunny*.

1926's *Another Adventure of Elsie and the Bunny* was a sequel that saw the bunny show Elsie all the improvements to the factory that had taken place since her last visit – the message was clear; Cadbury's did not stand still. Like *Visions,* the silent, advertising film *Elsie and the Brown Bunny* was framed by a dream narrative. It opens with a shot of Elsie reading outside while eating her way through a chocolate selection box. She notices a rabbit and, the intertitle tells us, wishes that he were like the white rabbit in the copy of *Alice in Wonderland* she is holding. She then drifts off to sleep and, in a moment of surreal film trickery, becomes two Elsies: one left curled up on the ground, while the other rises, wraith-like, from her body and runs off to find the bunny – who is now giant sized, and waiting close by, eager for adventure. The bunny introduces himself as a creature from Bournville, and Elsie asks if they can go and see the factory. They hop onto a Bournville-liveried steam train, driven by the bunny, and head to the site's station. When they arrive, Elsie is taken on a tour of the factory by a white-overalled woman employee, then reunited with the bunny and shown the Men's Recreation Ground, a section that includes relatively lengthy shots of the cricket and tennis matches that are taking place. Their final factory destination is the Girls' Recreation Ground, where Elsie and the bunny join in with the girls' rhythmic gymnastics drill class happening on the plant-covered pergola. The Bunnyorus fused this established industrial-pastoral imagery with a prehistorical/mythical creature, staging another facet of Cadbury's use of a fictionalised past to create a company story that underpinned its innovative, modern activity, and permeated the factory's theatre.

In the final scene of *Visions* Theo and Monte returned to the present day and encountered the 'realest' of commercial travellers, Gordon Bennett (1894–1960). James Gordon Bennett was a Cadbury's employee who took on a brief cameo role in the entertainment. Having started at the firm in 1911 as a chocolate moulder, he progressed to become one of their leading commercial travellers and sales personnel and was also a recognised factory actor, member of the dramatic society, and prizewinner at the 1921 duologue competition organised by the group. Onstage, Bennett (as Bennett) brought samples of current chocolate products – the working materials of his trade – to show to Theo and Monte. All were assortment boxes drawn from the firm's high end, fancy chocolate selection lines. As Bennett demonstrated his wares, tableaux vivants brought them to life, staging the marketing campaigns designed for the three sample products he had selected – the Sylvia, the Esmond, and the Mayfair. The tableaux backgrounds were designed and painted by Frederick Broome (1886–1963), a fellow Cadbury's commercial traveller who had started his working life in professional craftsmanship, as a jewellery maker. Images of the 'Sylvia' living picture give a clear sense of the attention to detail and to the creation of illusion that Broome crafted for the entertainment (Figure 6). Starting as a frozen image, Sylvia – played by Peggy (Margaret) Thompson (1905–1979), a member of the firm's record office staff, then stepped out of her painted backdrop frame to perform a fairy dance, before returning to take her place in the chocolate box facsimile.

Following 'Sylvia', an eighteenth-century-costumed lady and gentleman familiar from the Esmond assortment marketing campaign appeared against a backdrop reminiscent of the central Birmingham streets where the firm's first Quaker-district cocoa house was located, before coming to life and dancing gracefully to a minuet (Figure 7). Both 'Sylvia' and 'Esmond' were choreographed by Amy Forbes (1889–1941), an on-staff gymnastics instructor at Bournville who regularly produced dances for the factory's entertainments. A third, and final, tableau followed, inspired by a recent advertising scheme for the Mayfair chocolate box – 'Taking Mayfair to Betty'. Cadbury's commercial artist Olive Goulding (1908–1987) played Betty, dressed in contemporary fashion, flanked by six page-boys in eighteenth-century-inspired dress, there to supply her with her chocolate fix. The Mayfair press campaign was extensive and ongoing, focusing on the fashionable luxury of the chocolate selection and the pleasure

Figure 6 'Sylvia Chocolates', *tableau vivant*
Bournville Works Magazine, March 1928

Figure 7 'Esmond Assorted', *tableau vivant*
Bournville Works Magazine, March 1928. Cadbury Archives and Heritage Services.

of the product. One enamel sign set of advertisements captures the line. Headlined 'In Mayfairing Mood', the promotional text reads:

> The modern world loves chocolate but it never yet found chocolate so much to its liking [...] And that is why the holidaying crowd is Mayfairing – taking Mayfair chocolates into the partnership of all its holiday joys. (CAHS)

The text on the range of signs and press advertisements was accompanied by a range of black and white and coloured line drawings, which Olive Goulding herself might well have helped to design. References to seaside holidays and evenings of saxophone music, coupled with the 'jazzy' primary coloured design scheme of the Art Deco influenced box brought work and play to a new generation – the bright young things of the roaring twenties. Current fashionable cultural connections between the product and wider entertainment and leisure trends were further extended by the product's association with *Betty in Mayfair,* a long-running popular stage musical that opened at the Adelphi Theatre, London in November 1925, transferred to the Shaftesbury Theatre, and closed in April 1926, with a Pathé film produced mid-run further increasing its familiarity. The concept of the pleasure of leisure embedded in the Mayfair line was aligned with the ethos of work and play staged through the tableaux, albeit in a more reserved Cadbury's fashion at Bournville.

As with the 'Orinoco Assorted' tableau from the 1914 summer works party, with which this book opened, the employees who made Cadbury's products, designed the company's key images, and ensured the day-to-day running of the Bournville operation and its recreational provision, used their bodies to recreate the company's products and visual culture. Professional and amateur artistry and crafts intersected. Seamlessly. Together 'Sylvia', 'Esmond' and 'Taking Mayfair to Betty' brought together Bournville's production, administration, marketing, art, recreational, and legal departments to materialise the firm's products and values. Their bodies – essential parts of the process of the production of Cadbury's cocoa and chocolate lines – re-played and re-staged their working identities in spaces connected with recreation and play – frozen so their visual meaning could sink in and resonate. Within this industrial micro-culture of performance, the repeated presence of tableaux vivants within other entertainments – including *Visions* – was a well-informed and carefully made choice, one that speaks to the form's connection with Cadbury's. As a familiar leitmotif, the visual culture they created interlocked with advertising and recreation and actively co-produced

Bournville's identity as a real and romanticised space for both internal and external viewers. Watching performers spectators *knew* create and perform these frozen pictures increased their pleasure and power. Alison Griffiths has suggested that a key dynamic of the tableau vivant is the way in which it 'play[s] on [the] spectator['s] foreknowledge of a represented scene' (2002: 18). In the case of the *Visions* tableaux this referred to both people and product – the use of advertising images adding further overlapping layers of familiarity, knowledge, and recognition. *Visions*'s content fused current and past Cadbury's performances and advertising imagery with current local/factory celebrities playing key roles and the factory site to produce a style of his-story-telling that echoed and built on other visions of the North Birmingham landscape that were conjured and commissioned by Cadbury's. The next section of the chapter explores the crafting of these narratives through other indoor performances at the Bournville site and the ways in which the provision of space for performance underpinned and demonstrated its significance to the firm's operations and identity.

The Cadbury Concert Hall

Visions was staged in Cadbury's new flagship factory space – a purpose-built company Concert Hall, located within the firm's huge new, four-storey dining block that had opened in March 1927. Production efficiencies required by the challenging post-war economic landscape resulted in the demolition of several of the Bournville site's earlier Victorian factory buildings during the 1920s, and the construction of new spaces capable of accommodating the machinery needed to produce cocoa and chocolate on a mass scale. Alongside these developments came improved facilities for staff. Catering for up to 6,000 staff a day, the new dining block offered a range of services that far exceeded eating, including dental surgeries, a library, reading room, club rooms, and lecture room. The Concert Hall was fully licensed for song, dance, music, and cinematograph, and with a capacity of 1,050, an under-stage scenery store, good lighting technology, dressing rooms and an orchestra pit it marked a step change in theatrical production and entertainment at Cadbury's (Opening Week Programme, CAHS/353/001919; *Birmingham Daily Gazette,* 21 December 1926: 9). The Concert Hall – and the building as a whole – were held up as a beacon of company pride: a symbol of Cadbury's continuing industrial success, and a signal of the firm's ongoing commitment to its employees despite the economic challenges of recent years. Used repeatedly in advertising materials

Figure 8 'The Cadbury Concert Hall'
Bournville Works Magazine, April 1927. Cadbury Archives and Heritage Services.

of the 1920s and 1930s, the new dining block remains the most iconic of the Bournville site's buildings (Figure 8).

As noted above, the narratives that framed the *Visions* skit would have been familiar to the party audience in many ways. They had been at the heart of the pageants and outdoor theatre of the summer works parties (covered in the next two chapters) that had peaked a decade and a half earlier and become a key source of living cultural memories at the firm. More recently they had been invoked at the celebrations to mark the opening of the firm's new Concert Hall, and by default the opening of the new dining hall block, in March 1927. On the first evening of a full week-long programme of entertainments, the acclaimed Bournville research chemist Arthur Knapp (1881–1939) stood on the Concert Hall stage, in front of a full house. Costumed as Father Time, he reflected on the many wonders he had witnessed to date at Bournville. Telling and authorising his story through the familiar dramatic rhythm of Iambic Pentameter, Father Time/Knapp recalled the Pyramids of Egypt, the story-telling of Homer, the falls of Carthage, Rome and Spain, and the theatre of Shakespeare, before the kindly patriarch concluded that, looking back on all these 'spacious days of old':

> No greater marvel did I e'er behold
> Than this – / to find within a Factory's scope
> A stage so set that critics cannot hope
> To find a fault. / From now magnificent
> Will be your Drama / and more excellent
> Your Music!

And – as for those who had built this 'Welfare House of Dreams' in which they had all gathered tonight – *they*, he promised, would be remembered for all eternity (*B.W.M.*, April 1927: 99). Knapp was in his mid-forties in 1927, and a renowned, respected chemist both within the firm and in wider national and international professional networks. He was also a veteran of industrial communities; an early career move had seen him working in the Lever Bros research laboratory at Port Sunlight. Obituaries published on his death, just twelve years after the opening of the concert hall, note that he served as chairman of the Birmingham and Midlands section of the Society of Chemical Industry, and on the councils of the British Association of Chemists and the Institute of Chemistry (*Birmingham Daily Gazette*, 12 January 1939: 5; *Bournville Works Magazine*, February 1939: 1). Knapp was also the author of numerous articles and his most well-known work, *Cocoa and Chocolate: Their History from Plantation to Consumer* (1920), a playwright whose works were staged by Bournville Dramatic Society, and former Chair of the factory's theatrical group. To mark his early death, the works magazine carried a full-page obituary and photograph, in addition to a lengthy published eulogy written by his close friend, co-worker and fellow playwright Thomas Badger Rogers (1875–1956), of whom we will learn more later. As with Hilda Greaves and Arthur Whittaker, *who* played Father Time at the opening of the new concert hall mattered. Professional identity and fictional character were fused and performed simultaneously in this Welfare House of Dreams where work was play, and play was work.

The Concert Hall was an interesting development in the provision of entertainment spaces on Cadbury's Bournville estate. It was located on the ground floor of the building, with its own separate external access opening out on to Bournville Lane, the site's main business and public thoroughfare, close to the Girls' Baths and the Directors' offices. Management of the space was handed to George Margetts (1876–1967) a long-serving clerk at the firm who had previously served as committee secretary for the firm's largest entertainments, the summer parties. While it was primarily used for in-house Cadbury's events, the space was also hired out to local organisations from early on its history, including local amateur theatrical societies, and for charity fundraising performances. The front-facing entrance secured this function, but it was not just a functional entrance, it was imposing and celebratory – an advertisement of this new provision and space. Records of an early licence application hearing indicate the recognised commercial potential of the space. Emphasising that the venue was 'primarily intended to be used for educational and industrial meetings of the workers' and recreational society productions', it was noted that the hall had a very public face and that the firm's plans had prompted considerable concern and a formal objection from the local cinematograph exhibitors' association that was only withdrawn when it was officially stated that there was no intention to run regular film screenings (*Birmingham Daily Gazette*, 21 December 1926: 9).

Investing in the Concert Hall marked the firm's support of factory performance, indicating the warm reception of factory entertainments, and registering and addressing the need to improve the facilities available for them. The dining block and concert hall build had been significantly delayed. Initially proposed and taken to planning stage in early 1914, the outbreak of war, its economic impact and the changes in production these necessitated had resulted in the project being put on hold. As an interim measure the firm had constructed an alternative building – the New Dining Hall – to serve employees' immediate catering and recreational needs, a space promoted as 'the latest evidence of the Firm's regard for their workers' wellbeing' (*B.W.M.*, May 1922: 115). The New Dining Hall offered seating for 500 staff as diners, or audience members, and a stage, dressing, and cloak rooms, storage for costumes and props and a wooden dance floor. Designed to be multifunctional, for the following five years the space hosted most of Cadbury's recreational occasions and company events, including dances, plays, operas, and 'even a poultry show' (115). Despite the intentions behind the provision of this new, improved entertainment space, the result presented significant challenges for performers. The hall was reminiscent of a village, or school, hall. Some sense of the space, and its challenges, are captured by the view from the stage seen in Figure 9. Framed by a long, relatively low-height proscenium arch, doors and curtains, the fifteen feet deep stage (twenty-three with the apron) offered foot, head, and side lights. The firm's performers found it 'very practical though small' with 'simple but effective' lighting equipment (Cossons, 1933: 10). While the size of the stage, its backstage provision and storage were – as the works magazine rightly celebrated – of a 'design not possessed by many theatres, and certainly by few amateur organisations', the shared nature of the space came with concessions (115). There were clear limitations. Some were caused by the 'long slit of a proscenium opening

Figure 9   'The Hall, from the Stage' in the New Dining Hall
Bournville Works Magazine, May 1922. Cadbury Archives and Heritage Services.

and an audience below the actors' feet' (*B.W.M.*, December 1923: 476). The walls were half-tiled and the roof half-glazed – both acoustics and light control would have been an issue. The wooden dance floor that covered the main body of the hall would have been noisy underfoot, and the innovative, fan-based air conditioning system that changed the air in the hall four times an hour may have increased comfort levels, but it came at the cost of more background noise.

Despite these challenges, the Dining Hall offered space for performance and was given over entirely to factory societies for their use outside of work hours, providing they adhered to a clear set of expectations and spirit of quid pro quo. We 'are sure the Societies [...] will continue to produce such work as shall justify the Firm's faith in their ability to make worthy use of the magnificent facilities afforded' noted the works magazine, reminding users of the 'deal' – the unwritten recreational contract – that lay behind this offer (117). Cadbury's recognition that factory groups had been 'looking round for spaces to try their wings for stronger flights' for several years, while demonstrating in advance that 'work can be done worthy of the splendid facilities', framed a clear expectation that such performances would continue, and further improve (115). Further discussion of productions staged in the new dining room by the firm's dramatic society will follow later in this book, what is important to note here is that the entertainments staged in the Dining Hall must have met these standards, further affirmed the value of such performances to the firm, and played a key part in their decision to invest in the Concert Hall – which opened just five years later, and offered a bespoke performance space entirely focused on the stage and auditorium.

The significance of the 1927 Concert Hall to Cadbury's is clearly signalled by the week-long opening celebrations that Knapp had opened with his Father Time speech, a series of six evening events that were programmed by a small committee of individuals representing the factory societies involved. The six-page article dedicated to the opening festivities in April's works magazine suggests that attendance was high. 'Audiences throughout the week were very large', the author noted, 'on two or three occasions late comers were unable to get in'. Amongst these spectators were Company Directors, their families, and a group of representatives from Fry's at Bristol (101). Looking at reports of sell-out evenings and detailed accounts of the people involved in the performances on stage it seems likely that somewhere between 6,000 and 7,500 people engaged with the opening week of events – as either participants or spectators, or as both. The programme offered a mixture of music, theatre, and dance throughout the week. The opening night was the domain of Bournville Dramatic Society who presented a triple bill of previously staged, one-act plays – *The Locked Chest*, by John Masefield (1916), the Scottish historical drama *Campbell of Kilmhor* (1915) by clergyman playwright John Alexander Ferguson, and *High Tea* a maritime comedy (first production traced, 1914), by navy captain Hugh Edward Holme. Each short play was fully produced, with sets and costumes. 'It would have been nice to have some new work', noted the reviewer, but the late-running of the building project made such ambitions impossible. There had been no rehearsal in the space at all, with builders working up to the wire on the interior décor and technologies. 'Behind the scenes' we learn from the works magazine 'the work was at times strenuous' (101). A revival of previously successfully staged work was the only safe option under these conditions, and it did enable the showcasing of the theatrical potential of the new space – images show large sets and costumes, and accounts record musical accompaniment. We can safely assume that lighting was also a part of the spectacle – for, although it is hard to see this in any visual evidence, lighting technologies were a significant part of the hall's design, and had they been missing on the evening it is likely that their absence would have been noted. Arguably, the outcome of the return to these three short plays was a more collective repertoire for the firm's dramatic society, enabling more individuals to participate in a significant event designed to showcase the firm's recreational provision and the ethos of work and play that drove Cadbury's and had prompted the creation of the concert hall space.

The opening week programme's entry for Bournville Youth Club's performance on Monday makes no mention of a theatrical performance, but other reports make it clear that it did include one – Lord Dunsany's *The Gods of the Mountain* (1911). First staged at the Haymarket Theatre, London, Dunsany's short play had become popular fare for charity and society groups. Like *Visions* the play's plot was grounded in mythical worlds of gods and fairies. On this occasion, the production was praised for the aesthetic spectacle it presented, the result of the costumes created by the factory's design office. Thursday night's variety-based entertainment included two dance performances. The Bournville Centre of the English Folk Dance Society transported the audience 'back through the centuries to the Merrie England of village green and maypole', while a ballet performed to Grieg's *Peer Gynt* suite by Bournville Girls' Athletics Club – written by Amy Forbes (the member of the firm's gymnastics staff who had choreographed the tableaux vivants for 1928's New Year Party) – showcased a series of solo and ensemble dances in rustic settings on a central theme of fairy lovers. Considered individually, the acts contained in the opening week of performances showcased the concert hall's versatility and technologies. Acoustics were demonstrated through performances of community singing from the Youth Club, the soloists accompanied by Bournville's orchestra, and the works Choral Society. The generous stage dimensions were made clear in the group choreographies of the Folk-Dance Society's offering, and the sets and stage-spectacles of the theatrical productions. Further technologies – including the screenings of films and projection of images from the works Camera Club – were exhibited as part of every evening's entertainment. Together they presented a discrete mini-repertoire that invoked another version of Bournville's modern industrial world.

The content of each page of the concert hall's opening week souvenir programme is framed by selected theatrical quotes, with the vast majority taken from William Shakespeare's plays despite none of his works appearing in the entertainments (CAHS/353/001919). These quotes function in a meta-theatrical way, aligning the firm's performance activities with the canonically affirmed figure of Shakespeare. Page two of the programme presents the Dining Room Block's multiple spaces in extensive detail, emphasising the welfare provision the build represented for the firm, and offering a separate section on the Concert Hall. At the top of the page the quote, 'A Hall! A Hall! Give room' from *Romeo and Juliet* is printed; at the bottom, 'Here is a marvellous convenient place for our rehearsal' from *A Midsummer Night's Dream*. Through the positioning of these two quotes on this page, Cadbury's presents itself as responding to Shakespeare's call for space and for performance, and by extension the wider national and international debates around education, betterment, leisure, and theatre that shaped the firm's recreation and welfare schemes. In an opening week that offered music, opera, dance, gymnastics, and film, the 'staging' of the factory in this programme is acknowledged and foregrounded within a set of conditions recognised as theatrical. Other pages use 'The actors are come hither, My Lord' from *Hamlet*, and 'our revels are now ended. These our actors … are melted into air' from *The Tempest*. The actresses and actors who appeared on stage cemented this connection. Casts were dominated by Bournville personalities who had formalised the provision of drama at Bournville through their active involvement in setting up the first dramatic society in 1912, including Walter Pedley Hunt, Lottie Allen, and Arthur Whittaker (*Visions* lead character Monte), all of whom will feature again in performances explored across the following pages.

As the use of the Concert Hall became more commonplace, the challenges that the large-tiered, galleried space presented for Bournville's performers became more evident – or perhaps better documented. Reviews carried out by the works magazine include repeated comments about the inaudibility of the dramatic society performers cast in the early society seasons staged in the hall. Clifford Coope's (1898–1979) performance as the kidnapper in A. A. Milne's 1921 play *Dover Road* was praised, but it was noted that 'a little more attention to audibility in the first act' would have 'made it better still'. Hugh Weeks' (1904–1992) appearance in Luigi Pirandello's *Naked* (1922) was judged to be 'not so good as he was in *Joy*', at least in part because 'I found it difficult to catch his words' (January 1928: 24; 25). Weeks had been in post at Cadbury's as the firm's statistical and research manager for two years, and it is interesting to note that both he and Coope were well-known figures on the public lecture circuit: Weeks was a respected specialist in market research for industry, and Coope a leader in thinking around advertising and marketing (*Birmingham Daily Post*, 20 October 1939: 8). This other facet of their careers and professional identities has relevance both to their lack of audibility on the Concert Hall stage, despite their public speaking experience, and to the different ways in which they represented Cadbury's in the public arena. While voice projection had been identified as an issue in some performances staged before the move to this larger space, reported problems with hearing actors had been far less frequent and less consistent across cast members. In the Concert Hall, it was those that could be clearly heard who were identified as the exception. Secretary Alice Clara Hudson's (1904–1962) performance alongside Coope in *Dover Road* was warmly received, primarily for her acting being 'always so delightfully audible', the emphasis on this quality identifying the challenges that were faced by other cast members, and those who tried to hear them (24). Alice Hudson was a familiar face for Bournville's late-1920s audiences. She had been cast in the production of *Campbell of Kilmhor* during the concert hall's opening week, performing alongside many of the firm's most established and experienced stage performers, and she also played Puck in *Visions*. Professional speaker or amateur performer, there was no guarantee of sufficient voice projection from cast members, and the human-ness and differences pinpointed in these reviews serve as an important reminder of the complexity of this theatrical history and signal the risks of assumptions grounded in divisions between amateur and professional in work-based, factory theatre.

Cadbury's flagship Concert Hall was well used in the ten-month period between the opening week celebrations and the staging of *Visions* at 1928's New Year Party. Just two and a half weeks before Cossons's skit re-envisioned Cadbury's history and staged a clear vision of its present, the hall had housed a two-night run of Bournville Dramatic Society's production of Stephen Storace and Prince Hoare's late eighteenth-century romantic comic opera *No Song, No Supper!* (1790), preceded by a very current comic curtain raiser by the Manchester School playwright Harold Brighouse, *The Little Liberty* (1927). Reports from this performance suggest that factory performers were getting used to the space, its scale, acoustics, and large audience in stalls and balconies. Photographs from the performance show a large orchestra in the pit, indicating the increasing significance of musical accompaniment to factory productions – a factor that may have influenced the programming of the operetta, and resulted in the creation of a Dramatic Society Orchestra whose sole function was to support stage productions at the firm. Nonetheless, the ongoing challenges of the new space can help us to contextualise and understand why 1928's New Year Party entertainments – including *Visions* – were recorded as being notably 'simpler in form than that of previous' years (*B.W.M.*, March 1928: 71). The small-scale performances and plays may have been simpler, but they were no less significant. *Visions*'s staging of the outside – and its associations with fresh air, health, leisure, and fairy-tale or folklore – in Bournville's new, indoor Concert Hall space was a powerful moment of industrial performance, one in which Cadbury's showcased investment in their employees to their employees, and to the outside world, affirming the location of industrial theatre as both part of the factory's recreational and educational provision and a key means of publicising them. The pictorial narrative Cossons's skit offered re-told a very familiar visual story. That vague setting referenced at the opening of the piece was anything but vague, it was a projection of Bournville – a sophisticated construction crafted at least in part by the performances of Cadbury's employees, staged in a new space purpose built to support it.

Performing at the Pool: Entertaining at the Girls' Swimming Baths

Despite the challenges and the limitations that they presented for performers and audiences, the New Dining Hall and the Concert Hall were both specifically designed and created as performance spaces within the factory. Many other Cadbury's productions were staged in spaces that were not designed for performance, and in some cases were designed for entirely different and distinct purposes. In this next section we return to Christmas celebrations at the firm but, in this case, to entertainments produced in a high-profile, found space on the Bournville estate – the Girls' Swimming Baths. Drained of its water, and with the ramped floor of the pool used for seating, the narrow strip of poolside at the end of the baths was used to stage entertainments at staff occasions between 1905 and 1908.

The Girls' Baths (constructed 1904–1905) might seem an unlikely performance space. Built by William Alexander Harvey (1874–1951), the same architect who had led the development of Bournville Village, the facility housed an eighty by forty feet swimming pool (the same size as a standard twenty-five-metre pool today), showers, slipper baths for bathing and health, and hair dryers (Williams, 1931 185). Supplementing the outdoor pool used by male employees, the new baths increased the numbers of Cadbury's workers who were taught to swim by the firm, with lessons made available during works time, and compulsory for boys and girls when they began work at the factory (186). Theatrical entertainments staged at the baths were not the only occasions when swimming and entertainment were brought together as spectacle. The pool was regularly used to stage competitions which were open to the public, for an admission cost, and the firm's commitment to swimming was regularly showcased at factory events, with displays of swimming, water gymnastics, and life-saving – often framed by narrative sketches – forming popular features at parties and other occasions when large numbers of visitors were hosted at Bournville. Like the later Concert Hall, the baths had a prime location on the factory estate, sitting on Bournville Lane next to the Directors' Offices, and a separate public entrance. Productions at the drained baths saw the firm's recreational focus on sports and leisure come together in one place in a statement building for the firm and drew attention to its cutting-edge leisure and health provision.

With the water drained away (or occasionally covered by boards, both methods were used to create a performance space) and the interior draped in colourful fabrics and decorated with ferns, palms and evergreens, the baths made a spacious venue (*B.W.M.*, February 1906: 108). Photographs of the pool reconfigured for performance indicate a capacity of around 750, more seating than any other space on site at the time could offer. Thanks to Mondalez's estate manager I gained access to the Girls' Baths, now mothballed, and rich in large spiders! The site visit helped me understand the practicalities of staging party entertainments at the bath more clearly. It was immediately clear that the performance space offered by the end of the baths was very shallow. While audiences were large, space for their entertainers was very restricted. The stage depth in the area behind the two 'picture framed' performance spaces captured in Figure 10 was just under six feet. Getting performers on and off this long, thin stage would have presented a challenge: pieces with entrances and exits would have been at best inadvisable, at worse risky. In front, a wooden platform was built out over the baths for some of the performances. Acoustics would have been difficult, but despite the glass roof, lighting would have been less of an issue, as by the time the audience entered the baths for the entertainment part of the winter event the sun would have been setting. Taking all this into account, it is unsurprising that the entertainment repertoire staged in the baths was made up of a variety of appropriately small-scale performance forms, including dramatic scenes, recitations, illustrated songs, music, short films, and tableaux vivants.

1906's Christmas party supplies a good example of the type of entertainments that worked in this found performance space on the factory estate. After a welcome and tea in the Girls' Dining Room, partygoers walked out of the factory and a very short distance down Bournville Lane to enter the baths. The performance programme was structured around two series of tableaux vivants that restaged well-known narrative paintings within the stage front 'picture frames' (the similarities in images from the Girls' Baths entertainments suggest these were stored and reused each year). The first of the tableaux was 'The Star of Bethlehem', a representation of the local

Figure 10   'The Entertainment Hall in the Girls' Baths'
Bournville Works Magazine, February 1907. Cadbury Archives and Heritage Services.

Pre-Raphaelite artist Edward Burne-Jones's (1833–1898) painting that had been commissioned by the Corporation of Birmingham in 1887. Centre stage was confectionary coverer Maud Boylin (1885–1968) as Mary, alongside Clarkson Booth as Joseph, the three wise men – two of whom were played by women – and an angel. The still visual image was accompanied by the carol 'Bethlehem', sung by a quartet of factory employees, and praised both for its likeness to the original in 'colour, costume, and posture', and for the performers' ability to hold their positions and remain motionless (*B.W.M.*, February 1907: 109). Next up was a work in a similar aesthetic, 'The Dreamers' (1882) by Albert Joseph Moore (1841–1893). Both Burne-Jones's and Moore's works hung in Birmingham Museum and Art Gallery at the time of the Bournville Christmas party, and this very local connection with these tableaux was further deepened by the Pre-Raphaelite style and content of the paintings and their resonance with the Arts and Crafts influenced architecture and ideologies of Bournville. The complexity of the tableaux entertainments' sets, costumes and props necessitated an interval after the first two images, in order for the stage to be reset for a second half that included a tableau of the most recent painting presented, 'O Mistress Mine, Where are you Roaming' (1899) by the American artist and illustrator Edwin Austin Abbey (1852–1911). Abbey was known for his depictions of scenes and themes from William Shakespeare's plays. While this work was held by Liverpool's Walker Art Gallery, and less accessible for Birmingham's residents, the content – a depiction of the theme of Feste's song from Act two of *Twelfth Night* reflected the embryonic use of Shakespeare as an educational tool at Bournville in the first decade of the twentieth century, and represents the early production history of this play in various forms at the factory that we shall see in following chapters. Each of the stagings was accompanied by music and song performed by Cadbury's employees and had been designed and produced by staff, with much of the set and prop creation undertaken by those from the Card Box Making Room.

The evening's entertainment programme also included songs, short films, and recitations, but it was the tableaux that were presented as the main attraction. The overall effect was judged 'splendid', the hard work involved acknowledged and applauded and the articulation of a desire that more work in a similar vein be encouraged (*B.W.M.*, February 1907: 110). This wish was granted, with the following year's entertainments in the baths featuring tableaux that included representations of paintings by Albert Moore (1841–1893) and Marcus Stone (1840–1921). On this occasion, production and design were directed by Sophia Pumphrey. Hired by Cadbury's as a commercial artist in 1896, Pumphrey was a Birmingham School of Municipal Art trained artist with specialisms in Arts and Crafts style stained-glass making and metalwork who 'transformed' the firm's 'fancy box trade' with her designs (*B.W.M.*, January 1919: 14). Quickly promoted, by 1904 she was Head Forewoman in charge of all the girls' departments and business at the firm, and with leadership responsibilities around welfare and recreation. Birmingham's Municipal Art School was renowned for its radical pedagogical approach of Executed Design: students followed a programme of studio-based teaching, making their designs, not just producing them on paper (Hoban, 2013: 8). Women also attended life-drawing classes (8–9). Pumphrey benefitted from the skills-based training she received, and was clearly a skilled artist, with regular write-ups in *The Studio* (see October 1897: 338 for an example of this). In addition to her professional skills, she was a member of a prominent Birmingham Quaker family that also included her brother Spencer (1873–1913), also trained as an art metal worker, who had moved to work for Cadbury's shortly before his death, and sister Hilda (1867–1935) who was inaugural, long-serving headmistress of Bournville's village infant school. Sophia Pumphrey stayed with Cadbury's until her early retirement on grounds of ill health in 1918. She offers a clear model of the career and promotion opportunities available to unmarried women at the chocolate factory, and – alongside other Pumphrey family members – makes clear that the ongoing faith-driven focus of key management figures for whom 'the traditions' of old Quaker families 'were living things' comfortably co-existed with theatre and performance at early twentieth-century Bournville (*B.W.M.*, February 1913: 52).

1907's Christmas party tableaux were accompanied by a new performance form – the illustrated song: mimed, costumed action that played out the narratives of popular lyrics as they were sung (*B.W.M.*, February 1908: 101). Dramatic scenes were also introduced, including a restaging of five scenes from Charles Dickens's *Our Mutual Friends* featuring Elizabeth Cadbury (1858–1931) in the role of Mrs Wilfer. Joel Hoffman notes that far from being anti-theatrical, the Cadbury family were 'enthusiastic advocates of drama' who engaged in theatrical activity at home (1993: 737). This appears to have been true of particular types of drama in certain contexts, although – as we shall see in chapter four's discussion of the firm's connection with the playwright John Drinkwater – theatre continued to provoke thoughtfulness and reflection for members of the Cadbury family. The Dickens scenes had previously been performed at the family's Manor House Christmas party, an exclusive event at their home. Fashionable house party entertainment had been transported to the factory's temporary poolside theatre. Onstage in front of a large audience of employees, Elizabeth Cadbury's stage appearance in character and as herself, the wife of George Cadbury, affirmed the approval of theatre within – and for – Bournville's industrial community and extended the idea of the firm as family, with access to these re-staged, re-presented public domestic entertainments.

The use of the firm's swimming baths as a performance site was – at least in part – a result of the ongoing challenges of finding sufficient, suitable spaces to stage the factory's entertainments. Transforming the pool into a venue would have been costly. The investment of time and money incurred is testament to the significance of these social occasions, and especially the entertainments at these occasions, to the firm. Tableaux were a very practical response to the need to produce spectacle in the restricted space the baths offered. Whether by happenstance or consideration, the performance form also echoed the building's primary function. Christmas parties were not the first time the Girls' Baths had served as a backdrop for tableaux. Opening publicity for the building had used tableaux of posed, poolside swimmers in the same 'performance' space to advertise the firm's new facility, and showcase employees' healthy bodies – a key outcome of Cadbury's welfare investments (*B.W.M.*, November 1905: 4). When the popular staged paintings were presented at the only slightly later entertainments, they recalled and reframed these earlier snapshots of Bournville's employees. At the Girls' Baths, frozen in theatrical, rather than sporting, activity employees presented a clear visual signifier of the company. Yet, physical work was still demanded in this non-sporting endeavour: holding a pose and remaining motionless demands physical endurance, as anyone who has practiced yoga or pilates and experienced the strength required to maintain a posture for any length of time will have experienced. As we have seen above, the works magazine was aware of and noted this connection between stillness and strength, drawing attention to the performers' abilities to remain frozen. In stillness was strength and health, and in these pictures of pictures, a unified snapshot of the firm's sporting and cultural provision, networks and employee creativity, collaboration and skill were displayed. In a consideration of employees' bodies within Cadbury's wider visual culture, Hoffman argues that 'through physical fitness, adornment and ritual, the Bournville body represented and honoured the achievements of the Cadburys and their nation' (1993: 746). There was certainly an element of this in the bodies staged at the factory, but there was more at play in their play. A more nuanced, micro-historical focus on individual performances that took place at specific moments in the firm's history, in particular factory buildings or outside spaces, within wider entertainment programmes at events, and amidst the firm's theatre facilitates better understanding of the changing and evolving meanings of performing bodies at Bournville and reveals an adaptability and complexity that substantiates the rationale behind the firm's significant investments in making performance. Though grounded in the same core values, the bodies at the baths, those in *Visions*, in the Concert Hall opening entertainments, and in the outdoor entertainments considered in the following chapters offered different, complex meanings that were of value to themselves as individuals, as employees, and to the firm.

Modern Advertising: Chocolate, Theatre, and the Business of Promotion

The three factory spaces closely considered in this chapter to this point – the Girls' Baths, the New Dining Hall, and the Concert Hall – were part of a larger set of temporarily repurposed or specifically designed spaces for theatrical activity at Cadbury's. Several others will feature across the following chapters, but I conclude here with two buildings and performances that further uncover the function of theatre in place-making and community creation at Bournville. The first is another new build – T Block.

Opened in 1914, T Block was constructed to meet both production and recreation needs. Unlike previous builds, the structure had been designed in-house, and it was very much a functional, rather than an aesthetic *and* functional, building. Executed with no internal columns, the floor space offered by the 158 by 44 feet construction was vast. To give some idea of scale, Blackpool Tower is 158 feet high. The firm celebrated the build by using it to stage 1915's New Year Gathering, the first social occasion that occurred after its completion: showcasing the new space to factory employees and marking an early instance of a quickly established pattern of using theatrical entertainments to launch new onsite builds.

Cadbury's workers were not generally familiar with the whole factory site. Most members of staff would have had their own experiences of the Bournville estate, with their day-to-day working lives restricted to the areas that they worked within, those allocated for their sex, and the communal recreational spaces they could access during and after their shifts – for lunch, sports or other out-of-hours leisure activities provided by the firm. This typical individual, partial knowledge of Bournville was clearly articulated in the works magazine review of 1915's gathering. 'The party was to be held in T Block, and some of us wondered where 'T' Block was to be found' noted William Davenport (1867–1938). Davenport was a long-serving commercial traveller with the firm who had returned to Cadbury's headquarters because of the war. He noted his relative outsider status at Bournville and how this added to his awe at its 'possibilities' and 'all of which it is capable'. This position was carefully harnessed by the magazine, the outside/inside eye he offered further emphasising Cadbury's staff provision. While it is unlikely that the scale of the building project needed to construct T Block had not attracted staff attention, the more general lack of familiarity with the new space and access to it – shared by Davenport and others – had been anticipated, and once spectators made their way 'inside the [factory's] lodge gates all difficulty disappeared. Wrong paths were roped off, and the right way was indicated' (*B.W.M.*, March 1915: 67). The evening functioned in multiple ways, as part of the firm's social calendar, to inform and update key employees about the business, as a networking opportunity, a mechanism to familiarise employees with the redeveloped part of the estate and display the modern new building, and – signalled by the recourse to the label 'Gathering' – a means to offer a celebration and community event in keeping with the wartime moment in which it took place. Alongside their community building and promotional functions, such occasions worked on a very practical level to create knowledge of Bournville's layout.

At 1915's New Year Party, the entertainments were spread across T Block's three floors. The evening opened with a reception on the building's airy, light top floor that had been staged as a 'drawing room in a factory' with carpets and easy chairs. Here partygoers were treated to a musical programme, followed by a range of attractions on the middle floor including, the 'Fine Art Museum', 'Photographic Curiosities' and 'Symbolized Proverbs'. Next came a programme of songs, recitations, and 'The Cocoa Nibs' a Pierrot troupe who performed a short selection from their exclusive programme as performed – 'they claimed' – at Lifford-on-Sea, Dogpool, Dudley Port, and other 'health resorts'. The joke would have worked rather better then and there than it does here (for most of us) and now. These places were not seaside resorts, they were local, and the troupe a burlesque of seaside Pierrot performers. The Fine Art Museum presented a series of visual puns on the title of famous works of art. The audience perhaps expected the familiar Cadbury's form of the tableau vivant from the list of works that were to be displayed. 'Sweet Seventeen' had made Davenport anticipate 'a Gainsborough-like' image of some 'Bournville beauty' he noted. Instead, the display was of seventeen, carefully stacked sugar lumps. The other forty-four displays that made up this entertainment reflected this installation-style model of localised, knowing humour reminiscent, in many ways, of metropolitan cabaret and artist collectives from the turn of the century. Edward Organ's (1873–1922) recitation 'Rhymes for the Times' traced the past, present, and future of the firm, its site and values, and gently mocked the current number of committees that facilitated and governed work and play by suggesting that management consider setting up a M.C.C. a 'Matrimonial Control Committee'. These were not just rhymes for a time, they were rhymes for a place; part of an 'in-jokes' entertainment programme for Cadbury's community that was strengthened by the way in which they flipped audience expectations. A modern take for the firm's newest modern building also supplied the theme for the photographic display – an exhibition of trick photography where images captured objects disguised as other objects, for example, a close-up shot of a golf ball that appeared to be a thimble (*B.W.M.*, March 1915: 68). Refreshments were served back on the top floor of the block, while the middle floor was reset for a performance of J. M. Barrie's one act play, *The Will*. Accounts indicate that even though T Block was not furnished with a permanent stage, a temporary structure had been created that had some form of performance frame which enabled curtains to be drawn across the stage between acts. Featuring key figures from Bournville's theatrical activity including Arthur Knapp, Florence Showell, and Harry Bradbear, the play was seen as strong evidence that the factory's drama was improving every year (68). T Block's opening entertainments connected Cadbury's with modernity and entertainment through a range of performances that spoke to Bournville's audiences in both locally specific and more generic ways. As the firm, and its employees faced a war that was soon to go into its second year, performance was working on multiple levels to deliver, cement, and publicise the firm's recreational offer and shore up the factory's industrial community.

Audiences for entertainment programmes at Cadbury's Bournville factory would have anticipated theatre and performance as part of the evening's offer. As an exception from this model, the final example I consider in this chapter is a performance event that is likely to have taken most of its audience by surprise. 'Modern Advertising' was a lecture that formed part of the firm's regular on-site lecture series, delivered in the Youths' Dining Room by Clifford Coope in March 1931. It offers a clear model of how widespread theatrical activity was at the factory and reminds us that there are performance histories concealed in indoor factory spaces that did not have stages, were not kitted out for performance, and that occurred as part of events that we would not immediately identify as theatrical. We have already come across Clifford Coope earlier in this chapter, as a cast member in plays staged in the concert hall. His career path appears to have followed that of what we would today identify as a Marketing Executive or Advertising Consultant, and he was a well-practiced, frequently booked public speaker throughout the West Midlands. During this lecture on advertising, Coope drew on the participation of a troupe of at least six performers. Following his arrival at the front of the room, a dramatic moment of interruption was staged. A performer, in the role of an unethical retailer, stormed into the lecture room shouting out unrealistic claims for his 'Elixir of Life' product. He was quickly surrounded by a group of female performers, who giggled at the exaggerated claims he made for his product – a series of all-encompassing health benefits and curative properties that would be familiar to anyone who has encountered advertising columns in late nineteenth and early twentieth century popular print culture. The day, and the consumers' money, was saved by another performer playing Constable Clegg, who dragged the ungoverned advertiser out of the performance space.

The lecture's opening dramatic moment offered Coope the opportunity to present the benefits and importance of the modern, regulated advertising industry as an educational, protective, and economically beneficial force that worked in the favour of buyers, manufacturers, and retailers, and to alert consumers to the risks of poor practice. Simultaneously its message,

Figure 11 'Modern Advertising'
Bournville Works Magazine, March 1931. Cadbury Archives and Heritage Services.

and Coope's status as a Cadbury's employee, evoked and affirmed the firm's ethical advertising approach and rejection of non-evidencable claims and hyperbole. Later in the lecture, the performers returned to play out scenes/ explaining how good advertising deals were struck, to create tableaux that visualised the best way in which to use human bodies and gestures in advertising images, and to explain the technologies of modern advertising photography (*B.W.M.*, March 1931: 84–85). The lessons Coope laid out in language were reiterated and strengthened through practical, applied demonstrations, made possible by theatrical performance. The interventions and tableaux built into the lecture were considered interesting enough to be captured by a photographer for the firm, and for several of these images to be published in the works magazine. This was not common practice in coverage of the regular lectures that took place at Bournville, the appeal was in the novelty of Coope's approach. Visually, these moments of performance were connected to Bournville's wider theatrical activity. Figure 11 records costume and plotting reminiscent of still images of dramatic society productions from the same period, and the performers themselves would certainly have been familiar, Coope included. 'Modern Advertising' fused education, entertainment, and industry in ways that were relatively routine for Cadbury's by this moment in the firm's development and indicates engaged audiences who were literate in the factory's theatrical culture, style, representatives, and multiple functions and meanings.

The performances, performers, and performance spaces considered throughout this chapter disclose clear synergies between the factory's theatre and Cadbury's advertising imagery, promotional strategies, and people management. Together (often on the same entertainment programmes) the re-creation of marketing campaigns through employees' bodies, the embodiment of core values realised through humorous, knowing references to Cadbury's life, the production of plays familiar from theatrical and amateur circuits, and the staging of romanticised, fictionalised histories of Bournville and its founders, served to affirm, materialise, animate, and publicise the firm's position as an industry leader of both production and human relations. Direct connections between place, product, people, and theatre were created, explored, and shared through performance, materialising the rationale behind the firm's significant resource investments in theatre. These dynamics were arguably stronger still when Bournville's theatre was staged outside, in Cadbury's Factory in a Garden, and it is these performances that the next two chapters move on to explore.

PART II

Theatre in the Factory Garden

CHAPTER 3

Marketing Fresh Air
Outdoor Performance at Bournville's Factory in the Garden

Cinema audiences watching the story of *Elsie and the Brown Bunny* (1921) play out in front of them would have been very familiar with one of the film's few intertitles: 'Come Along to Bournville – to the Factory in the Garden'. This well-known reference to Cadbury's business headquarters had emerged during the firm's early years at the greenfield production site, and become increasingly familiar and well-used over the following two decades. 'The Factory in the Garden' captured a vision of Cadbury's landscaped estate as a carefully crafted, industrial-pastoral world; a cutting-edge modern industrial site nestled in a quasi pre-modern rural idyll. 1902's investment in the Visitor Department had clearly signalled Bournville's prevailing role in the firm's strategic management of their ever-closer relationship with the press, and other external groups: the team's remit was to nurture, display, and promote Cadbury's ethos through onsite visitor experiences. Journalists invited to tour the factory and its grounds on press days, or those who visited independently, were fed this image along with their cocoa and chocolate samples. In turn, their reports and illustrations shared and promoted it more widely. From the 1884 representation of Bournville as 'a charming valley which might have served for Rip Van Winkle's "Sleepy Hollow", but for the hive of industry it contained' (*Leicester Mercury*, 29 March 1884: 7, also printed in the *York Herald* and *Manchester Times* on the same date), to the fashionable *Illustrated Sporting and Dramatic News*'s depiction of the site as 'a Worcestershire Eden' (8 February 1896: 835), and *The Bystander*'s description of 'A Workshop in a Garden' (2 February 1906: 46), newspaper columns strengthened and distributed images of Cadbury's industrial-pastoral world in descriptions that interwove manufacturing processes, cocoa and chocolate products, the factory landscape, employees, and recreation. Images of the Factory in the Garden sat at the core of Cadbury's culturally, socially, and economically powerful company identity. The repeated use of the phrase was deliberate and during the 1910s it served as a repeated strap line in high-profile advertising campaigns across national and regional newspapers including *The Illustrated London News, Sheffield Daily Telegraph, Portsmouth Evening News,* and *Nottingham Evening Post*. In this two-chapter section on Bournville's outdoor theatre, I step outside of the factory walls into its garden, in search of performances that were staged amidst the site's landscaped grounds, identifying the masques, Robin Hood plays, Ancient Greek tragedies, pageants, productions of Shakespeare, burlesques, and revues that were produced in these outdoor spaces as events that embodied, entrenched, and promoted Cadbury's core values, and served as integral elements of the firm's visual culture, public identity, people management, and marketing.

Cadbury's advertising activity is at the core of understanding outdoor performance at Bournville. The history of the firm's theatre transcends the category of recreation. It was a widely used organisational tool. From the Cadbury's Caramel Bunny and the Mini Eggs parrot to the Dairy Milk Gorilla drumming along to Genesis's 'I Can Feel it Coming in the Air Tonight', Cadbury's innovative media marketing campaigns are imprinted as familiar cultural memories for many today. Such creative advertising techniques were the latest in the firm's long history of skilled, pioneering marketing strategies: activities that had been central to their operations since the Bull Street shop was fitted with Birmingham's earliest plate-glass window displays in the 1820s, and staffed by costumed salespeople weighing and packing tea for customers – acts that marked the earliest iteration of performance in the service of promotion at the firm (Williams, 1931: 8). The first decades of the twentieth century at Bournville synched with a rapid growth in consumer culture and interconnected developments in an increasingly professionalised marketing industry. Cadbury's management team were quick to respond, with a series of careful, planned investments in novel print- and events-based advertising models that optimised 'first-mover advantages that were impossible [for others] to imitate', developing 'a business model perfectly in tune with the new consumer opportunities of the day' that still adhered to Quaker-guided company values (Fitzgerald, 2005: 512; Bradley, 2008: v). Positioning nature at the core of advertising schemes was one such response; a means of balancing Quaker business ethics with a need to respond to the faster, larger, increasingly competitive global marketplace of the new century. As the twentieth century progressed, the established advertising focus on Bournville's cocoa and chocolate health giving properties that had been introduced through medical endorsements was expanded to include images and references to the healthy, fresh air lifestyle offered by the factory – claims that were increasingly evidencable through emerging ideas from sociology, urban planning, nutrition, and exercise studies. The social reform energies that had directed Quaker businesses towards cocoa as an alternative to alcohol continued to reverberate in the advertising strategies that sustained Cadbury's diversified, expanded operation. Data around the good health of Cadbury's employees was documented and promoted through the press, publications, and academic and professional conferences, some of which included Bournville site visits. Products were advertised as containing health-giving properties and the fresh air that surrounded the firm's factory became a symbolic, invisible ingredient. 'It is important that Food Products should be manufactured under clean and healthy conditions' read a characteristically wordy 1919 advertisement for Bournville's chocolate. 'This essential has been fully observed at Bournville where every detail to promote cleanliness and the good health of the workers has been considered. Such ideal conditions ensure ideal production' (*The Sphere*, 77: 188). International audiences and consumers received similar images of this ideal British countryside production setting. An Australian newspaper carrying a report from a British journalist's visit to the factory noted the healthy girls working with focus and energy in rooms where 'breezes [were] blowing in at the open windows, breezes laden not with the impurities of the town, but with the sweetness of the trees and the country' (*The West Australian,* 25 January 1907: 7). The sweetness of the trees, the presence of the countryside, and the factory's working conditions were also to become key ingredients in making Cadbury's outdoor entertainments, particularly those that were staged at the firm's summer works parties.

Investing in Fresh Air: Performance at Cadbury's Summer Works Parties, 1902–1914

Staff parties have featured in Chapter 2, and it is clear that indoor factory events were established features of Bournville's calendar by the early twentieth century. The first years of the 1900s saw the introduction of outdoor events, including day-long summer works parties that entertained thousands of employees, their families, and a small number of invited guests. Edward Cadbury recorded the significance of these occasions in his 1912 book *Experiments in Industrial Organisation,* highlighting the entertainments they offered: 'no pains are spared to provide an entertainment worthy' of the parties, he stated, marking the key role performance played in 'a function with which memories and traditions are associated' (239). Bournville's first outdoor staff summer works party had been held in 1902, a decade before Edward Cadbury's words were published, and they were to continue until 1914. Their longevity, despite the costs they incurred, can be attributed to their capacity to materialise ideas about working culture, recreation, and health that were central to the firm, offering an ongoing, updated presentation and experience of Bournville as 'a wonderful place to visit, all holiday [...] a sort of fairyland fantasy', as Chief Engineer Louis Barrow (1865–1948) nostalgically recalled in his contribution to a 1929 reminiscence of the factory's early decades at the new site (*Personal Reminiscences of Bridge Street and Bournville*, CAHS/000/003270). Outdoor theatre and entertainment contributed to, created, and refreshed images of Bournville as a 'wonderful place'.

The summer parties were made possible by Cadbury's substantial investments in outdoor factory spaces. By 1935, the firm's industrial estate spanned 208 acres, a significant increase from the 14½ acres of land originally bought by George and Richard Cadbury in 1878. This expansion was the result of major land purchases: The 1895 acquisition of the adjacent Bournbrook Hall estate that more than doubled the size of Bournville's footprint and enabled the creation of the Girls' Recreation Ground, and the 1919 addition of a further 120 acres of land at Rowheath. The use of this extra land is of particular interest here: 64 per cent of the expanded site was devoted to staff recreation and public entertainment. Expansion was driven by the firm's desire to increase space and amenities for sports and performance, and to accommodate factory staff, visitors, and spectators in out-of-work activities (see Williams, 1931: 280–283; Chance 2017: 49). Reflecting the centrality of fresh air to employee welfare schemes, and the importance of Bournville and Cadbury's employees as visual representations of the firm's image, a carefully designed landscape was carved from these outdoor spaces. The most high-profile and visible of them – the large Girls' and Men's Recreation Grounds – lay on either side of the main factory thoroughfare, Bournville Lane. With their carefully designed and maintained gardens, water features, lawns, sports pitches, glasshouses, temporary and fixed seating, shelters, and sports pavilions, these grounds offered practical, pastoral scenery that framed the factory buildings and served as a living backdrop for the firm's staff, production, and recreational pastimes. The Bournbrook Hall land had enabled the creation of a greenbelt of outdoor space, sheltering the factory from other developments in the adjacent area. It was on this green space that outdoor theatre was provided for, with a large amphitheatre constructed in 1910 (discussed fully in Chapter 4) as part of a capital project designed to make the recreation grounds 'much more valuable for games' and to enable the firm to 'entertain visitors more conveniently' (*B.W.M.*, June 1910: 268). The importance of this moment to Cadbury's remains visible in Bournville today. The large areas of open space and green lawns owe their continuing existence to the early twentieth-century commitment made by the Board to protect a large percentage of their land from any building and development; the legacy of a fin-de-siècle business-driven recognition that landscape 'has meaning', 'associates people and place', and is not a 'passive backdrop to human theatre' (Bournville Publications, 1936: 3; Spirn, 1998: 16–18; Readman, 2018). It was on these two recreation grounds that the summer works parties were held.

The origins of Bournville's outdoor summer works parties can be traced back to a new style of staff gathering that took place in the factory in December 1902, eight weeks after the first issue of the works magazine had appeared containing the definition of Bournville's Spirit. In place of the regular small festive gathering for senior management, this occasion aligned the company party format with innovative people management practices being explored by the firm. A greater focus on staff inclusivity resulted in a much larger guest list. Although it remained 'a matter for regret' that the entire staff body, which numbered 3,600 at the time, could not be invited, employees from all departments who had been with the company for seven or more years could attend (*B.W.M.*, February 1903: 79). 1902's event followed a format that will be familiar from the previous chapter, George Cadbury welcomed the guests, Edward Cadbury gave an address, refreshments were offered, and partygoers were entertained by the factory's orchestral and choral societies, a piano solo played by Dorothy Cadbury (1872–1950, Edward Cadbury's wife), a gymnastic display by employees, a cinematographic exhibition of local subjects, and lantern slides of images taken by members of the camera club. More speeches and the distribution of prizes to staff by Elizabeth Cadbury followed. The prize-giving was for winners of the Suggestion Scheme, a Cadbury's initiative that rewarded employees who proposed useful changes to factory production or welfare practices with both public recognition and small cash prizes. Like the later New Year parties, the occasion was presented as a reward for the winners, and for those who had accrued relatively long periods of service with the firm; a treat that functioned as part of the creation of a culture, community, and identity at Cadbury's. The evening closed with a hymn, echoing the framework of the Quaker gatherings that had shaped earlier, smaller factory events at Bull Street and at the Bournville site (*B.W.M.*, February 1903: 79).

1902's December party offered a new model, a clear adjustment to the format and function of Cadbury's social occasions that fitted the firm's growth, development, and new level of investment in community and the Bournville Spirit. A prototype outdoor party had taken place earlier in the same year, marking the opening of the Men's Pavilion on the factory's recreation grounds, integrating a prizegiving, and featuring sporting displays as entertainment (Williams, 1931: 179). 1903 saw an expanded outdoor event, still framed around the prizegiving and demonstrations of sporting prowess, but with the inclusion of athletics. Despite the change in location, these two parties were still arranged to recognise senior management and employees who had contributed significantly to the firm. They continued to represent a reward agenda. Interestingly, there is no record of any religious content at either of these occasions. While the firm's morning readings continued until 1912, it appears that the move away from very limited guest lists and indoor venues also marked a move away from the partial religious framing of these events. A month after the 1903 party, a second outdoor event was staged – the Girls' Athletic Club Gymkhana – with a more diverse entertainment programme that offered a mixture of sport, performance, and participation, including fancy dress competitions, a tortoise race, potato race, water-carrying race, serpentine race, chariot race, a men's versus girl's cricket match and the grand finale, a Lantern Cycle Maze, that had to be abandoned because of the wet weather – marking the first occasion on which Cadbury's outdoor performances encountered the perils of heavy rain, but certainly not the last (*B.W.M.,* September 1903: 336).

In 1904, these two developments – bigger invite lists and outdoor entertainments – came together. All factory employees were invited to the party, shifting the purpose of the occasion from a reward and recognition format to a community-building occasion that celebrated the firm and its workers. Tried and tested entertainments from the previous year's athletics gymkhana featured during the afternoon, including a relatively small fancy dress competition during which twelve 'enthusiastic' costumed competitors, all women aged from their late teens to late twenties, paraded around the recreation grounds on bicycles. Several of their outfits were fancy dress representations of Cadbury's products or institutions, including 'Milk Chocolate', a costume reminiscent of banner advertising girls, 'A Bournville Nurse' and 'The Bournville Works Magazine'. Others reflected fashions in fancy dress from other social events, including 'Caller Herrin' a Cornish fishwife inspired by the popular song, 'Summer', and the fairytale character 'Mother Hubbard'. Nellie Knight (c.1887–1906), who was seventeen years old and employed as a chocolate box maker claimed victory. Cycling around the recreation grounds dressed as a lady gardener, she embodied Cadbury's investment in horticulture, nature, and health against a backdrop of the firm's landscaped outdoor space. Nineteen-year-old Kitty (Catherine) Ann Noon (1885–1953), a clerk from the wages office, dressed as a Geisha, also won a commendation for her costume (*B.W.M.*, August 1904: 360). The feature marked the origins of performance at the Summer party programmes, staging an element that was to continue, repackaged as tableaux, in future outdoor and indoor factory events and symbolising the clear connection between sports and performance that was to continue in Bournville's entertainments for many years to come. A new culture of staff participation in performance emerged at the 1904 party, one that was acknowledged in the works magazine's conclusion that the event had made it clear 'there really is good talent at Bournville' (August 1904: 359). It was talent that was to be drawn on time and time again over the following years: talent that would draw wider public attention to the firm and its employees. By 1905, the summer works parties were large and notable enough to attract the attention of the fashionable, illustrated newspaper *The Sphere,* which praised the occasions as part of Bournville's wider identity as 'a wonderful place' (8 July 1905: 30).

Employee events became of increasing importance as Cadbury's business boomed, and staff numbers continued to grow. It is no surprise, perhaps, that this aligned with an acceleration in theatrical activity – both as an entertainment offer at factory occasions, and as a recreational pastime. 1906's summer party was plagued by bad weather again, with only a brief break in the downpours. Admitting defeat to the elements, the event was called off early and the grounds cleared by seven o'clock, but the works magazine reported that the curtailed occasion was nonetheless enjoyable. A large crowd gathered on the prettily decorated factory grounds and watched a familiar programme of sporting displays. Other entertainments featured external performers, who had been hired in for the party. This had happened before at smaller events; accounts suggest professional entertainers were occasionally hired for staff parties as early as the final decade of the nineteenth century, but 1906 represented the peak of external entertainers being used onsite (CAHS/350/002610). One of these 'new attractions' was offered by 'the engagement of Madame Fontainebleau and her Performing Dogs'. A temporary stage was built on the Men's Recreation Ground for an act that included a solo agility routine in which she balanced, juggled, and walked on a gigantic wooden globe, as well as the choreographed spectacle of her with her canine co-performers. Alongside Fontainebleau, Willis Crisford (1867–1921), a well-known Birmingham-based self-styled Professor of Elocution and 'Society Entertainer', appeared on the programme. Crisford had performed at other Cadbury's events, and on this occasion presented a range of his 'at homes'; songs, dramatic sketches, and recitals. During the afternoon a dramatic recital by Edgbaston-based amateur actress Margaret Chatwin (1878–1937) was also staged. Chatwin was to become one of the first permanent members of Birmingham's Repertory Theatre Company, and we will encounter her, and her important connection to Bournville, again in chapter five. The last of 1906's four external performers was the most famous. Dr John Byrd Page (1854–1916) was a society conjuror, known for drawing room, garden party, table magic, and At Home entertainments and his sleight of hand magic that 'baffled' audiences (*Times,* 18 June 1906: 1). His performance at Bournville in his act 'The Arts of Deception' was a programming coup: well-known on the London magic scene since the 1890s, he was an early member of the Magic Circle and moved in elite, fashionable networks (*B.W.M.,* August 1906: 351). By 1904, he had performed for royalty on several occasions and two years after his Bournville appearance he was to appear at Buckingham Palace to celebrate the birthday of Prince Henry of Wales (*Leader,* 23 May 1908: 50). Internationally renowned, *The New York Clipper* noted that from early in the century this 'very witty and skilful conjuror' was known for his refusal 'to take any but swell engagements' (11 September 1915: 47). Byrd Page's act was distinctive, with his 'austere' appearance, 'caustic wit', and 'biting sarcasm' noted as the most characteristic features of his performance in an obituary in *The Magazine of Magic* 'Magicians of the Past' series, that aligned him with conjuring greats Professor Hoffman and Alexander Hermann. The tribute was written by his friend Captain O. Bowen, who recalled the 'cleverest drawing room conjuror we possessed in this county'; one who worked in the 'intimate sphere of society drawing rooms and clubland' where he shone and scintillated'. 'So many conjurors are mere performers with tricks, but he was a superb actor playing the part of the magician' (July 1916: 30–31). Together Margaret Chatwin, Willis Crisford, and Dr Byrd Page represented drawing room style entertainment, wit, and fashionable popular culture that were perfectly aligned with the spirit of Bournville, embodying the useful connections wider trends in popular performance offered Cadbury's. They represented the external (local or national) celebrity performers who were familiar, welcome fare at the factory: records of discussions about the summer parties strongly suggest that the provision of fireworks, with the temporary spectacle and significant cost they presented, prompted more debate amongst senior staff than the careful engagement of current, well-known entertainment and theatrical personalities (see, e.g., CAHS/CMM/7 February 1911: 126).

After a year's hiatus in the summer parties to mark the death of Emma Cadbury (1846–1907, the wife of Richard) in 1907, 1908's event was celebrated as 'the most successful' held to date (*B.W.M.,* August 1908: 293). A large part of this positive reception was due to the production of *May Day,* the first of Bournville's outdoor pageants, and a performance that will be covered alongside other outdoor pastoral plays and masques in the following chapter. 6,000 spectators were invited to 1908's party and entertained by a second acknowledged 'new departure' – a continuous programme of attractions with acts repeated to allow partygoers to see everything that they wanted to across the afternoon and evening. Employee partygoers were spread widely across the outdoor spaces, taking part in sports, performing in the pastoral play's large cast, having tea, or watching or participating in other entertainments. The resulting distribution of staff made it logistically impossible to hand out Suggestion Scheme prizes at the party, and this – the last remnants of the reward agenda that had defined the earlier occasions – was deferred to a later date. 1908's party further developed an ambitious but viable, large-scale outdoor event model and, as the works magazine reminded its employee readers, served as a clear reminder to Cadbury's staff of 'advantages we enjoy [...] which we do not really forget, if we do at times take them for granted' without which 'the social life of Bournville, of which the Summer Party is the chief expression, would be quite impossible' (*B.W.M.,* August 1908: 293). By 1908, the crowds and casts of Cadbury's summer parties created a simultaneous moment of recreation, community building, and promotional activity that was in close dialogue with the firm's industrial pastoral visual culture, and created memories, traditions, and stories about the firm that strengthened the company's image for both internal and external audiences.

Taking Part: Performance and Participation at the Summer Parties

Looking closely at these early summer outdoor party events signals a direct link between the amount of factory theatre they included and their perceived success as community functions. By 1909, active engagement with the summer works parties – as either a musical, theatrical, or sporting performer or spectator – was an expectation, and it was clearly articulated as such. 'Any who failed to find enjoyment' in the 'large and varied' entertainments at the year's works party was deemed 'dull indeed' (*B.W.M.,* August 1909: 293). Not participating in, or enjoying, the party was judged a personal – and, by extension, a professional – failure; an absence of the

Bournville Spirit. When the firm's travelling sales staff – who were invited 'home' for the summer party – contributed to the event for the first time in 1909, the works magazine reflected that:

> we might here remark that we are glad the Firm's representatives were induced to take a part in the day's proceedings beyond that of spectators; perhaps they will be so emulated by the many evidences of the active imagination at Bournville as to figure at the next Party, say in a fancy dress parade of their own, or in some other event transcending in originality anything yet thought of at home. (August: 295)

Taking part at Bournville meant <u>fully</u> taking part. The travellers had put on some races, but it was made gently, yet firmly and publicly, clear here that that was not sufficient and – now they had learnt from attending the event – a more original contribution would be expected from them next year. Expectations of staff creativity were high, and there was increasing evidence of this creativity, and of performance, at 1909's party. Building on the success of the previous year, a second pastoral play was staged. Sports continued to be a popular item on the programme, with the intersections and similarities between sports and performance noted by the works magazine report on the fancy dress parade, judged by Elizabeth Cadbury, as a competitive item 'which may be classed with the sports' (*B.W.M.*, August 1909: 297). The time and money invested in spectacular entertainments is clear in attractions including the Water Carnival, a sound and light display staged on the streams and pools of the Men's Recreation Grounds at dusk. Trees and boats were lit with fairy lamps, performers aboard the boats and on the banks carried torches, and the factory's male choir provided a musical accompaniment to a spectacle that transformed the work environment into a fairyland. The piece was the work of the firm's electricians' department, whose involvement in the creation of the illusion was visible only from 'the obtrusion here and there, by day, of electrical wires' (298). While the pastoral play had two ticketed performances, the Water Carnival had been classed as an attraction, or sideshow, and admission was not controlled, while the time of day and light levels required resulted in just one performance. Combined, these elements led to crowd management issues in what were (by report) typically well marshalled and planned occasions. 'An unpleasant crush' was recorded when the flickering reflections from the lights off the water indicated that the performance was about to start (298). The sophisticated operational and production management typical of the summer parties is here revealed through this unusual account of its absence, as is the popularity and appeal of this installation.

While the water carnival was an elaborate, outdoor, sensory spectacle, examples of an increasing use of more low-key theatrical devices also featured on 1909's entertainment programme. Narrative became increasingly important to sporting demonstrations. Cycling's history was told through a series of bicycles from across time, ridden by costumed employees with a narrator telling the story of the sport's development. The firm's fire brigade division were praised for their 'originality' as they put aside their standard display of drills and manual exercises and instead played out extinguishing a fire in a lightly erected wooden house constructed for the occasion on the grounds, showcasing Cadbury's new fire engine in the process. Some creation of dramatic tension through the narrative is clear. 'A wreath of smoke curled itself up from the open window of the cottage, and the crowd stood on tiptoe' the works magazine recorded. Performers were located within the house: 'the cries of [these] inmates were awful to hear, and their writhing forms were actually seen silhouetted against the flames at the window'. Just as 'it began to seem a really serious matter' the fire brigade arrived and put out the blaze. With some audience members concerned that they had waited too long for the sake of the spectacle, the reviewer noted, 'this may have been so, but to have been sooner would have been to quench prematurely a really magnificent bonfire', to everyone's disappointment 'with the possible exception of those in the cottage' (299). In a theatricalised scene evocative of a high sensation moment from stage melodramas, the bravery of the firm's employees – fire brigade members and those trusting them within the cottage – and the firm's care for staff through the provision of the new engine (if not through the risk assessment of this entertainment!) were displayed. Details of the attractions at 1909's summer party evidence both an increase in the number of employees playing roles in a greater range of theatrical narratives and spectacles, and in the production complexity of the attractions staged.

1909's event demonstrates that, although expanded in scale, summer works parties continued to offer programmes of sideshows and attractions that echoed those of their earliest years, alongside increasingly extensive entertainment programmes. By this time, each of the occasions ran for eight hours, from half past two in the afternoon to ten thirty in the evening, with performance becoming an increasingly important feature. The acts and activities staged at the parties between 1909 and 1914 are listed in Table 1. Considered together they reveal in- and cross-year repertoires that were heavily influenced by popular performers and performance styles drawn from across music hall, fairground, pageants, concerts, and theatre. As the culture of participation strengthened, there were notably fewer

Table 1 *Entertainments at Cadbury's Summer Works Parties, 1909–1914*

Year	Number of tickets	Entertainments
1909	6,000	Pastoral Play; Gymnastic Displays; Fancy Dress Parades; Dances; Aquatic Sport; Water Carnival at Dusk; Races; Strolling Players.
1911	6,000	Fancy Dress Parade; British Empire Tableaux; Burlesque Cricket Match; Gymkhana; Masque / Pageant; Human Chess; Ham Cutting Competition; Organ Grinding Competition; Hat Trimming Competition; Driving Competition; Water Carrying Competition on Cycles; Potato Race (cycles); Tug of War; Fireworks.
1912	7,000	Toboggan; Coker-nut Shies; Aunt Sallies; Pipe Shies; Swing Boats; Punch and Judy Shows; The Burlesque Man-agerie; Masque / Pageant; Football Burlesque; National Dances; Mandolin and Banjo Band, Male Voice Choir, The Musical Dons, Aquatic Display; Daylight Fireworks; Bowls Tournament.
1913	8,000	Helter Skelter; Roundabout; Swing Boats; Coker Nut Shies; House of Mysteries (home-made); Departmental Tableaux; Masque / Pageant; Burlesque of Street Life; Old English Country Dances; Torch Swinging Display; Daylight Cinematograph; Dancing (for all); Fireworks.
1914	8,000	Helter Skelter; Roundabout; Departmental Tableaux; A Bournville Review; Masque / Pageant; Folk Dances; Gymnastics Display; Dancing (for all)

non-Bournville performers. While the outdoor pastoral plays/pageants and huge tea tents took over the Girls' Recreation Ground, the Men's Recreation Ground (with the factory buildings behind them) were home to the other attractions, staged across two, temporary platform stages and a large arena constructed for each year's event. Programming involved some dialogue with staff, and a desire to please party goers is signalled through evidence that organisers listened to staff feedback and made changes. As one example, employees stayed later into the evening at 1913's party because of the introduction of more fairground-style attractions. Recognition that the audience was made up primarily of young people who were seeking more to do, as well as more to see, had prompted this development. The resulting 'provision of roundabouts and swing boats and helter-skelter lighthouses and houses of mystery was a popular move […] evidenced by the fact that they were patronised no less than 15,000 times during the day' noted the works magazine, while simultaneously cautioning against any disapproval of such frivolity:

> If some few thought this strange machinery of joy 'hardly Bournville' [...] they probably learned a deep and forcible truth after they had been up-and-down, and round and through, on the day of the party – and that truth was there is sanity in abandon. (B.W.M., August 1913: 256)

Finding sanity through abandon sat at the extreme end point of Cadbury's spectrum of work and play, but it was accepted and encouraged within these controlled, time-limited conditions. Recognised connections between fun, laughter, and mental wellbeing are clear here in a distilled vision of the key impetus that lay behind the factory's day-to-day educational and recreational activities. Indeed, elements of these participatory events echo Wil Gesler's definition of 'therapeutic landscapes', a 'geographic metaphor for the process of creating health and wellbeing in places', through places, and the creation of the interlocked physical, social, and symbolic environments that Clare Hickman identifies as important to early twentieth-century creations of outdoor space (2018; Hickman, 2018). While therapeutic landscapes were more commonly linked with healing properties, at Cadbury's they were designed to create and foster wellbeing, to prevent a need for healing. Delivering all in work/out of work activities with this level of abandon would have been unsustainable for the firm, but a temporary annual 'twelfth-night' model of relaxed factory rules and routine identifies an understanding of the benefits of such release to employees. There were other positive outcomes, of course. One that did not go without notice was how the red and white candy stripes of the helter skelter and the flags, mirrors, and lights of the roundabouts added to the temporary creation of the factory's recreation grounds as pastoral idyll by evoking images of village fetes and presenting Bournville's industrial factory estate as a 'charming picture' in its 'rightful' rural 'setting' (*B.W.M.,* August 1913: 253). Each occasion saw conscious marketing, management, and production strategies blend with happenstance outcomes and moments in a complex balancing, and re-balancing, of work and play, labour and leisure, duty and pleasure that was the kernel of Cadbury's people management schemes in this period. And, amidst this series of parties, the role of theatre in the places and activities created for employee health and wellbeing, as well as the firm's public identity and promotion, was growing.

1910's groundworks – including those that created the new amphitheatre on the Girls' Recreation Ground – had made it impossible to stage a summer party, but the following year's event, in 1911, harnessed the success of the increased theatrical activity that had marked 1909 and extended it further. Cadbury's summer works parties peaked between 1911 and 1914, and these four annual events remain the largest entertainment programmes staged at Bournville. They represented a time-specific flurry of recreational activity and demonstrated the role theatre played in the firm's business strategies within a set of wider dynamics that reflected a particular moment of flux. It was not just the buildings, outside spaces, size, and management of the firm that shifted during this period, the first decade of the twentieth century had also marked major shifts in the firm's business practices and organisational structures. Writing in the early 1930s, the earliest historian of the Cadbury business, Iola Williams, identified 1911 as a significant year in the development of the firm to date – the point at which earlier changes were firmly established and came to fruition (1931: 91). He also noted a side effect of the changes that the firm's leaders had had to contend with over the previous decade – a concern from some employees that 'the new order that was to replace the old, almost patriarchal, conduct of the establishment, might not be less human, less understanding, than its predecessor' (77). Their fears were largely unfounded at this point. As we have seen already, as the firm grew recreation and staff welfare were positioned as increasingly important to the business, but the crossovers between this staff perception of change and the large-scale summer party with its focus on performance pinpoint a moment at which theatrical entertainments at the factory were clearly slotted into the firm's new organisational structures and business drivers and realised as a means to showcase the new factory and its landscapes, and to contribute to a new model of industrial community that could reassure those members of staff concerned by the loss of the 'human'. 1912 was to bring another significant change to the organisation, with the private company going public. Throughout these developments – and the anxieties they prompted – theatre and entertainment supplied continuity, identity, and community.

As outlined above, by 1911 the summer parties had grown into time-consuming, annual occasions, entertaining between 6,000 and 8,000 employees and their families, offering them mixed programmes including the annual pastoral play, alongside burlesques, parades and visual spectacles, refreshments, sports, and sideshows. *Bournville Works Magazine* laid out the 'many weeks of elaborate preparation' demanded by these 'costly days' (*B.W.M.*, August 1912: 228). The outlay was indeed high: refreshments, marquees, fireworks, costumes, props, sets, and the staff time needed for preparation, rehearsal, and attendance were all covered by the firm. In 1911, the Board agreed to authorise a significant budget of 795 pounds for the party, with permission to allow the spend to reach 1,000 pounds once all costs connected to the day were met (CAHS/CMM/7 February 1911: 21). Currency conversion is a methodologically difficult area, but rough ideas of equivalence do remain helpful and London's National Archives cost-of-living based currency conversion tool, last updated in 2017, estimates the agreed sum to be the equivalent of 78,000 pounds. A more useful comparison still, perhaps, is that the party was given the same budget as the firm's visitors department annual expenditure, a clear signal of the level of investment (and recognised return) in this employee event. Committee of Management minutes clearly signal that generous summer party funding did not represent Cadbury's throwing financial caution to the wind. Records reveal careful event-budgeting by the Girls' and Men's Works Committees, the Summer Party Committee and its five subcommittees, evidencing the scale of the work connected with the annual event, and the significance it was accorded. This was a business activity and as such was subject to tight financial control. Membership of the five party subcommittees increased from thirty-eight in 1912, to fifty-one in 1913, with the additional roles charged with planning, catering logistics, and managing stewarding, entertainments, the masque, and the music. Accounts from these multiple committees involved in party planning, from the most senior management to operational staff evince that Cadbury's could, and did, balance the books in relation to these large-scale events. Regular meetings ensured planning was on track, within budget, and that the parties would be well organised and presented. Their outcomes were reported to the highest-level company boards. In 1911 the event came in under budget, with the final costs totalling 959 pounds (CAHS/CMM/7 November 1911: 856). On top of recorded outlays, the costs of staff time redirected to preparation of the party and those associated with the half-day factory holiday are not traceable. But these events were not accounted for wholly through columns of figures. While expenditure was carefully monitored and tracked, the parties were understood to be part of the social and economic benefits of the firm's ongoing business commitment to the nexus of staff, recreation, leisure, and productivity, which they understood to be the foundations on which the positive columns of figures that represented Cadbury's business were built, and remained stable.

The most heavily pre-publicised events at the 1911–1914 summer parties were the Bournville masques – a series of large, pageant performances written and produced by local poet, playwright, and actor John Drinkwater. These form the subject of the following chapter. What is simultaneously revealed by party accounts, programmes, and other evidence is that the popularity of the summer celebrations was at least as much connected with the many other entertainments and attractions they offered to partygoers. After all, the masques were no more than an hour and a half in length and embedded in a wider event and entertainment programme. Spectators would have watched them before, or after, something else. Not considering these other entertainments – albeit acts that might be considered less conventionally theatrical, like the Water Carnival or fancy dress cyclists – would produce a very different understanding of theatre and performance at the summer works parties, and as part of Cadbury's business operations. In the remainder of this chapter, I consider three other performances that took place over the four peak summer years, while emphasising that it is critical that we register and keep in mind that each of the acts listed in Table 1 contributed to a complex web of performances, ideas, and humour at the parties. They functioned as stand-alone entertainments and opportunities to recognise colleagues and friends, and intersected as parts of a wider programme of entertainments that spoke to each other and to the day-to-day experiences of work and play at the Bournville factory.

1911: The British Empire Tableaux

While the foregrounded event in 1911's summer party pre-publicity was John Drinkwater's first masque, partygoers were also promised many other entertainments. As part of the lead-up to the occasion, May's edition of the works magazine reported 'extensive arrangements are being made for the pleasure of visitors' on the men's grounds' (155). What is also made clear from the details in this account is that 1911's coronation year programme had been deliberately designed to offer a new scale of fun and distraction. Participation was expected of employees, but there is a sense in both this account and in those cited above, that tangible efforts were made to secure this staff engagement by providing a good day – rather than 'enforcing' fun at an event designed solely to fit the tastes of the Board or the firm's senior management. Two large performances created for the 1911 party were presented as key features of the fun on offer: the British Empire Tableaux and the Burlesque Cricket Match. Of the eighteen entertainments that were included in the seven-page party programme (the masque had its own separate programme), these two were given the greatest amount of space, with three of the seven pages dedicated to them. Together they offer a snapshot of the factory's cultural and sporting activities and priorities, further illustrate the idea of fun that was a clearly articulated desired outcome of the works parties, and signal a distinct, ongoing relationship between Cadbury's performances and the popular entertainment industry.

The 'British Empire Tableaux' was promoted and reviewed as a major attraction of 1911's summer party. The synopsis for the tableaux published in the party programme offers some detail of the staged action:

> Britannia, as typifying her chosen race, receives an oration from Neptune, God of the Sea. Surrounded by characters representing the leading industries and the four home counties of the British Isles, she receives representatives of her Colonies, Dependencies and Protectorates, who are introduced by Neptune and who bring as tributes to Britannia gifts of fruits, mineral products etc., typical of the various countries. (CAHS/350/002134)

Billed as tableaux, in practice, the entertainment was a pageant with a final tableau scene, accompanied by a performed commentary reminiscent of those delivered by magic lantern professors, and other public lecturers. Neptune's speech was the work of Arthur Hackett (1878–1945), a mechanical engineer on Cadbury's senior staff team who had worked at Bournville since 1900. It was printed, in full, in July's works magazine, serving as both a memory of the recent performance and a stand-alone piece that emphasised clear links between Cadbury's ethos, ideas about industrial leadership, and the entertainments offered at the parties. Written in verse, Hackett's oration connected Bournville's display with the coronation of King George V and Queen Mary – the new heads of the British Empire – that would take place two days after the summer works party, and with the associated 'week of pageantry' that had drawn visitors to London from around the globe (*B.W.M.*, July 1911: 210).

The party programme reveals the entertainment was performed twice during the afternoon, had a running time of around half an hour, and concluded with a huge group tableau created by the bodies of the 200 plus employees who participated, alongside many horses that were used in the procession. The action took the form of an extended scene framed as part pilgrimage, part homage. Each country – represented by a single performer, or group of performers – entered the arena and offered gifts to Annie Grange Hyslop (1890–1972), the Scottish-born Cadbury's clerk who played Britannia. Spectators were left with a final-staged picture depicting representatives of Empire gathered around Britannia and leading industry figures, performing symbolic deference to her, and to her position of authority, and by default to the leaders of industry who stood with her (*B.W.M.*, July 1911: 210). As a spectacle, it marked a step away from the local histories and fairy or mythic narratives that tended to be produced at Cadbury's, in favour of a colonial parade that drew far more heavily on conventions from exhibitions and other popular pageants and displays. The order in which representatives of countries appeared was significant.

The British Isles, Gibraltar, Canada and New Foundland, were followed by Australia and New Zealand, South Africa, Egypt, the Soudan, Cypres, Aden, West Indies, East Africa, China, India, Ceylon, Burma and Singapore. As their bodies became parts of the scene they created a visual hierarchy, later arrivals appeared not only before Britannia but – by default of their positioning in the evolving picture – before her already present representatives from the British Isles, industry, and other nations. The dominant model of established racism this staged underpinned the whole content of the entertainment and its visual and verbal narratives, as might be expected from a synopsis that stated Britannia represented the chosen race. Countries were reductively identified through skin colour in Arthur Hackett's speech, which included the line 'here, white and black, and yellow, here red and brown are seen'. Race became visual spectacle. Two Cadbury's employees, Maud Gallimore (1882–1973), a factory forewoman, and forewoman and chief clerk Beatrice Duke (1872–1966) were responsible for the costumes, using some items created in-house, and some borrowed from employees who had travelled on behalf of the firm, including clothing and accessories from William Cadbury's collection and from local missionary societies. The 'dazzling colours' these brought to the tableaux were noted and praised (210). Representations of other cultures and races had been present in Cadbury's recreational events for some time. As early as 1903 the factory staged a lecture in the Girls' Dining Room by the journalist James Budgett-Meakin (1866–1903) on Morocco. Meakin delivered the lecture in 'costume' and performed 'street cries, calls to prayer, and chants'. Content ranged from exoticism – with discussion of snake charming – to quotidien, with guidance on correct courtesy and etiquette. Elizabeth Cadbury accompanied the lecture with incidental music played on the organ (*B.W.M.*, December 1903: 44). Such entertainments disclose the tensions in Cadbury's attempt to stage the world. The works magazine report on the visit of a contingency from Jerusalem, Damascus, Smyrna, and Baghdad in 1909 rejected visions of Empire and superiority of the 'West' promoted by Rudyard Kipling and others, recording the visiting party members' 'intelligent grasp and appreciation of the most progressive social ideals'. In the same article, the representatives were described as 'most remakable' with red fezs that 'gave just the magic touch which revealed their Eastern origin' (*B.W.M.*, September 1909: 341). The British Empire Tableaux was one in a series of educationally framed spectacles that played out the gap between ideas about race and representations of race in practice.

Through the use of costumes *Bournville Works Magazine* claimed a style of documentary realism for the Empire tableaux. 'The costumes, the customs and the forms of homage had been for a long time a matter of the closest study, so that the whole formed a liberal education to the insular British spectator' the report noted (*B.W.M.*, July 1911: 210). Performance had long been employed as a space to create and cement ideas and images of race and identity that supported and promoted empire, with international exhibitions, music hall acts, circus shows and stage drama playing key roles in ideologies and popular understandings. Prarthana Purkayastha's exploration of the mistreatment of touring nautch dancers in London, performing a style that had been modified and reduced in British popular performance culture of the fin-de-siècle offers a powerful model for the complexity and endemic nature of these practices by the turn of the twentieth century (Purkayastha, 2019). Within the context of Bournville, the references to educational content held particular weight and resonance. Theatre's role in Cadbury's educational agendas is the subject of chapter six, but it is worth noting here that this performance was assigned the power to teach. It was defined as education. Concurrently, surviving images and descriptions make it clear that the pseudo-anthropological expertise and educational approach laid claimed to here was unsettled by caricatures familiar from theatre, music hall, wider popular culture, and other party entertainments. Photographs show cast members performing in blackface (see Figure 12). While the appearance of the performers suggests there may have been some attempt to stage different skin colours, rather than wholly replicate the grotesque 'comedic' image of the minstrel familiar from the popular stage, the presence of blackface in Bournville performances identifies a moment of tension between Quaker ideals around race, education, and humanity, and practices in performance.

Cadbury's industrial ethos sought to foreground equality and working conditions across the globe. As Quakers, they held strong anti-slavery positions as individuals and industrialists, but the firm was not immune to failures on either of these fronts. Cadbury's cocoa and chocolate manufacturing production depended on the colonies and trading routes of the British Empire, with the firm's overseas posts in West Africa critical to the business operation. Earlier generations of the Cadbury family, and the Quaker movement actively supported the abolitionist movement, but that support did not equate to an absence of racism or Quaker involvement in the slave trade, as ongoing research reveals (see Quaker.org). As an early-twentieth industrial organisation the Bournville firm aligned itself with the Third Party. Identified by Kenneth Dike Nworah as a 'small but perceptible sect which identified itself with the development of a true colonial conscience in Britain' (349), and by Anandi Ramamurthy as a

Figure 12 'An Empire Selection'
Bournville Works Magazine, July 1911. Cadbury Archives and Heritage Services.

group that found its roots in the work of Mary Kingsley and was 'mainly sustained by the humanitarian idealism of John Holt and E. D. Morel', the Third Party 'condemned both the predominant racist creed and the patronising condescension of traditional philanthropy', asserting that 'the interests of Africans would be best served by allowing them control over their own resources, so as to encourage development through "free trade"' (Ramamurthy, 2003: 63). Third Party members were close to businessmen, including William Adlington Cadbury, who sought to apply the ideologies they created and shared to their industrial or commercial operations, and financially supported E. D. Morel's political campaigns (70). At Cadbury's action around global production conditions increased following the exposure of enslaved labour on the islands of Sao Thomé and Principe, sources of the firm's raw material, in 1901 and ensuing questions surrounding delays in the firm's withdrawal from those markets (24–25). Silke Hackenesch evidences the ongoing coverage of the accusations of racism and slave labour against the firm this prompted, and positions Cadbury's chemist Arthur Knapp's (who was to go on to play Father Time at the 1927 Concert Hall opening performance) 1920 book on production, *Cocoa and Chocolate*, within ongoing attempts by the firm to reassert their ethical credentials in the face of the scandal.

1911's summer work party took place almost exactly at a midway point between the 1901 revelation of enslaved labour in Cadbury's island cocoa sources and Knapp's *Cocoa and Chocolate* – two clear marker points in early twentieth-century histories of the firm and race – and at this moment racist imagery and ideas pervaded some entertainments staged at Bournville, particularly those staged at the works parties that appropriated music hall, exhibition, and variety culture, rather than those that staged dramatic texts. As Anandi Ramamurthy has revealed, images grounded in race were also connected with the advertising industry, and its habitual use of empire as a key motif in marketing of British brands (2003). Hackenesch identifies a language of 'adventure, excitement and exoticism' in these descriptions that can be aligned with factory burlesques and tableaux, and Ramamurthy identifies a painting hung in Bournville's Girls' Dining Room depicting an eighteenth-century coffee house scene that included 'an exotically dressed black boy' sitting and playing as another example of devices that enhanced 'the exoticism of the chocolate house and its produce' (2017: 35; 2003: 64). Knapp's *Coca and Chocolate* mirrored Third Party discourses and objectives, celebrating the skill of the cocoa producers, praising the stamina and health needed for the labour involved, and presenting the support for their business that Cadbury's production offered, and later advertising images increasingly focused on images of 'peasant production' of cocoa that fitted more clearly with Third Party positions on trade and labour, Hackenesch's reading of Knapp's work indicates the endurance of earlier imagery and patterns in Cadbury's literature that connect with the stereotyping and racism present in summer party entertainments (35).

Other elements further unsettled the educational claims made for this entertainment. In an impromptu performance moment in the second performance of the afternoon, the tableaux cast were joined by the group of around 100 employee dancers who had performed their 'Four Seasons' dance earlier at the event. They gathered around the edge of the arena, framing the final tableaux. Still clothed in their costumes as Spring, Summer, Autumn, and Winter they brought evocations of the mythical and pastoral to the pseudo-anthropological frozen performance moment, a picture familiar from other images of the pastoral staged through the firm's theatre. In this happenstance spectacle the tableau of characters chosen as representative of the British Empire, who appear also to have been all – or at least dominated by – women employees, were surrounded by dancers embodying a pastoral idyll; the Green and Pleasant land of Bournville, and more widely of Britain. This was an accidental motionless display surrounded by an animated frame that spoke to the staging of colonial hierarchies played out before the audience. Bournville's factory landscape can be interpreted as a materialisation of ideas around British national identity, most clearly through its reflection of political and cultural constructs of the Back to the Land movement that was prominent in the early twentieth century. In her study of American company towns Margaret Crawford categorises Bournville and Port Sunlight as more 'overtly self-conscious' evocations of the traditional English village than either the garden cities of Letchworth and Welwyn Garden, or the American case studies that she explores (1995: 73). Robert Burden and Stephan Kohl have argued that such images and the dynamics that created them produced a sense of a 'false universalism', a pastoral utopianism (2006: 14). The summer parties' visual references to village fetes can be read as a model of this, with performance – and the objects of performance – feeding into representations of Cadbury's industrial site as a pastoral idyll. In relation to outdoor performance's, kinetic, embodied imagery, this approach can be read as overly simplistic. Paul Readman has reminded us that while artistic and social understandings of land, landscape, and the rural as utopian visions were 'too extensive to be regarded as culturally marginal', there are persuasive arguments (he cites Peter Mandler) that present them as protests 'against prevailing trends' rather than as the dominant consensus (Readman, 2018: 12). Reading these positions as in flux, and as potentially resistant, opens up the complexity of Cadbury's choreographed, performing bodies, and the ways that their familiar identities and presence, and the diverse events and spectacles they participated in, temporarily changed Bournville's landscape, disrupted its vistas, and changed its meanings, working as part of what Anne Spirn has identified as landscape's active presence in meaning making, as a backdrop re-presented, re-made, by the scenes staged against it (18).

1911: The Burlesque Cricket Match

A cricket match provided the outer frame for 1911's other summer party large-scale entertainment, bringing together the most quintessential of rural British sports with a series of caricature characters familiar from the wider world of popular entertainment and images of a Green and Pleasant land. Staged on the factory's sports pitches, the lengthy burlesque reflected the importance of recreational sport to Bournville's progressive industrial culture, conjured an image of the countryside, and showcased resources funded by the firm. Against this backdrop – an industrial version of the village green idyll evoked by the sport, further indication of how the

Figure 13 'The Burlesque Cricket Match'
Bournville Works Magazine, July 1911. Cadbury Archives and Heritage Services.

industrial-pastoral disrupted images of the countryside idyll – the staged action introduced and lampooned a cast of character-players familiar from current literature, visual culture, popular performance, fashion, politics and, to some extent, from the British Empire Tableaux, with spectators expected to follow both the game and the loose comedic action. Facing the white-flannel clad Bournville team, embodiments of sporting prowess, a series of figures straight out of the plays, musicals, music halls and circuses of popular culture were fielded. The educational/anthropological edge of display claimed by the Empire Tableaux switched to a set of more reductive representations of celebrity, gender, and race in the cricket match. In a reductive, romanticised vision of the 'orient', 'Lo-Fing-Lu' walked to the wicket, re-staging the still popular Chinese magician figure performing 'with his perfectly acted ceremonies and illusive bat'. An Indian prince, Broncho Bill from the Prairies, the Australian Victor Thumper, Baron de Bourne 'one of the old [French] stock' whose 'ancestor came over with the conqueror', Bounding Bison, a Canadian Sioux Chief, and Shamus O'Connell from Tipperary were among the other characters who followed (1911 Summer Party Programme, CAHS/350/002134). The appearances of these cricketing characters were greeted with 'roars of laughter' from party spectators, likely prompted by the blended experience of familiar caricatures and the spectacle of their friends and colleagues in disguise.

Overt connections with celebrities from the world of popular performance were also present in the Burlesque Cricket Match (Figure 13). Scoring the game were David George Lloyd – a clear reference to David

Lloyd George (1863–1945), whose political career was on the rise and whose social reform Liberal politics were very much on home turf at Bournville – and Eugene Sandoe – a direct parody of the celebrity physical culturalist Eugen Sandow (1867–1925) whose act was formed from a series of 'spectacular and highly developed' bodybuilding poses Nick Havergal has defined as 'iconic representations of masculinity' (2020: 18; 27). Both – spectators were told – were scoring as they were 'good at figures' (1911 Summer Party Programme, CAHS/350/002134). Sandow is of particular interest to theatre's staging of wider Cadbury's culture. The relationship between Sandow and the firm was tense. Sandow had published Cadbury's cocoa advertisements on the front page of his own *Sandow's Magazine* during the early years of the twentieth century; placement that realised the link selling benefits of his physical strength and fitness, and the health properties of cocoa. Ever the entrepreneur, Sandow saw an opportunity to market this connection for himself, releasing his own 'Sandow's health and strength' 'Drink Diet' nutritional cocoa onto the British market late in 1911, accompanied by advertising that replicated much of Cadbury's health-based marketing strategy and formats (see *Truth Christmas Annual*, 26 December 1911: 7 for a strong example of this). In retaliation, Cadbury's and other leading manufacturers cut their prices, eventually driving Sandow's operation into bankruptcy by 1916 (Chapman, 1994: 170). At the time of the 1911 summer party, Sandow's cocoa was yet to reach the stage of mass production, but his purchase and refit of a huge-abandoned factory site in Elephant and Castle, London was general knowledge in business circles. While his entry into the cocoa market was met with growing disquiet, indications are that his competitors did not take him wholly seriously at this point, a dynamic that might suggest a secondary, humorous set of meanings in his identification as 'good at figures' within an industry that doubted his abilities as an industrialist. Stagings of the firm's deteriorating relationship with Sandow featured again two years later at 1913's summer works party as part of the staff tableaux vivants competition. By this point the celebrity's cocoa production business was up and running, nonetheless the depiction of a Sandow-esque figure created by the F Block Tablet team shows him posing and flexing on top of an advertisement for Cadbury's cocoa, surrounded by white-clad Bournville factory girls (see Figure 14). In this image Cadbury's products underpin his strength and wellness, not his own cocoa brand, in a creation that might be viewed as playing to the crowd. As we have seen, tableaux staged strong connections between performance and advertising and the smallness of their format made them practical performance forms, ubiquitous across Cadbury's events. Open, competitive summer party

Marketing Fresh Air 119

Figure 14 'Purity and Strength', *tableau vivant*
Bournville Works Magazine, August 1913. Cadbury Archives and Heritage Services.

tableaux events showcased the commitment and ingenuity of Cadbury's workers, affirming the firm's welfare policies, celebrating the individuals who staffed the factory on a day-to-day basis, and offering what was considered to be a healthy element of competition amongst employees. 'Such rivalry is good', reported the *Bournville Works Magazine*, 'it stimulates the best kind of feeling in the departments represented [and] fosters both ideas and ingenuity'. Healthy competition was considered good for business, a way of developing, motivating, and inspiring staff members. 1913's competition was judged by an external invited visitor for the first time. A board member of booksellers, W. H. Smith decided on the winner, demonstrating how even these small, seemingly peripheral moments of performance were used to showcase the firm (August 1913: 254).

Returning to 1911's cricket pitch stage, The New Woman was fielded in the semblance of Dulcibel Spankers, a 'famous lady cricketer', played in drag by thirty-five-year-old Cadbury's invoice clerk George Margetts. The New Woman was 'a cultural icon of the fin de siècle'; 'not one figure, but several. In the guise of a bicycling, cigarette-smoking Amazon [...] she romped through the pages of Punch and popular fiction' embodying fear and progress (Richardson and Willis, 2019: 12). George Margetts was at the heart of delivering the firm's entertainments. He was secretary to the summer party through the first two decades of the twentieth century and was later appointed manager of the Concert Hall. As Dulcibel Spankers he 'tripped to the wicket […] in a hobble skirt', fell repeatedly, powdered her/his nose after every bat, and was, eventually, taken off the pitch by an ambulance (*B.W.M.*, July 1911: 211). For industrial and recreational contexts that were relatively supportive of women's work, this was an oddly reductive caricature. Cadbury's engaged with, shaped, and promoted intellectual, representative debates on suffrage and women's rights, and were progressive employees in relation to current gender equality. As the next section will explore, Cicely Hamilton's suffrage drama *Votes for Women* was staged at Bournville and suffrage events by factory performers, and local women education leaders and political figures were impassioned, activist speakers at Girls' Continuation School events. The factory had a clear, unapologetic, gently radical political edge when it came to questions of women's rights. Many of the women employees who featured in the performances covered in this book, and whose professional histories I have managed to uncover achieved management roles and good career development, although that ceased if they chose to marry. Only men played the roles in the Burlesque Cricket Match, there was no women's team at Bournville at that time (although 1903's event had seen a girls versus boys cricket match), but this comedic sending up of the cultural archetype of independent women strikes as quite distinct from the presence and roles of women at the firm, many of which were being played out in different entertainments taking place at the same occasion. In the gaps between these entertainments and the characters they staged wider current tensions around gender become clear.

Fusing sport and theatre was a characteristic of Bournville's party programmes. I have not traced similar burlesque cricket matches in other industrial spaces, they appear to be more commonly linked to community event and charity occasion programmes since the 1860s and 1870s, one had been included on the Crystal Palace 1910–1911 Christmas holiday entertainment programme, and the format appears to have gained some traction over the following years. Interestingly, while there were an estimated 6,000 plus employees at the party, the photographic image of the Burlesque Cricket Match selected for publication in the works magazine suggests there were not a huge number of spectators at this entertainment. There were two performances, so it might be that this was the less popular of them, but it should also be considered that accounts make it clear that the action was chaotic, and difficult to follow, with no sustained narrative above that of the Bournville team being better at cricket, and the staging of a series of various familiar 'characters' or 'types'. Party organisers were not dissuaded. A football burlesque was staged the following year, with Bournville competing against the 'Gentlemen of England', a team of players that comically referenced football teams from around the country, including 'Robin Hood, the Nottingham Forester' and the 'Aston Villa Lion'. Again the works magazine reviewer could make no sense of any plot but did admire the 'brilliant play' that took place despite 'the unconventional rules' (*B.W.M.*, August 1912: 236). Sporting burlesques were dropped after 1912, reflecting the sense that the participants perhaps gained rather more than the spectators of this entertainment form.

1912: The Burlesque Man-Agerie

By 1911 entertainments that foregrounded mass employee participation were prioritised at the summer works parties, establishing a pattern that was to continue throughout the next two decades of Bournville performances. This model was adaptable. 1911's party corresponded with coronation celebrations, resulting in a kaleidoscopic suite of staged images that intersected with wider national patterns and events, while 1912's summer party offered entertainments that were far less moulded to a national, outer frame of reference. One of these was The Burlesque Man-agerie, performed in an arena on the Men's Recreation Ground, in front of a large crowd. It began with a faint humming – a 'noise like that made through combs and tissue paper' – heard from a distance. The volume gradually increased as a slow-moving line of animals came into view, advancing across the purpose-built, temporary performance space. Elephants, giraffes, dromedaries, lions, tigers, bears, and monkeys processed alongside the more native bulls, horses, monkeys, donkeys, and the Bournville Bunny. The humming ceased and the works band struck up. Bears wrestled and danced. Lions and tigers performed acrobatic routines. The monkey performed a series of poses that mimicked the strong men popular on the musical hall stages of the time (including, of course, Eugen Sandow). The bulls fought a matador (*B.W.M.*, August 1912: 232). There are no surviving records that tell us what the Bournville Bunny did, but her presence amidst this wider menagerie supplied a clear visual reference to Cadbury's world-leading branding and marketing. Reinvented on regular occasions, here she reminded audiences of the current popular children's book character and prefigured the cinematic rabbit amidst the factory's garden that would star in *Elsie and the Bunny* a decade later. The Burlesque Man-agerie was rooted in fairgrounds, travelling circuses, and zoos. Simultaneously it was a very local entertainment; delivered with a Cadbury spin; typically Bournville.

Figure 15 'The Burlesque Man-agerie'
Bournville Works Magazine, August 1912. Cadbury Archives and Heritage Services.

The Man-agerie animals were all played by factory employees, dressed in costumes that were 'a little worn' (235). Comments on this wear and tear suggest the costumes might well have been borrowed for the occasion, for those created in-house were consistently praised for the skill of their design, construction, and creativity. Never ones to hold back on the talent of the firm's staff and their creativity, the works magazine captured the picture as 'an amazing and amusing aggregation of active, awe-inspiring and antediluvian animals' (235). The tiredness of the costumes paled into insignificance against the 'life and spirit' of their performances. Of course, life and spirit are precisely what a photograph depicting a frozen moment of action (such as that captured in Figure 15) cannot capture, but audiences were impressed and amused and, for the works magazine's reviewer, the entertainment was a 'capital take off' of the wild beast show and a 'true burlesque'. 'The ease with which the impersonators revert[ed] to type' was noted, 'proving beyond question the theory of the origin of species' the reviewer joked (235). The party's audience laughed, a lot, we are told, with attempts to guess which of their colleagues was hidden in which part of each costume supplying a large part of their enjoyment: 'who was the hind legs of the elephant was one of the prevailing questions of the day' (236). Of course, many amongst this audience knew, which added to that pleasure of spectating. Further evidence indicates that the entertainment also worked for wider audiences. Sections of the Man-agerie performance were filmed and screened at the Birmingham Picturedrome in Sparkbrook at a later date, where they were well received by the cinema's mixed spectatorship (236). In this extra-factory space, the performances served as an advertisement for the firm's recreational provision and employee creativity. For a firm recruiting from local areas – as a standard within a three-mile radius of the factory – this offered a potential publicity tool on a second level, promoting Bournville life and its leadership, and attracting future employees. Records of discussions around advertising clearly set out the rigour with which Cadbury's managed and controlled their marketing campaigns, particularly new investments in film promotional materials, so this screening affirms the location of these entertainments as endorsed features of part of the firm's public identity.

Like the previous year's cricket match, The Burlesque Man-agerie reflected other entertainments staged at local and more high-profile fairs and garden parties across the country. There are notable synergies with the annual Actors' Orphanage Fund Garden Party, a spectacular, fashionable, well-publicised event organised and staffed by theatre's leading celebrities that attracted significant national press and newsreel coverage. Detailed programme notes for the Man-agerie highlight other reflections of wider cultures: the monkey/strongman hybrid I referenced above can be easily read as another 'appearance' of a Eugen Sandow model, with trained lions, the matador (a popular character from musical comedies), and the invocation of the Ringmaster or Fairground Barker in the description of 'an amazing and amusing aggregation of active, awe-inspiring, antediluvian animals' offering an eclectic mix of images and references from the popular theatrical and variety stages. Arguably the success of the Man-agerie would have depended to some extent on the audience being up-to-date with current variety trends and performers, as well as enjoying the sight of friends and fellow employees performing. The procession of slightly worn animals across Bournville's entertainment grounds brought together city, countryside, and production and publicised them more widely through screenings in Birmingham cinemas. While the Drinkwater masques received the majority of the press's attention, other entertainments were powerful agents for the firm.

Playing in the Fresh Air

Summer party entertainments at the Bournville factory site created an active palimpsest of the firm's key advertising imagery, animated by the bodies of performing employees and drawing on tropes from business and stage cultures. The reach and influence of the summer works parties were significant. This was a firm that thought carefully about its external image and meticulously controlled it. Reports of the annual events were carried by the national press and regional publications, by daily newspapers and fashion magazines, and short films of entertainments and the crowds that watched them were screened at local cinemas. Together this publicity clearly signals that party performances were endorsed by the firm and identified as representative of Bournville's values. The theatrical and sporting activity entertainments showcased was fuelled by the firm's drive to cultivate participation and increase spectacle: 'Bournville is ever striving to surpass itself – to go one better than the time before', noted an editorial in the works magazine in April 1931. 'Whether it be a better year's trade than the last, or a jollier and more original New Year Party than ever' (97). No one rested on their laurels at Bournville. Each of the entertainments considered here fitted into this culture and modelled and promoted it, and outside spaces were key to them. Practically, because there was insufficient space inside. Symbolically, because of the health benefits connected with fresh air, and the relationship between the local landscape, the industrial pastoral and Cadbury's identity. The same set of dynamics were at the core of the firm's outdoor pastoral plays and pageants, and it is these performances that are the focus of the next chapter.

CHAPTER 4

Serious Play
John Drinkwater's Masques at Bournville

'Without undue pride, we have considered ourselves an important opening in that tendency towards a new out-door theatre which began with the revival of the pageant in many parts of the country', reflected the works magazine author of 'Community Drama', locating Bournville at the heart of early twentieth-century dramatic developments (June 1920: 165). Experiments with large outdoor-theatre productions began at Cadbury's summer works parties in 1908, escalating in both scale and ambition over the following six years, and peaking between 1911 and 1914 with four outdoor plays written and produced by a local theatrical personality, John Drinkwater. In its entwining of recreation and fresh air, the firm celebrated Bournville's open-air factory theatrical activity as 'one of the healthiest forms of people's art' (*B.W.M.*, August 1913: 252). Outdoor performance was harnessed to create, foster, and promote industrial community, realising Edward Cadbury's publicised understanding of theatrical activity as key to Bournville's identity and cultural memory-making (Cadbury, 1912: 238). To explore and understand these dynamics, and the importance of outdoor theatre to the business, in this chapter I focus on Drinkwater's four productions for Cadbury's – *An English Medley* (1911), *The Pied Piper: A Tale of Hamelin City* (1912), *The Only Legend: A Masque of the Scarlet Pierrot* (1913) and *Robin Hood and the Pedlar* (1914)– contextualising them within a series of earlier pastoral dramas staged on Bournville's factory grounds.

The First Pastoral Plays at Bournville, 1908 and 1909

1908's summer works party organisers had grand ambitions to produce a masque staging Bournville's history. Pageants had been the subject of some discussion amongst the factory's key cultural players. Clarkson Booth's article 'About Pageants' published in November 1907's works magazine noted that he had 'heard and read this summer about pageants here, there, and (almost) everywhere ... most of them very successful', but he questioned why they 'should be confined to places' with 'mouldering abbeys', or castles rather than 'our modern towns, which have sprung up as centres of industrial life'. Over the following two and a half pages Booth set out his vision for an industrial pageant at Bournville, performed 'at the foot of the bank on the men's grounds' (20). Interestingly the performance he proposed did not centre on local history. His dream pageant was far closer to the costumed spectacles of the other pageants he critiqued, offering a global industrial history of the 'peaceful victory' of cocoa in a structure he aligned with the 'durbar' ceremony, appropriated by the British Empire (20–22). Ideas about pageantry had clearly been under discussion, but the eventual 1908 outdoor play did not follow either of these models. Challenged by the 'paucity of [available] historical material' (or knowledge of its whereabouts) a creative compromise was necessary, one that retained the overarching vision of a large-scale outdoor performance to celebrate the new works party format and tackled the difficulties with its planned content (*B.W.M.*, August 1908: 295–296).

The day was saved by (John) Robert Quinton (1870–1958), a carpenter at Cadbury's who was to become a leading representative of factory theatre during the 1910s and 1920s. Sticking with the organising theme of history, Quinton created *May Day,* a visual spectacle inspired by drawings of old village views that fused tableaux and short acted scenes staging traditional May-Day celebrations. Its scale was larger than anything Bournville audiences had previously seen. Performed against 'the magnificent background of forest trees on the rising greensward' of the Girls' Recreation Grounds, the play conjured the atmosphere of an 'old-time fete' (295). Its focus would have been familiar, for Bournville had its own traditions. In an oral history recording Herbert Davey (1902–2000), who was to marry Quinton's daughter, Miriam, recalled how the village's delivery carts and horses were decorated on the first of May each year (Birmingham Museum/ Sound Cloud). Quinton's outdoor production also foregrounded maypole dancing – a pastime favoured and to some extent resuscitated by George Cadbury. Accompanied by music and featuring a cast of around 170, *May Day* satisfied the firm's desire for a more ambitious form of outdoor performance: 'that such a production could be the work of those pursuing their daily vocation in connection with an industry' was 'astonishing', concluded the works magazine. 'In all probability no more brilliant spectacle has been seen at Bournville before' (August 1908: 293). *May Day* may have staged a more generic set of images of the countryside than was originally planned, and it may not have been about Bournville's history, but it nonetheless staged and animated key elements of day-to-day life at Cadbury's,

Figure 16 'A View of the Audience at *May Day*'
Bournville Works Magazine, August 1908. Cadbury Archives and Heritage Services.

in particular imagery associated with the industrial-pastoral and with the party's fete-style attractions set out on the Men's Recreation Grounds, just across Bournville Lane (Figure 16). 1908's pastoral play set the standard for a series of outdoor dramas that featured at the firm's summer works parties for the next six years and prompted the firm's thinking about the creation of an outdoor performance space.

The shift in Bournville works parties from indoor to outdoor occasions and the staging of the firm's first outdoor plays coincided with a peak in pageant making as a popular national leisure activity, with the verb '"to padge" or "to paj" meaning to participate in a pageant coming into popular usage during the first third of the twentieth century' (Bartie et al, 2020: 4). Pageant director and playwright Louis Napoleon Parker (1852–1944) – recalled by *The Times Literary Supplement* as 'the first and greatest of the Edwardian pageant-masters' – had created his first pageant in 1905, at Sherbourne in Dorset (30 September 1944: 472). With a cast of 900, and an estimated audience of 50,000, Ayako Yoshino's study of Edwardian *Pageant Fever* identifies this Sherbourne event as the 'first popular pageant'; a performance that 'seized the popular imagination' and triggered a series of pageants staged in towns and cities in a 'vogue [that was] genuinely nationwide' and lasted for several years (2011: 50). It was this culture that Cadbury's saw their open-air theatre contributing to and developing. The following year, in 1906, Parker staged a pageant at Warwick Castle, a historical site relatively close to Cadbury's Bournville factory. It is not inconceivable – although at present not evidencable – that some factory employees witnessed this event. It would have been difficult for them not, at least, to be aware of it. In *Restaging the Past: Historical Pageants, Culture and Society in Modern Britain,* Angela Bartie, Linda Fleming, Mark Freeman, Alexander Hutton, and Paul Readman position these Edwardian pageants as important community spaces that were 'always primarily concerned with the past and its representation in the present'. To achieve those representations the events frequently blended 'fact and fiction' in the stories of people and place they staged (Bartie et al., 2020: 3). In many ways, Bournville's pastoral plays and masques adhered to these common patterns. Synergies between pageantry and Bournville's theatrical representation of its people and places are clear.

The factory's outdoor theatre productions did not mark the birth of a new cultural phenomenon in the villages to the north of Birmingham's city centre. Local green spaces had been used as performance sites long before pageant fever swept the country and before al fresco theatre became connected with Cadbury's. A clear earlier model can be discovered in the regular outdoor music and theatre programmes offered at Edgbaston's Botanical Gardens (around three and a half miles from Bournville) from the 1880s onwards. These summer entertainments were produced in connection with the local commercial entertainment industry and included military band programmes and performances by orchestral string bands made up of resident musicians from Birmingham's Prince of Wales's Theatre (*Birmingham Daily Post,* 4 August 1883: 4). July 1887 saw open-air theatre added to the Botanical Gardens programming, with the arrival of Mr Poole (of Cambridge) and his company in a production of the forest scenes from *As You Like It,* staged with the permission of Ben Greet (1857–1936) (Programme/UOBTC/M&M/REF/TH/RE/3/BE2). Greet's name was closely connected with pastoral theatre. His company 'The Ben Greet Players' had been founded in 1883 and had popularised national touring schedules of plays performed in regional green spaces, including parks, colleges, and village greens (O'Malley, 2020: 68–69). Poole's Edgbaston production included dances arranged by London's Lyceum and Princesses theatres, and promotional materials that highlighted Greet's current position in the Lyceum company. Marketed as a 'Pastoral Play', this countryside *As You Like It* was heavily seasoned with fashionable, London West

End theatre, and the appeal of this recipe is indicated by the cost. Standard admission price for Poole's *As You Like It* forest medley was four times more expensive than the promenade vocal and instrumental concert that had taken place the week before; this was a novelty with fashionable status targeted at relatively affluent audiences, at a ticket price that also reflected the heightened costs of producing theatre (*Birmingham Daily Post*, 21 July 1887: 1). Further theatrical events took place at Edgbaston Botanical Gardens over the following years. In 1900, the well-known actor-manager Frank Benson's company appeared for a three-day run of, again, *As You Like It*, performed next to a large pond with a wooded backdrop. The report from the *Birmingham Daily Post* clearly signals that regular outdoor performance had taken place between these two recorded productions. Mr Benson is always lucky, it notes, when he visits Edgbaston, for he manages to avoid the 'contagious fog' that seems to plague many of the botanic garden performances (29 August 1900: 4).

Padg-ing and local touring outdoor theatre productions supplied an outer frame for Bournville's activity, but no local pageant appears to have pre-dated Cadbury's party plays. The perceived benefits of a pageant designed to celebrate Birmingham's identity had formed the subject of an extended feature – 'Why not a Birmingham Pageant?' – in a 1906 edition of *The Birmingham Illustrated Weekly Mercury* that included contributions from Louis Napoleon Parker and the Local Mayor but, despite this call for a city-wide event, only small pageant-style performances took place over the following years (July: 6). 1908's Dudley Castle fete saw a cast of local children perform a thousand years of the site's history (*Birmingham Daily Gazette*, 8 June: 6). The following year, the 'Birmingham Historic Pageant' was staged under the auspices of Birmingham Sunday School Union at the Town Hall (Library of Birmingham/AxPamphlets/Vol 45/123777). Birmingham's *Daily Gazette* coverage of a procession of children in costume as historical and religious personalities, staged to raise funds for the children's hospital in 1914, opened with a note that the city still saw 'little of pageantry except in the form of parochial procession' (13 June: 5). Local outdoor performance in the Bournville area was most clearly connected with touring pastoral drama and marked by a relative absence of pageant-making, but both theatrical forms would have been familiar to amateur and professional theatre-makers at the factory, and to many audience members.

The success of *May Day* prompted a second outdoor production, staged at the following year's Summer Works Party, *Sherwood's Queen*, a dramatic adaptation of the tales of Robin Hood (Figure 17). 1909 was accorded 'special significance' in Cadbury's in-house crafted history. It marked the

Figure 17   'Sherwood's Queen, A Tableau in the Pastoral Play'
Bournville Works Magazine, August 1909. Cadbury Archives and Heritage Services.

thirty-year anniversary of the firm's relocation to Bournville and was the first staff occasion to take the place of the Christmas-time gathering that had been held for forty-one years, before it was discontinued in 1908 in favour of a new event that could accommodate all employees (*B.W.M.,* August 1909: 293). Reflecting the importance of this significant anniversary year, aspirations for the party's main entertainment increased again. With an ambitious two-hour running time, the Robin Hood – themed pastoral play brought together Thomas Mee Pattison's 1885 cantata for mixed voices 'Sherwood's Queen', with Alfred Tennyson's 1892 play *The Foresters or, Robin Hood and Maid Marian*. The outcome was a production that the works magazine deemed 'a delightful pageant'. As with 1908's *May Day,* the play was performed on the Girls' Recreation Grounds twice during the afternoon to ensure the maximum number of people from the crowd of 5,000 to 6,000 thousand partygoers could watch it. Featuring 170 Cadbury's employees, a musical accompaniment supplied by the works orchestra, acted scenes, strolling players, jugglers, acrobats, and a live donkey, 1909's play was identified as a clear step change in the scale, quality, and potential of works party performances (*B.W.M.,* August 1909: 293). Concurrently, while the achievement represented by 1909's pastoral play was lauded by the works magazine, there was also an interesting response from the reviewer to the polish, or the 'professionalism', of this outdoor, home-grown production, and it was one that marked a new dynamic in discourses around Bournville's factory performances. Notwithstanding praise for producers and performers, the write up recorded that the final production suffered from a lack of full rehearsals (an understandable issue when the size of the cast and their diverse production and administrative roles across the firm are considered). It also passed comment on moments in the performance when cast members were clearly being amused by each other, and were consequently out of character. While the charm of the piece was, at least in part, to be discovered in its home-spun qualities and industrial-amateur nature, what emerges in 1909 is a recognition of the potential for more polished outdoor performances at Cadbury's, building on the success of that year's production, and of *May Day*.

Space to Play Outside: Cadbury's Outdoor Amphitheatre, 1910

Outdoor theatre was staged on the Girls' Recreation Grounds, which lie slightly further away from the site's main factory buildings than those used by the men. Casts performed against the green backdrop provided by the space's grassy banks and trees, the 'magnificent background of forest trees on the rising greensward', recorded by the works magazine reviewer of *May Day,* which offered occasional glimpses of buildings through their leaves and trunks (*B.W.M.,* August 1908: 295). This choice to routinely stage the outdoor productions amidst the factory ground's industrial-pastoral views, rather than against a backdrop that included the factory's buildings, or village architecture positioned open-air spaces as important ingredients in the series of site-specific productions represented by the pastoral plays and pageants. In 1910, still two years before the firm had an in-house dramatic society, opportunities for outdoor performance were further increased by the construction of the factory's amphitheatre. Helena Chance's work on the gardens of Cadbury's Birmingham factory estate has revealed how 'landscaping and recreation became part of the discourse of factory reform and the modern industrial outlook', a meeting point of multiple agendas that resulted in beautiful outdoor spaces that held considerable 'socioeconomic significance' (2007: 197; 209. See also Chance, 2012). The socioeconomic significance of fresh air was firmly identified by 1910, and publicised as 'one of the many factors that go to make everything from Cadbury's garden village absolutely pure' (*Eastern*

Daily Press, 17 October: 9). Such advertising tropes built on images of nature had been located at the core of Cadbury's large-scale marketing experiments from their earliest days, including the firm's first advertising logo. In 1905, William Adlington Cadbury (1867–1095), son of Richard Cadbury, had visited Paris. Like his father, who was a skilled watercolourist whose paintings had been used on chocolate selection boxes from the 1860s onwards, William had a keen interest in art. During this visit to the French capital, he commissioned Art Nouveau artist, designer, and poet George Auriol (1863–1938) to produce the first Cadbury's logo, an image that depicts a stylised cocoa tree in bloom capturing the firm's core, raw, natural ingredient and simultaneously evoking the blossoming fruit trees that lined Bournville's streets.

Typified by curves and organicism, Art Nouveau was inextricably linked to mass production, modern domestic and industrial architecture, metropolitan life, and interior design entangling natural forms and lines with industrial production opportunities, changing urban lifestyles, and a burgeoning consumer culture. Auriol's art bridged fashionable networks, the avant-garde, and commercial culture, and was imprinted on Paris's landscape through his lettering on the city's iconic metro signs. Both artist and style were ideal fits with Cadbury's brand and the firm's ongoing project to create and stage Bournville. Art Nouveau resonated with similar ideological and social reform potentials of the visual arts to Arts and Crafts, the movement with which the first two generations of management at Cadbury's Bournville enterprise had the greatest affinity, and whose influence was inscribed onto architecture, landscaping, educational and recreational provision, and a focus on creativity and making as well as the family's ongoing patronage of artists, architects, and designers. Clear overlaps and intersections between the Arts and Crafts movement and Art Nouveau had been showcased on the international stage at 1902's First International Exhibition of Decorative Arts in Turin. The distinction between them that is of greatest significance here was the positioning of Art Nouveau within consumer-led arts and commerce, with Arts and Crafts more clearly identified as artist-led: a shift that reflected changes on the ground at Cadbury's in many ways, as the company expanded (O'Neill, 2007). Art Nouveau, represented by both Auriol's identity and the logo he designed, was of the moment, a cutting-edge design for the day that aligned with Cadbury's dependence on the fast 'emergence of a consuming class', while looking back to the style and ideological values of Arts and Crafts imprinted on Bournville's buildings and open spaces and more widely throughout the city of Birmingham (Bradley: v). Despite this currency, it was not licensed for six years after Richard Cadbury's return from Paris. When finally used in 1911, Auriol's stylised tree became a keystone image in an expanding, enduring visual advertising culture focused on cornfields, blue skies, rich green cricket pitches, milkmaids, and woodland creatures. Later marketing tools, including the Cocoa Cubs – fifteen collectible, small, lead clothed creatures including rabbits, geese and squirrels that came free with Bournville Cocoa in the mid-1930s and featured in their own annual- signal long-lasting use of the countryside as a marketing tool that spans the whole period covered in this study.

Individually and consolidated, countryside images presented the outside world with a mood-board style collage of Bournville as a hyper-real, industrial-pastoral landscape that was imprinted on to and fostered by the factory's expansive green spaces. Theatre rapidly became an ephemeral, yet key, contributor to this catalogue of countryside imagery, creating, staging, and sustaining the firm's guiding motifs at the firm's outdoor entertainments. We have seen in previous chapters how imagery drawn from nature defined the firm's marketing activity, representing product purity, healthy work conditions, and the resulting wellness and happiness attributed to its employees. How better to promote this healthy, pure place, and its products than through the representative healthy, pure bodies of Bournville's workers in a space created for them to play and tell stories connected to the factory's site, people, and ethos? Through the creation of the amphitheatre in 1910 outdoor theatre was carved into Bournville's carefully designed landscape, housing productions of outdoor plays that cemented and animated the wider functions of factory landscapes identified by Chance, and creating dynamic engagements between Cadbury's space and Cadbury's people that were integral to the fulfilment of the Bournville grounds' potential and socioeconomic significance.

The amphitheatre was the first bespoke performance space Cadbury's funded, but it was – at least in part – camouflaged, taking the form of a set of earthworks that gave the impression they had always been there. As Cadbury's 1921 in-house publication 'Drama and the Worker' explained 'in a grassy hollow a bank was levelled for the stage, and the opposite bank was raised in a half-circle, forming an auditorium' (14). Explaining the lack of a summer party event in 1910, *Bournville Works Magazine* clearly stated that the rationale behind the estates' project was to put in place 'adequate seating accommodation for any further outdoor plays or pageants that may be held' (June 1910: 26). The result was a space that – when the temporary seating used for performances was not in use – resembled natural undulations in the landscape. This was a theatrical facility that blended into the landscape, simulating an environmental feature. An auditorium carved out of the earth that belied the significant engineering project behind it, making it notably distinct from the interruption to the landscape that W. H. Lever's monolithic, more architecturally ambitious neoclassical stage build presented in Port Sunlight. Led by people and recreational priorities, the design of Bournville's amphitheatre manifested Cadbury's developing approach to factory theatre. Its creation was not primarily a statement about the firm, its innovations, and capital investment, instead, it was a planned resource. With this driver in mind, it is no surprise that the design of Bournville's outdoor venue placed a clear emphasis on creating a large-scale, functional space for performance. Edward Cadbury's 1912 *Experiments in Industrial Organisation* makes it clear that sightlines and acoustics for the 3,000 to 4,000 spectators it would accommodate were prioritised (238). This was a working space and a work-space, intended to become a part of the firm's material and recreational landscapes. As Chance has argued, the provision of this space signalled new ideas about employee welfare approaches driven by 'altruistic and commercial purposes' (2017: 2). In a second contrast to Lever's equivalent space in Port Sunlight, the construction of the amphitheatre was not used as publicity for the firm; only the events that occurred within the grassy venue were drawn on for Cadbury's promotional materials. It was the theatre – the temporary play – that the outdoor space enabled that was considered significant, not its pastoral architecture.

Fresh air performance was a fundamental part of the journey of acceptance of theatre as an activity at Cadbury's Quaker-led Bournville business. Just how important outdoor spaces were to support for theatre at Bournville is illustrated by Alfred Gardiner in his early biography of George Cadbury, where he delineates a clear distinction between theatre and outdoor theatre in his remembrance of the first-generation of leadership at the factory estate. 'Though George Cadbury was but once in a theatre in his life, and had little taste for the intellectual drama, he delighted in the pageantry of the open air', Gardiner recalled, noting further that open-air theatre was a form that 'was cultivated as industriously as the roses and the apple' at Bournville (1923: 304). This direct connection between the factory's 'pageantry of the open air' and its industrial horticulture captures the amphitheatre's location on the Girls' Recreation Grounds, adjacent to kitchen gardens and glasshouses, and firmly positions theatre within a sphere of healthy, beneficial activity. The belief in the 'redemptive power of gardening' that Adrian Bailey and John Bryson have identified as a driver in the design of Bournville village also influenced the landscaping and use of the factory grounds (2007: 101). In Gardiner's recollections outdoor theatre is presented as an activity that – like horticulture and its products – had the power to make Cadbury's employees grow and flourish, physically and mentally. George Cadbury may, as Gardiner notes, only have been to a theatre once, but the progressive Quaker capitalist appears to have accepted that the stage could function as a wholesome and productive leisure activity. Gardiner's recollection continues with the statement that 'even when his tastes were narrow, his tolerance was large', and that, atypically, this liberal paternalism grew as George Cadbury aged and gradually handed over management of the firm to a new generation of the family and the senior managers who supported them (324). A similar evaluation of George Cadbury's character and liberal politics and religious practice emerges from Bailey and Bryson's consideration of how the development of Bournville Village departed from traditional Quaker practices. 'As an evangelical Quaker', the authors note, 'Cadbury attempted to influence the lives of those beyond the practising Quaker community. The construction of a Quaker-led community in Bournville, therefore, involved significant departures from established patterns of Quaker worship' (2007: 103). Theatre was one such departure.

Gardiner's bucolic image of Bournville's outdoor theatre should not prompt an underestimation of the step change in thinking that this staging of large-scale outdoor performance at Cadbury's represented. In the second volume of his autobiography, John Drinkwater recalled that 'by the Quaker tradition of the Cadbury family the theatre was forbidden ground, and this departure from old custom [through the staging of the masques at the summer works parties] caused something of a sensation at the time' (1932: 194–195). The open-air plays were the first large-scale performances at Bournville. They could not be packaged as skits, sketches, tableaux, or drawing room style entertainments. They were undeniably theatrical productions. The reputation and cultural status of theatre may have improved over the late nineteenth and early twentieth centuries, but an aversion to theatre had formed a strong tenet of Quakerism and, while the turn of the twentieth century witnessed a gradual reduction in this anti-theatrical sentiment, considerable reluctance to admit or endorse stage performance remained (Lloyd, 2007; Underiner, 2011). Drinkwater hints at the discussions that preceded agreement to the open-air dramas he produced, remembering that 'once the decision had been made [to go ahead, George Cadbury] took to the project very kindly' (195). It is clear that there was nothing in George Cadbury's public, professional response to the firm's outdoor theatre that detracted from, or contradicted, his eldest son Edward's belief in the benefits theatrical activity could offer to industry. Crafting a sense of distance between Bournville's theatrical entertainments and those that took place in the wider theatre industry can be identified as a core factor in early experiments with large dramatic performances at the factory, and it was the outdoor performance space offered by the grounds and the amphitheatre that supplied the most significant of these distancing techniques. Simultaneously, the deliberate carving of a performance site into Bournville's landscape materialised the engagement of both family and firm with liberal, progressive New Quakerism and their commitment to the social reform potential of theatre as a recreational activity. The amphitheatre offered an effective way to experiment with and mould a Cadbury's style of theatrical activity, one that could co-exist with the firm's fundamental religious and social convictions and embody them. Incongruous though it may seem, social reform, and Quaker business practices were at the core of Cadbury's large-scale outdoor theatre.

The John Drinkwater Masques

John Drinkwater's four Bournville masques built on the potential of outdoor performance that had been identified in 1908 and 1909's theatrical experiments, *May Day* and *Sherwood's Queen*. Cadbury's major capital investment in the amphitheatre was coupled with a recognition that experienced theatre professionals were also needed to support the development of outdoor theatre at the factory. Drinkwater was an ideal candidate. Describing himself as an actor, producer, manager, and odd job man, this theatrical all-rounder wrote and produced his first masque for Cadbury's in 1911 – a performance that was the first, important moment in his longstanding connection with Bournville's theatre, the story of which will unfold over the following chapters (Drinkwater, 1925: v). From 1904 (aside from a brief hiatus when his work in insurance sales had taken him to Manchester), Drinkwater had been a key member of Birmingham's Pilgrim Players; the amateur theatre group that evolved into the Birmingham Repertory Theatre Company in 1912. Under the leadership of Barry Jackson (1879–1961), the Pilgrim Players began their activity in Jackson's father's home in Moseley, with pastoral plays staged amidst the family's extensive lawned gardens. The group later performed at the nearby Edgbaston Assembly Rooms, a venue also connected with Cadbury's and its recreational activities. Members socialised together, and took annual trips to Stratford on Avon, where they watched the Benson company performances at the festival (the same Frank Benson who had performed at Edgbaston's Botanical Gardens at the turn of the century) (Kemp, 1948: 94–140). Their presence and success was abetted by active, vocal support from local vicar and social reformer Reverend Arnold Pinchard (1859– 1934). Based at St Jude's Church in the heart of one of Birmingham's poorest areas, Pinchard lectured on the plays the group staged, later produced new versions of Medieval mystery plays for the Repertory company, and supported his daughter – Betty's (1895–1984) – founding membership of the group as an actress (Ibid.: 3). Pinchard's involvement affirmed the potential of drama as a tool for social change, and offered a strong, approved connection to Birmingham's wider culture through his role in the formation of the Birmingham Repertory Theatre. These civic networks were to prove key to theatre at Cadbury's. Under the stage name John Darnley, Drinkwater acted, wrote, produced, and adapted plays for the group. By the time Cadbury's commissioned him to write and stage *An English Medley*, the first of the works party masques, John Drinkwater was a familiar and well-established figure in north Birmingham's suburban cultural life and beginning to carve out his place as an important figure in the history of regional repertory theatre.

An English Medley, 1911

A month before 1911's summer works party, Bournville's works magazine apprised its readers that 'it may not be generally known that the pageant to be played at the summer party in the Girls' Grounds is to represent the history of Birmingham'. There is 'immense scope in the subject', the article continued, and this year's 'event promises to outdo all past occasions' (May 1911: 155). To some extent, Drinkwater's first Cadbury's masque returned to the unfulfilled ambitions for Bournville's first outdoor play, 1908's *May Day*. As the works magazine noted, *An English Medley* was to be a 'historical pageant with a local setting' that tightly entangled its two parts (July 1911: 205). The end product was a masque divided into two distinct, stylistic sections. Its first scenes depicted imagined moments from Bournville's past; recreated histories of the space employees and their families now gathered on. Opening with the arrival of the Romans and construction of the Roman road Ryknield Street, which stretched across the factory's recreation grounds, attention was drawn to the material histories layered on the familiar factory site (see Figure 18). Speeches delivered by Roman characters highlighted the road 'passing' 'here through your home', inscribing the past on to the firm's recently reconfigured landscape – a landscape that

Figure 18   'The Coming of the Romans', from John Drinkwater's *An English Medley* *Bournville Works Magazine*, July 1911. Cadbury Archives and Heritage Services.

been temporarily transformed again by the summer works party stages, arenas, tents, performers, and spectators (253). Later scenes moved forward in time to the 'Middle Ages' and sought to recreate Birmingham's traditional Gingerbread Fair, with wagons, booth performance spaces, jugglers, wrestlers, wandering minstrel musicians, and dancers. These itinerant forms mirrored those populating the other entertainment and sideshow spaces at the party event. Subtitled a 'story of the people', these local narratives created and told stories about the factory landscape. The final third of the masque's action was an extended scene watched over by the Spirit of History, who carried a set of tablets on which she inscribed the stories she watched played out before her. The content of this section was much closer to the large-scale civic pageants popularised by Louis Napoleon Parker and – like the British Empire Tableaux staged on the same day – it prematurely commemorated the coronation of England's new King, George V, who was crowned two days after 1911's party. Beginning with the Spirit of History's reflection that she has 'seen the coming and crowning of many kings, and watched them pass into the shadows, leaving behind them a name and a story', this lengthy scene staged a procession of representatives from the eleventh to the nineteenth centuries, all of whom recounted short stories about the monarchs they had served (266). Through the storytelling, the behaviour of each was narrated, evaluated, and judged.

The theme of good leadership pervaded *An English Medley*, and its local focus outweighed its national messages. The production opened with a three-stanza, sung chorus dedicated to George Cadbury. Invoking the gods of classical civilisation to guide their labour and story-telling, the chorus ended:

> And of this green land of our dwelling
> How sweet is the story to build.
> As we shape the new vision, compelling
> All hearts to the hopes unfulfilled. (Drinkwater, 1925: 247–248)

Through these lines 'Bournvillean' culture modelled and idealised a site-specific vision of 'Englishness' in a modern, progressive factory community rooted in a timeless pastoral vision of a green and pleasant land. Across Bournville Lane, on the men's recreation ground, other visions were offered through the Burlesque Cricket Match and Empire Tableaux. Opening with a hymn to George Cadbury and closing with a reflection on leadership and its legacies, Drinkwater's first masque focused on people, their stories, and what they leave behind. Each character in the final scene was inscribed into history by the Spirit of History as their moment in the spotlight passed into the shadows of time, leaving only their stories to be judged by the people of the future. These messages were for the factory, for its managers, its workers, and its wider audience. Drinkwater's *An English Medley*'s classical choric device, tree-set stage, and hymn to a 'new vision' was a salient moment in the creation and use of theatricalised visual cultures at Cadbury's and in performer-employees developing roles as often intangible, yet powerful, agents in the firm's ongoing operational and commercial successes.

Factory plays, speeches, and publications regularly turned to the subject of local history, or histories of the Cadbury family. They were themes that had been placed at the core of the firm's image and creation of Bournville's Spirit since the earliest stages of their development. The first issues of the *Bournville Works Magazine* featured a series of articles on 'The Historical Associations of Bournville and District', generating shared knowledge about the identity of the area surrounding the factory amongst employees. Later in the same year, entertainments at the Christmas party included a cinematographic display of local historical sites, with the slides and printed catalogue made widely available after the event (*B.W.M.*, February 1903: 79). Similar local history content continued during the following years, attracting praise and acknowledgment of its educational function from public figures. In 1909, the works magazine carried a note from William Duignan, F.S.A. (1824–1914), a 'well-known Staffordshire antiquary' and local politician who wrote to Cadbury's

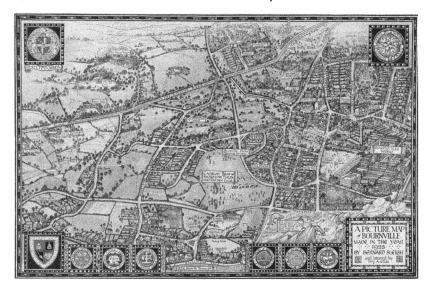

Figure 19   'A Picture Map of Bournville', 1923. Bernard Sleigh and Ivy A. Ellis Cadbury Archives and Heritage Services.

board to praise the 'great deal' they were doing to 'please and instruct all ages of the rising generation'. 'The love of antiquity is a very desirable sentiment to cultivate', Duignan continued, 'it inculcates the spirit of reverence and the spirit of humility, which are so conspicuously lacking and so often despised, but without which no one can be really good or great' (*B.W.M.*, January 1909: 89). Similar local history themes remained key content for entertainments and activities well into the 1920s – as we have seen in the case of *Visions* – contributing to the firm's visual culture and to the creation of Bournville as a palimpsest of people, stories, and homespun myths. Creating stories, or his-stories, at Cadbury's was part of the business. Drinkwater's first masque slotted into a dynamic, ongoing cultural project that was captured visually by local artist Bernard Sleigh (1872–1954) in his 1923 picture map of Bournville (Figure 19).

Bernard Sleigh was a Birmingham-based Arts and Crafts woodengraver, painter, muralist, and stained-glass maker, and a well-known member of local professional artistic networks that connected him with the Birmingham School of Art (where he both studied and taught), the informal Arts and Crafts collective the Birmingham Group of Artist Craftsmen, the Bromsgrove Guild of Applied Art, and the Birmingham Guild of Handicraft (Cooper, 1997; Hickman, 2018). It is likely that these networks would also have brought Sleigh into contact with Cadbury's forewoman, commercial artist and Birmingham School of Art trained artist Sophia Pumphrey (1865–1923), factory draughtsman and exhibiting artist Harry Northway Bradbear (1882–1917), and other Cadbury's employees who were key players in the firm's theatre and within the city's wider cultural fabric. He had also worked for the Cadbury family before, as the designer of the Cropwood Open Air School in Moseley that they funded, a build that materialised the alignment of Arts and Crafts with education and social reform (Hickman, 2018: 171–172). By the time he produced the Bournville map in the early 1920s, Sleigh had carved out an international reputation for fantastical book illustrations and woodcut prints. The most familiar, and commercially successful, of these fantasy works was 'An Ancient Mappe of Fairyland, Newly Discovered and Set Forth' (1918); a colourful cartographic image of a collaged world of landscapes from children's literature inhabited by fairy-tale characters. Produced amidst the aftermath of the First World War, Sleigh's fairyland map offered a powerful visualisation of the good and bad, trauma and fantasy, horror and magic of fairy-tale worlds and, by default, of their human creators. The map was widely reproduced as prints and on fabric, with each item accompanied by a written text that explained and contextualised the fantasy world and its inhabitants. Anne Carol Moore's 1920 *Roads to Childhood* records that a copy of the map was gifted to, and displayed in, the children's room of New York Public Library:

> This unique map is in color, measuring five feet or more in length by about twenty inches. Children and grown people are completely fascinated by it. "Isn't it great?" exclaimed a boy of twelve. "There's Rockabye Baby square on the treetop, The Three Blind Mice, Humpty Dumpty sitting on that long wall, and down here are King Arthur's Knights, the Sea King's Palace, Dreamland Harbour, and the Argonauts. There's the Rainbow Bridge, Hansel and Gretel – everything and everybody you ever read about in Mother Goose, Fairy Tales, or Mythology. (165–166)

Moore was a writer and advocate for children's literature and universal library access. Her interest in Sleigh's map and its content resonates with the educational and recreational agendas that moulded Cadbury's staff provision, and the family and firm's wider social engagement and cultural patronage. It also clearly indicates Sleigh's established international reputation at the time he produced Bournville's map.

The Bournville map was not the first time Sleigh had focused on Birmingham. He had previously been commissioned to produce picture maps of other city districts by its Civic Society: a 1920 map depicted Bournville's adjacent suburb, Northfield, and an imaginative historical representation of Birmingham as it might have looked in 1730 was created in

1923 (the same year as the Cadbury's map). The commissions were fitting. The three Birmingham maps signalled the city's artistic reputation and networks through their form, media, and makers. The style, techniques, and artists were Birmingham-based – Ivy Ellis (1897–1984), the calligrapher, was also an artist based in the city – and they reflected the city's strong Arts and Crafts history and the ongoing influences of its practices and materials. In its content and artistic cartography, Sleigh's representation of the firm's industrial pastoral world is closer to these other two Birmingham maps than his fairy-tale land of 1918. The three Birmingham works are more documentary in style, grounded in a place and in landmarks that are used as stimuli for artistic, historically guided imagination. Nonetheless, his fantasy worlds creep into the Bournville image. The bottom right-hand corner depicts an area of land close to the site's boundaries as a prehistoric, frozen world inhabited by woolly mammoths, dinosaurs, and three tiny male figures. Prehistoric boulders still present on the Bournville site likely served as inspiration: a caption tells us that 'stones' record these as creatures that previously inhabited the area, but there is a second message, one concerned with progress, development, and the frozen wastes of the lands that had become Cadbury's industrial community. From pre-history to the present, this was a visual statement about how far activity on the landscape had come, reminiscent of the move from past to present staged twelve years earlier by factory employees playing the Romans who built Ryknield Street. In his creation of local artworks, Arts and Crafts aesthetic, folk and fairy-tale narratives, and depictions of imagined histories Sleigh's artistic outputs synched with Bournville's activity in many ways. His map of the Cadbury's site fused his reputation and the iconographic language characteristic of his artistic works with the factory, its landscape, and visual culture, invoking similar themes and imagery to those that were staged in the earlier outdoor plays, in the later production of *Visions,* and in multiple other moments of factory theatre between 1900 and 1935.

Interlacing John Drinkwater's first masque with Cadbury's wider visual culture is a deliberate decision on my part. As is the case with many large-scale, huge-cast outdoor dramas, *An English Medley* is, for the most-part, a terrible read, but I would hazard a guess that not many of the lines employees spoke were heard by most of the spectators, aside from the words delivered by the chorus. A photograph in the works magazine indicates that this group was made up of around ninety members, with women strongly outnumbering men to a ratio of around three to one (207). Their collective voice, with its range of pitches, is likely to have travelled. Edward Cadbury may have celebrated the acoustics of the factory's outdoor amphitheatre, and the works magazine reviewer did praise the beauty of the speeches in the historical pageant section, but when the background noise of the number of people at the party and the other sports, entertainments, and sideshows taking place at the same time is considered, alongside the sheer size of the crowd, it is difficult to argue that any unamplified performance could have been clearly heard consistently throughout by all. The performance was accompanied by an incidental music score, composed for the occasion by Rutland Boughton (1878–1950) from the Birmingham School of Music. While this instrumental sound, often with vocal sections performed by the chorus members, would have had a better chance of carrying to spectators, what the script, reviews, and Drinkwater's recollections capture are the prioritisation of the pageant's visual effects, its motifs, and the strong sense of locality that were positioned at the core of the piece. The Romans acting out building the road would have communicated with the audience more clearly than the Romans explaining their presence and their activity. Visual elements would have served as the most important meaning making devices for the pageant's audience. The words were not the main thing; a statement that is, arguably, the case for any theatrical script, but is very much the case here.

Alert to the importance of visual culture to the success of his Bournville productions, Drinkwater spent a considerable amount of time working as an active producer. Producing was a term that he used to describe his work, with descriptions implying his activity was closer to what we would identify today as directing (a less familiar term in this period). One such example can be found in the obituary *Bournville Works Magazine* published on his death in 1937. It is lengthy, but worth citing in full for the insight it offers into Drinkwater's practice and his work with Cadbury's:

> Those associated with the pageants and the Bournville Dramatic Society in its early days – and many of them are still connected with Bournville Dramatics – will recall his care and thoroughness in production – how at the hot summer evening rehearsals of the masques he tirelessly persevered in getting some effect, whether in the spoken word, or in crowd movements – for in these new outdoor dramas he was aiming at something new in pageant-making, and succeeded in giving this branch of drama a new simplicity and compactness of structure, constituting an important achievement in dramatic art. Many will remember his wonted anxiety at a final rehearsal as he paced along the path between our tree-set stage and the grass-banked auditorium – an anxiety he would suddenly throw off to become again the cheerful, inspiring companion of all, for friendliness and good fellowship with those working with him seemed a necessity of his nature, and were the secrets of his success as a producer. (May 1937: 168)

A considerable part of the action John Drinkwater created in the four outdoor Bournville masques took the form of choreographed group movement. In the introduction to his first volume of collected plays, published in 1925, he recalled that directing these large-scale productions taught him the importance of the 'greatest simplicity of mass effect in the open air'. Those 'crowd movements' he was remembered for allowed him to develop 'a technique that would be within the acting resources of a large and enthusiastic but unskilled company of amateurs' (vii). The challenge Drinkwater faced as a writer/producer entrusted with key theatrical events at Cadbury's remains palpable in the gaps between these words over a century later. Each of the masques he produced had 6 or 7 principal roles and other (mainly non-speaking) parts for anything between 200 and 300 hundred extra performers, from the young children of Cadbury's staff to the factory's eldest employees, occasionally supplemented by local residents, family members, and hired-in performers. The industrial ensemble approach he outlines here became a key motif of Cadbury's theatre, one that is clearly seen in the group of factory employees dressed as chocolates who froze within, and then rose out of, the box of 'Orinocco Assorted' at 1914's summer works party. Bournville's tableaux vivants, skits, and masques shared visual and embodied languages that Drinkwater drew on and expanded.

Individual performers further heightened *An English Medley's* visual impact. The employees playing parts would have been familiar to many audience members, despite their costumes. With the number of staff members in the cast, it is likely that each spectator would have been looking out for at least one or two faces they would recognise amidst the staged scenes. The 'added delight of seeing familiar faces in different guises' has been identified as a key dynamic of amateur performance (Nicolson et al., 2018: 3). Some faces in *An English Medley* were very familiar from other events, and from factory and pageant management. The Spirit of History was played by Lottie Allen, a clerk in her early forties. On her retirement from Cadbury's in 1926 – after twenty-three and a half years and promotion to management of the wages team – Allen was remembered for the 'dramatic talent that long ago made her a prominent figure in Bournville social life. She was the Ellen Terry of our stage' (*B.W.M.*, January 1926: 29). Her appearance in Drinkwater's first pageant marked one of her first steps in a career-long dramatic sub-career at Cadbury's, one that settled into the firm's collective memory (29). The three chorus leaders included factory clerk Beatrice Price (1885–1978) who, alongside Allen, was a member of the pageant sub-committee charged with organising the party's main entertainment. Other cast members included (John) Robert Quinton – the firm's carpenter who had stepped in to save the *May Day* pastoral play three years earlier, Ralph Moorhouse (1872–1944), a full-time gymnastics teacher employed by the firm who was also responsible for the displays of rhythmic gymnastics that were a regular feature of Bournville events, Walter Pedley Hunt (1874–1957), a storekeeper at the beginning of a long career at Bournville, and Thomas Baldwin (1876–1946), a member of staff from the factory's in-house printing team. Several of these members of staff eschewed guidance from the management committee that 'as far as possible the inclusion of foremen and forewomen in affairs such as the pageant is to be avoided', advice most likely grounded in concerns about the time commitment and workload involved, but perhaps also in recognition of the more informal social interactions that rehearsals and performance created (CAHS/CM/2 May 1911: 355). This first generation of Cadbury's staff actors carved out and occupied a space in between themselves at work, themselves out of work, themselves as characters playing entertainers from the past, and themselves as representative of the collective body of Cadbury's employees entertaining others across the site in the different attractions on offer at the party. The models these early theatrical events established endured for decades.

Local press coverage of *An English Medley* included accounts in the *Birmingham Mail* and the *Birmingham Daily Gazette*. While the *Mail*'s dependence on pre-circulated style stock text indicates that they did not send a representative to the party, the *Gazette*'s account suggests that their journalist was present at the event (20 June 1911: 6; 21 June 1911: 6). Both signal that Cadbury's summer party performance was considered worthy of the public's attention – a novelty, and an insight into a place and occasion that was usually off-limits to all but employees. These indications that Drinkwater's first Bournville pageant served as an advertising device do not detract from the firm's intention to provide a good day out for staff. A focus on making this an event to remember is clear from souvenir items produced and distributed in-house, including party programmes, bound scripts, tea tokens and tickets, all 'beautifully got up' in a way that 'might have been furnished for a Cook's Continental tour at least' (*B.W.M.,* July 1911: 205). Local and national dynamics and internal and external audiences coalesced in the 1911 works party main entertainment. Referring to this coronation year 'pageant', Joel Hoffman has concluded that Cadbury's outdoor productions 'served to create a sense of community identity, while inscribing Bournville in a narrative of national ritual' (1993: 742). These forces were at play in *An English Medley,* but local narratives appear to have been more prominent, and it is important to register that much changed in and between the outdoor theatrical productions that followed. This was an adaptable, evolving form that absorbed some elements of civic pageants and pastoral plays, but prioritised adapting and staging versions of the past and present that directly reflected the firm's values, engaged employees in creative, participatory activities, and strengthened the factory's identity and community. As a distinctive subset of nationwide pageant activity, John Drinkwater's masques were not only required to represent the local landscape and its stories, they also had to serve an equally important industrial function. By 1911, outdoor theatre was business at Bournville and this – the largest of the firm's outdoor theatrical productions – was intended to offer something new, a theatrical form that would stick in both employees' memories and the firm's history. Noting that there had been two pastoral pageants before, the works magazine concluded that to 'compare the three efforts would be idle. With the beauty of its conception and the perfection of each uttered line *An English Medley* is destined to stand alone in our memories' (205). 1911 marked a clear step change in approaches to outdoor performance at Bournville, and this masque and the following three large-scale, site-specific community performances written and produced by Drinkwater, burrowed in to and lingered in Cadbury's constructed collective memory.

The Pied Piper: A Tale of Hamelin, 1912

An English Medley's success affirmed John Drinkwater's status as a trusted pair of hands at Bournville. On rehiring him for 1912's outdoor production, minutes from the Committee of Management record, he was instructed to 'proceed as last time in regard to engaging artists', signalling both the hiring in of some non-Cadbury's employees in the masques, and the relative autonomy Drinkwater was granted to make such decisions (CAHS/CMM/14 November 1911: 875). This autonomy had its limits, however. Drinkwater's proposed productions continued to require clearance by the firm's board before he could move forward with writing, casting, and producing. Minutes from 1913 reveal that a 'rough scenario' of the following year's masque (*Robin Hood and the Pedlar*) had to be submitted and approved by the firm's senior management team before the event was given clearance (CAHS/CMM/17 December 1913: 920). The timescale stipulated here – six months in advance of the party – further evidences the significance of these annual productions to Cadbury's, and the seriousness and rigour with which they were managed. In 1912, the pageant was given its own sub-committee within the summer party's organising committee structure, indicating a recognition of increased work associated with the performance (CAHS/350/002134). Hiring Drinkwater was a business decision, and the agreed fee for writing and producing the Bournville masques was not inconsiderable. Committee of Management minutes document that Drinkwater received 50 guineas for the 1912 event (a sum roughly equivalent to 3,500 pounds in 2017). Useful context for this fee is supplied by the resignation of the firm's part-time Musical Director, Frederick William Sylvester (1872–1934) in June 1912 (interestingly to take up a position as Musical Director at the New Cross Theatre, London), and details of the search process that replaced him. Recommendations were sought from the composer and University of Birmingham Professor of Music Granville Bantock (1868–1946) and potential candidates directly approached with the committee authorising a salary of 130 pounds rising to 200 pounds a year for the right candidate (CAHS/CMM/2 July 1912: 496). After a search period of two months, an offer was made to the Bradford-based musician, brass band conductor, orchestral and vocal music instructor to Bradford Education Authority, and competition judge James Brier (1868–1944) at an annual salary of 250 pounds with no minimum length of contract (CAHS/CMM/15 August 1912: 583). Drinkwater's masque fee was equivalent to just over 52 pounds. Of equal significance to the amount of money is the discussion of this commission and fee at the most senior of the firm's committees (CAHS/CMM/12 March 1912: 185). The sum reflected the masque's promotion as the leading attraction of each party; negotiations at the senior level indicated both the amount of money involved, and perhaps contended with any lingering concern around theatre.

1912's outdoor play was *The Pied Piper: A Tale of Hamelin*, dedicated by Drinkwater to 'the workers of Bournville'. It was a cleverly crafted piece that acknowledged the playwright's strong relationship with the firm and illustrated his growing awareness of its people, place, and theatre. His choice of narrative was praised, with the 'suitability of the subject to outdoor presentation' 'at once apparent' to the party audience, but it was the adaptation of this story to Bournville that drew the greatest appreciation (*B.W.M*, August 1912: 228). Responding to his brief and his awareness of the strong reception of *An English Medley*'s local content, Drinkwater 'somewhat altered' the familiar fairy-tale to fit its factory recreation ground setting. The most obvious of these narrative changes was found in the return of the village children at the end of the play; the most familiar conclusion, with Hamelin's villagers remaining childless, 'would hardly do in the happy pastoral play' style that fitted the occasion of the summer party noted the works magazine (230). A second and more generalised modification to the tale can be discovered in the evaluation and critique of leadership that permeated Drinkwater's script, repeating a core theme of 1911's play. Early on in the masque's action the mayor's failure to deal with the rats plaguing Hamelin is called out by the village blacksmith, Peter, who jumps up on a bench and 'eloquently turns the people's grumbling into action' by demanding to know (and simultaneously reminding the villagers) 'whose business is it to look after the city?' (229). Peter's craft as a smith resonated with the importance of making at Bournville, connecting the strongest moral and social voice in the play with that of a worker-craftsman, and echoing the use of theatre and other recreational activities as substitutes for industrial factory jobs' loss of 'the joy and satisfaction' historically 'experienced in the practice of a craft' at work (Cadbury, 1925: 3–4). Later the mayor is directly confronted by angry villagers, who demand he takes responsibility for, and actively address, the loss of their children, leading to a deal with the returning piper that if he brings the children back to the town both the mayor and his councillors will willingly go to the mountain for a month, a week, and a day, to 'learn how to be better men for Hamelin' (Drinkwater, 1925: 23). The piper agrees, the children are returned, and the mayor and councillors are led away in a moment that the works magazine identified as seeing 'their humiliation complete'. 'Under the spell of the Piper, and divested of the dignity of their office, they [were] made to dance away like the children to the great garden in the mountain' (*B.W.M.*, August 1912: 230). Great gardens were presented as the site of better leadership; great gardens like those on which the masque was performed.

Bournville was not alone in harnessing the slightly sinister fairy-tale character offered by the Pied Piper. Two months after Drinkwater's factory masque, another charitable rewrite of the character was staged in Birmingham, when Joseph George Pentland (1851–1914) adopted the role to lead 5,000 children out of the city slums on foot to Sutton Park for a day of picnicking and fresh air. Pentland was a printer and philanthropist who the Cadburys would have known through his role as Vice Chairman of Birmingham School Board. His (self-identified) appearance as the piper, dressed in a long white cloak and carrying a crook, presented a hybrid version of the folktale character and the shepherd of religious iconography. As founder of the Bull Ring Mission in 1893, Pentland was committed to offering impoverished city children (referred to as Street Robins, or Pentland's Street Robins) food, fresh air, and fun (Library of Birmingham/L/./41/23; 302084). In this city, at this moment, the figure of the Pied Piper had lost the ambivalent location between good and bad that he evokes in many representations of the tale, and had been affiliated with welfare and philanthropy; a representation of leadership and integrity connected with the countryside and intent on confronting the industrial and social status quo.

As John Drinkwater's experience with the firm grew, so did the fit of the masques he created for their location, audiences, and performers. At the core of this theatre was an understanding of the need for action and words to mirror performance conditions and contexts; a recognition, in his own words, that while the poetry he is better remembered for was a timeless and static form, theatre was in its very nature interactive and engaged. '[T]he drama is a more empirical affair', he explained, 'more subject to outside influences and created more in relation to external necessities [...] poetry is written by the poet to please himself and drama to please himself and audiences' (1925: vi). Bournville's works magazine concluded that *The Pied Piper* represented the peak of the factory's theatrical activity to date. Its success was understood to be the combined result of its beautiful setting, the simple but realistic scenery, the 'freshness of the actors' who were 'thoroughly immersed in their parts' (unlike those earlier outdoor performances where it had been noted that performers had been distracted by each other), and the play itself. As with the 1911 pageant, the performance was accompanied by a musical score, written for the occasion by Frederick Sylvester, who had managed the musical accompaniment to the earlier masques, and performed by employees involved with Cadbury's musical societies, further showcasing the firm's out-of-work-hours activities. There is clear evidence Drinkwater learnt on his feet at Bournville. 1911's masque was lengthy and complex with multiple scenic requirements. This does not occur in the pieces produced over the following three years. Noting Louis Napoleon Parker's death in 1944, *The Times Literary Supplement*'s obituary writer remembers the pageant director amidst vast open-air performance spaces with a megaphone and ear trumpet managing and rehearsing huge casts and large-scale action (20 September: 472). It is a recollection that shines light on why 1912's *The Pied Piper* might have offered a piece of outdoor theatre that drew on a simpler narrative and stage actions. Photographs of the four Bournville Drinkwater masques indicate an ongoing pattern of improved clarity in the productions' visual story telling year on year. Yet, despite the streamlining of staged action that this indicates, the scale, spectacle, and spectatorship of Drinkwater's second Cadbury's masque was greater, supplying what was in many ways the perfect combination for the firm – spectacle simplified and distilled.

Figure 20 'The Pied Piper', John Drinkwater's *The Only Legend: A Masque of the Scarlet Pierrot*. Photograph
Cadbury Archives and Heritage Services.

Set was an important part of *The Pied Piper*'s success. Minutes from a Committee of Management meeting in May 1912 record the board's agreement to spend forty pounds on scenery, on top of the budget that had already been agreed for the production. The set was designed, constructed, and painted onsite at Bournville by Harry Bradbear, a draughtsman, artist, and member of Cadbury's advertising staff, aided by local artist, Sidney Currie (1870–1930). Currie had been Chair of Birmingham Art Circle from 1908 to 1909, and was a well-known, prolific painter at the time. Alongside Drinkwater, he offers an interesting early example of the connections between the firm's theatre and Birmingham's wider cultural networks. Figure 20 shows the set Bradbear and Currie created, representing Hamelin's walls and buildings within them, including a prominent house that the works magazine understood to be a 'somewhat altered' version of the German Renaissance painter Albert Durer's house in Nuremberg, with the costumes (also designed by Bradbear and Currie) following a similar Renaissance theme. Like the earlier tableaux vivants staged in the Girls' Baths, the visual spectacle of performance simultaneously offered cultural education. Durer was known for his landscape paintings, a visual model that aligned with the incorporation of the factory grounds into the play's setting. At one point in the masque the villagers emerged 'out of the landscape' – from behind the trees and the mounds where they had waited unseen; positioned as products of both the pastoral ideal the grounds represented, and Cadbury's recreational space provision (*B.W.M.*, August 1912: 229). The *Birmingham Daily Gazette* found *The Pied Piper*'s set to be an 'excellently designed' canvas that 'realistically depicted the ancient city' and complemented the 'ideal [wider] setting' offered by the recreation grounds (29 June 1912: 6). Spectators recognised that they were presented with a set within a set: the recreation grounds again offering an outer visual frame for the performance and serving as a part of its meaning making. In many ways, outdoor performances can be understood as being grounded in workers' and visitors' more general multisensory experiences of Cadbury's. In his 1903 book *The Food of the Gods: A Popular Account of Cocoa*, the author Brandon Head recorded the moment he stepped off the train at Bournville station and was 'greeted by a whiff of the most delicious fragrance' (47). Depending on the day you visit, the smell of chocolate still fills the air around the side of the Men's Recreation Ground. Once experienced, it forms part of the memory and future experiences of the space. Inside and outside were connected through aroma. Flowers, gardens, fresh air, and the smell of chocolate were accompanied by the noise of the factory, the smoke from its chimneys, and the activities on the grounds, railway tracks, and roads that surrounded the site. Any performance at Bournville had a changing, sensory outer frame that was integrally connected to the experience of the factory, and its theatre. Drinkwater's masques suggest that he knew this and drew on it.

Like *An English Medley*, the staging and content of *The Pied Piper* materialised and conveyed core Cadbury's values, holding up the poor civic leadership displayed by the Mayor and his councillors against the firm's leadership that was modelled through staff-performers' bodies and the summer party as a whole. The narrative's successful resolution in favour of the villagers, and the consequent shutting down of the potential for insurrection that is present in Peter's early cries for action – 'whose business is it to look after the city?' – were powerful messages in this large industrial, managed community that highlighted the firm's commitment to education and adherence to ethical industrial management. Cast members playing key roles further solidified these meanings. Most employees playing lead roles were not listed in the general party programme – conveying the industrial ensemble function of the large performance that focused on collective identity, rather than individual gain or local fame – but as senior staff at the firm, most would have already been familiar to spectators, and their presence would have been felt. Tom (Thomas, 1867–1945) Davies, as the Mayor, and Walter Pedley Hunt, as the Pied Piper were already well-known from the factory's early drama, and the citizens of Hamelin included other recognisable members of Cadbury's management teams. The village mothers included factory forewomen, displaying matriarchal leadership that was familiar from the working day, and that has been under-considered in definitions of Cadbury's leadership style as a form of industrial paternalism. Appearing alongside these more senior members of staff in the entertainment is likely to have reminded the cast members that they were performing as themselves, bringing both their individual bodies and skills, and their identities as factory employees, and performing for (and with) friends, family, colleagues, and managers. Site, performers, set, costume, and story came together to convey a strong message for Bournville's factory culture, far stronger in production than on the page and one that had clear connection with the business. Charles Dellheim has noted that 'trade unions were weak in light industry before the war, and Cadbury's was no exception'. A 1918 estimate (several years after the Pied Piper masque) suggested that 'only 50 per cent of the men and 10 per cent of the women at Cadbury's belonged to unions, although the proportion among skilled workers was higher' (1987: 22; see also Smith, Child and Rowlinson, 1990: 65–70). In this industrial context, and for a firm that strongly favoured internal resolution of issues, *The Pied Piper* identified and played out essential values, often through the bodies of individuals identified as representatives of management. Drinkwater's second masque finished with a scene of celebration; villagers feasting and dancing at a large outdoor party, in front of a crowd eating and being entertained at a large party. The metatheatrical meanings were cemented, and the dedication to 'The Workers of Bournville' and the local political and social messages the pageant circulated materialised. In this 'true achievement of people's art' lay a 'development of the new drama and a manifestation of the immense possibilities that lie before such' (*B.W.M.*, August 1912: 229). While these possibilities were connected to recreation and development, they were also entwined with successful industrial leadership.

The Pied Piper reached a much wider audience than previous outdoor plays. In the same meeting in which they approved the extra money for scenery, the management committee had accepted a proposal that the pageant be re-performed the day after the summer party 'to some of the public in aid of a charity' (CAHS/CMM/21 May 1911: 391). The fund chosen was the Selly Oak branch of the Cripples' Union, and a note of thanks sent from the charity recorded that the second performance of *The Pied Piper* had raised enough money to fund a bed for one child for a full year (*B.W.M.*, October 1913: 317). This wider, external audience endorsed and publicised the firm's recreational schemes and employees' creativity in an aligned philanthropic space – the fundraising performance – in which theatre continued to 'do good'. It is of note that this was a year in which the guidance that forewomen and foremen should not be involved had also seemingly been retracted. 1912's pageant was positioned to attract a greater level of attention, which it achieved. In early July, the *Dundee Evening Telegraph* told its Scottish readers of the masque concluding that 'folks who are in quest of an attractive open-air pageant scheme should requisition the aid of the enterprising people of Bournville' (3 July 1912: 1). These external audiences were to grow further in the following year.

The Only Legend: A Masque of the Scarlet Pierrot, 1913

The Only Legend: A Masque of the Scarlet Pierrot, John Drinkwater's third outdoor play for Bournville offered a more symbolic narrative addressing the importance of love, self-care, and community. The immortal Scarlett Pierrot fell in love with a human woman, with his refusal to abandon her resulting in her being beaten and left for dead on their wedding day, and his banishment from the community. At the start of the masque, a thousand years of the Pierrots rejecting kindness and love in favour of want and selfish need had passed: their inhumanity conveyed by the opening scene, which depicted an exhausted Old Woman on her way to market to sell a small basket of homegrown flowers and fruit collapsing, and a Pierrot taking the opportunity to steal her wares, leaving her for dead. Music signalled the arrival of the Scarlett Pierrot disguised as a Peasant on the scene, 'glimpses of scarlet' visible under his 'rough clothes'. Bringing water and care to the old woman, he confronted his fellow Pierrot's callousness: 'The Peasant: Have you a heart? The Pierrot: No' (Drinkwater, 1925: 307). As their conversation continued, the tale of the Scarlet Pierrot surfaced: the cruel Pierrot telling the disguised Scarlet Pierrot that no-one in their group had been capable of love since the events of a thousand years ago. Feigning ignorance, the Pierrot decides he needs help to tell the story properly, and whistles for others to help him narrate it. In a moment reminiscent of 1911's pageant – and identified by the works magazine as 'marvellously effective' – cloaked figures who had been lying still on the ground around the performance space rose and surrounded the three central characters in a semi-circle, ready to sing the legend of the Scarlet Pierrot (*B.W.M.,* August 1913: 253). At the heart of the tale they told was the legend that a leafless, flowerless tree close to where the Scarlet Pierrot's bride was attacked would blossom on his return. Having told their story, the Pierrots' brutality is emphasised further in a scene in which one Pierrot assaults another to claim ownership of the Pierrette he desires. Watched over by 'The Master Pierrot', the assailant is declared the victor. 'Pierrette is Bought, Your will shall be', the leader states (Drinkwater: 314). As the victim lies injured and unable to protest on the ground, the winner collects his 'poor broken prize' (316). Questions of marriage, gender, love, and consent are clearly articulated within the wider narrative of love, care, and hope. As the fight ends, the tree of the legend blossoms. Amidst the ensuing surprise, the Scarlet Pierrot exerts a mystical influence on the assailant, whose behaviour changes, causing him to care for the Pierrot he has hurt and regret his actions towards the Pierrette. Pierette takes centre stage, demanding recognition that love is more than a legend. The masque ends with the Scarlet Pierrot and the Old Woman left alone on the stage; a moment in which she drops her ragged cloak and, turning to the audience, reveals herself as the beautiful young woman the Scarlet Pierrot sought to marry one thousand years earlier. Love had made her, too, immortal.

Of all four of Drinkwater's masques, *The Only Legend* was the most removed from Bournville's immediate landscape, factory culture, familiar characters, and stories. Its more generic parabolist narrative laid out a simple way of being – care for others – as a route to happiness. Synchronously, messages about community, love, self-care, and tolerance centred in the production were enmeshed with the Bournville Spirit but, despite these connections, this outdoor play was not as well received. The works magazine noted that the crowd scenes were 'further advanced', but 'in certain other respects' the production 'falls short' of the previous year's *The Pied Piper*. Its narrative was considered too general, with subtleties of thought and action less clear within 'such broad treatment of the action' in an unfamiliar story. Solo speeches were also critiqued, with a clear indication that the audience were disengaged, tending 'to wander back to the vanished crowd' when they were delivered; a lack of engagement that seems likely to have been connected with an inability to hear clearly, for none of the speeches in the play are overly long. Concluding their thoughtful, gentle critique, the reviewer suggested that perhaps the style of the masque did not quite fit the location. Referring to the works of the symbolist playwright Maurice Maeterlinck, 'the perfect master of that brief and simple native speech which is so telling in its suggestiveness in tense situations', it was acknowledged that even he 'might himself fail were his stage not an indoor one [...] with all the facilities of such for concentrating the attention and emotions of the audience' (253). Drinkwater was developing his understanding of Bournville, its performers, its audiences, and his outdoor play style, and expectations for the summer masques were high by this time. Nonetheless, elements of 1913's *The Only Legend* appear to have missed the mark.

The reservations expressed in the works magazine account of the party indicate the ongoing support for and investment in outdoor theatre at Cadbury's, and the significance of it to the firm. Growing membership of the pageant sub-committee, in its second year of operation, signalled the importance of this art form 'of which we are so proud', and the impetus to reach the point when its 'significance is fully realized' (252). Unapologetic acknowledgment of *The Only Legend*'s flaws was testament to how 'we take our annual pastoral play very seriously' at Bournville, and it also had many recognised strengths. The costumes, again designed by Harry Bradbear, were 'genius'; the music, composed by the firm's new musical director James Brier, was 'beautiful', and one of the productions' 'most important features' (253). Journalists from local and national publications agreed. Detailed, different newspaper accounts of 1913's masque suggest journalists attended the party, including representatives from the *Nottingham Journal, The Sphere,* and *The Sketch,* alongside the local press (12 July 1913; 19 July 1913: 5; 19 July 1913: 53). External reviewers all praised the music, costume, spectacle, and performances, and identified the masque as the highlight of the afternoon's entertainments. These strengths were important: *The Only Legend* was seen by more people than any previous pastoral play, and by far greater numbers of more diverse external spectators. In addition to a second fundraising performance of the masque for the Cripples Union, prompted by the success of the 1912 charity event, the masque had a third staging to entertain the 2,000, home and international delegates who attended the British Association of Science Garden Party at Bournville, an audience that included the scientist Marie Curie (1867–1934). The charity and garden party performances took place on successive days in September, two months after the original production at the summer party – a period of time that likely required additional rehearsals of the piece to ensure it ran smoothly, particularly when the profile-raising opportunity of external audiences is considered. The conference entertainment attracted significant coverage: *Birmingham Daily Gazette*'s account of the British Association of Science performance exceeded that of any other outdoor performance and included a large photograph of some of the 160 costumed cast members (13 September 1913: 6). Other newspaper reports were published as far afield as Australia (*Brisbane Courier,* 5 November 1913: 15) While the third masque was deemed less successful than *The Pied Piper* as a summer party entertainment, in terms of profile raising it worked hard for Cadbury's.

Robin Hood and the Pedlar, 1914

Drinkwater's final Bournville masque, *Robin Hood and the Pedlar*, was staged in 1914. Praised for its 'artistic achievement', 'popularity', 'dramatic complete[ness]', balancing of humour, beautiful spectacle, and 'suitable' theme, the production was celebrated as a return to form, and the pinnacle of outdoor performance at Cadbury's (*B.W.M.*, August 1914: 232). After clear reservations around the more oblique symbolism of *The Only Legend*, *Robin Hood* was closer to Drinkwater's 1912 treatment of the *Pied Piper*, foregrounding the comeuppance of poor leadership. 'In the drubbing handed out to the Sherriff and his men, we had the humiliation of officialism, an ever-popular theme', noted the works magazine, and one that replayed a display of bad management in a space renowned for industrial innovation and good management (232–233). The familiarity of both narrative and characters were identified as key elements of the masque's success. Foreknowledge enabled character recognition and made the storyline simple to follow, a critical factor of outside performance, where noise cannot always be controlled, and strong voice projection across a wide amateur cast cannot be guaranteed (233). This masque positioned action as of greater importance than words. Maid Marian's role had been reduced to just half a speaking line it was noted, 'but Miss Maggie Cox more than made up for this in her doughty use of the quarterstaff against the Sherriff, her humiliating of that worthy evoking enthusiastic applause' (234). Cox (1887–1973) was an accountant, working as a clerk at the factory. Her adversary, Will Clack (1883–1955) in the role of the Sherriff, was a fellow member of the clerk team. Female staff members may not have made up much of the core cast, or been given many lines in this masque, but their presence was centred in stage action. Maggie Cox, it is clear, owned the grass stage at this moment in the masque's narrative.

While core cast numbers were lower in *Robin Hood and the Pedlar*, stage time was secured for a large cast through a series of interludes and dances inserted into the narrative. The 'Interlude of the Night' attracted the most attention and praise. As the outlaws settled down to sleep for the night in a woodland glade, groups of fairies and elves emerged from the trees around them and danced. Identified as one of the moments of beauty created in the play, the dancers were reported as being able to evoke a sense of moonlight in the bright sunshine of the afternoon through the choreographed movement of their gauzy costumes (Figure 21). The aesthetic influence of skirt dancing and modern dance is clear here, the scene offered a different vision of dance to the may-poling, folk and historical costumed dances that

Serious Play: John Drinkwater's Masques at Bournville

Figure 21 'The Dancers in the Interlude of the Night'
Bournville Works Magazine, August 1914. Cadbury Archives and Heritage Services.

were common fare at works parties. Reviewers noted that there was virtually no set for the 1914 masque; the recreation ground's landscape offered a forest backdrop, with the night interlude offering a clear model of how this outdoor setting was used to best effect. *Bournville Works Magazine* concluded that 'one of the first essentials of pastoral drama is simplicity of theme and breadth of treatment [...] there must be no intricacy of plot, no subtlety of thought' (232). Like the Pied Piper before it, Drinkwater's Robin Hood masque pivoted on its audience's ability to follow the action, bringing together the folktale's moral storytelling with familiar characters, performers, plot, dance, choreographed fight scenes, and humour. The play's comedy was important. Happiness was in demand, unsurprising considering the political climate of the moment and the increasing likelihood of Britain's entry into the war. This masque was considered 'essentially suitable for the happy occasion' the summer party supplied, amidst increasing uncertainty and concern (233). Alongside this local function of providing fun and lifting spirits, *Robin Hood and the Pedlar* also attracted national attention. The *Illustrated London News* account noted that 'there is apparently a wealth of dramatic talent at Bournville', with *The Sphere* publishing a photograph from the performance alongside its report (11 July: 39; 11 July: 38).

Taking Outdoor Play(s) Very Seriously

A conservative estimate suggests that Bournville's four Drinkwater summer party masques attracted around 30,000 factory spectators, with re-stagings entertaining large influential, external audiences. In addition to the impact of the live performances, their scale and innovation also drew the attention of international commentaries on industrial management and welfare, including 'Welfare Work' published by the Australian

Council for Scientific and Industrial Research in 1919. Nothing on their scale was staged at the factory again. While the outbreak of the First World War might seem a logical reason for the end of these pageant-based outdoor events, there had been discussions amongst the Cadbury's board about their ongoing logistical and financial viability for some time before the war broke out. A proposal that they shifted to biennial summer party events was mooted in June 1914, following an earlier motion in 1913 that in 'order to reduce costs' future summer works parties would finish earlier and fireworks be restricted to once every three years (CAHS/CMM/24 June 1914: 501; 16 July 1913: 525). Records of these extended conversations indicate a growing in-house realisation that the events had served their purposes of transition and community cohesion and that, going forward, the entertainment and leisure costs weighed up against the benefits for staff and business did not balance out. Smaller outdoor theatrical productions continued until the summer parties ceased in 1920, but their ending does not undermine their significance and impact. There are more archival holdings connected to the four Drinkwater masques than any other Bournville performance during the period I cover in this study. Accounts and documentation include both organisational records, local and national press reports, and numerous photographs that have found their way to the archives through collections held by individuals. Part of this is the result of the sheer number of people involved, but the importance and legacy of the firm's pastoral plays and masques are further indicated in the minutes referenced above. There was something distinctive about Bournville's fresh air summer party plays, for both Cadbury's wider community and for the outdoor theatrical form more widely.

Cadbury's business operation hinged on employee participation in the model of work and play that lay at the core of the firm's ethos, activity, and identity. In many ways this driver neatly aligned with the burgeoning national interest in civic pageantry that marked the early decades of the twentieth century; as Ayako Yoshino has argued, 'in the communal co-operation fostered by pageantry, a new kind of group emerged, which was defined neither by gender, nor class, but by region and nationality' (51). Local identity was fuelled by the outdoor productions staged between 1908 and 1914 at Bournville, with each play drawing heavily on the factory's landscape and the ideals they represented to inscribe stories onto the local industrial space and into the firm's cultural memory. A useful comparison can be found in *The Garden of the Leech: A Masque of Letchworth*, the first Letchworth Garden City masque, staged in 1914, the same year as *Robin Hood and the Pedlar*. Letchworth was an early model of the Garden City

Serious Play: John Drinkwater's Masques at Bournville 159

Movement. Founded in 1903, it materialised the urban planning ideals envisaged by Ebenezer Howard (1850–1928) and realised by the architects Barry Parker and Raymond Unwin, who had also been responsible for the design of Rowntree's New Earswick. Bournville's village had influenced and driven the Garden City movement forward – the inaugural conference of the Garden City Association, with over 1,500 delegates, was hosted by the firm at the factory in 1901 – but it was distinct from it (Fishman, 1982: 60). Cathy Turner has considered the Letchworth Garden City masque in depth in her study of dramaturgy and architecture, focusing on the dynamic relationship between dramaturgy and urban planning it represented (2015: 65–71). Staged by a cast of around 200, and produced by the Arts Club, the masque was performed in front of The Cloisters, a building dedicated to education. Letchworth's masque was grounded in allegorical representations of history and the future. It presented 'a vision of things that have been, and some bright foregleams of what shall be' (The Arts Club, 1914, cited in Turner: 67). The content was rooted in the 'now' of its social reform message, moulded by an Arts and Crafts grounded ideology and finished with a socialist edge.

As might be anticipated, there are multiple intersections between outdoor theatrical activity at Letchworth and Bournville. Cathy Turner argues for the 'industrial workforce as a kind of motif in garden city design' and the 'workers' procession' as a 'persistent', 'even indispensable element of garden city architecture' (71). The position can be productively mapped onto Bournville performances to an extent, but is simultaneously complicated by the production and employee contexts that shaped the Cadbury's masques (and the factory's theatre more widely). At Bournville, performers were employees in the first instance. This was factory theatre, not model – or garden – village performance. Theatre happened to benefit industry and employees performed in this interest. In front of the pageant's audiences of thousands, staff members played out a distinct set of multiple identities: as performer/character, as employee and as colleague/friend/family member. While these ephemeral occasions at Bournville's cocoa and chocolate factory have been occluded by history, they are central to the story and success of Cadbury's, feeding into the development and promotion of the firm's visual culture and employee recreational and educational provision, and affirming the significance of the factory site and its green spaces to both. Documentation of Cadbury's work parties allow us to begin to repopulate the factory landscape. The pastoral plays and Drinkwater masques reanimate the recreation grounds as significant parts of Bournville's industrial and cultural heritage outside of sport, for which material culture – pavilions and pitches – remain. Outdoor theatre was both recreational activity and a branding exercise. It demanded resource and incurred some (recognised and accepted) risk. Accounts refer to the ambitious scale of the dramas, the logistical challenges around securing adequate rehearsal time for the entire cast to come together, and poor weather that impacted the days of the parties. Balancing out this risk was the clear opportunity of sharing key values and messages about the firm to huge numbers of people. While the summer party was a private occasion – with tickets limited to staff, their families and a small number of local dignitaries and representatives from other firms – increasingly the plays also functioned as outreach and promotional tools for different audiences. Understanding the scale and content of outdoor performances offers a different angle on the dynamics of the social production of space at Bournville and the role of employees' bodies within it.

By 1921, when the article 'Drama and the Worker' was published in *Bournville: A Review,* the firm felt entitled to claim part-ownership of industrial theatre:

> Drama is coming in to its own again as a live art, and a people's art. The people are claiming that the art of 'make-believe' is not alone the preserve of what is called the legitimate theatre, but a field in which the joy, the vitality and the art-instinct of the community at large may rightly seek to find expression. Bournville workers are a little proud of their part in this movement. (14)

The article goes on to discuss Cadbury's dramatic society, plays staged by other factory groups, and the use of drama and play in the company's forward-thinking educational provision. And in 1922, the works magazine returned to the masques again, identifying them as Bournville's key 'pioneer work' in drama and events that 'lifted the English pastoral play to a higher plane' (*B.W.M.,* May: 129). Stories, mythologies, and memories materialised through outdoor theatre were inscribed onto the Bournville factory site, creating visual and verbal narratives that secured and showcased Cadbury's external public identity and local identity, functioned as community-building activities within the factory's staff body, cemented recreational and educational schemes, and contributed to the economic performance of the firm.

The previous two chapters have explored Bournville's garden theatre, exploring a wide range of large-scale outdoor performances and entertainments produced on the factory's recreation grounds for audiences of employees, visitors, and villagers and absorbed into local folklore and cultural memory. Theatre was key to creating and sustaining Cadbury's industrial pastoral, a set of ideas that were regularly invoked through artistic, marketing, and community activities at the firm that sustained the business and materialised its ideologies and working practices. The repetition of these motifs across different areas directed consumers, industrial peers, and social commentators to understand Cadbury's as more than a series of products, imbuing chocolate and cocoa with the firm's healthy and forward-thinking working and production practices. The next, and final, section of the book looks in depth at these two areas to evaluate the use of theatre across the organisation and how drama was aligned with Cadbury's work and play approach to the business of people management and the firm's emphasis on wellbeing and creativity, and social and industrial reform.

PART III

Theatre, Education, and Worker Well-being

CHAPTER 5

Keeping It on the Right Lines
Making Theatre in Bournville's Recreational Societies

Bournville's first dramatic society might well appear to be the most obvious of starting points for an investigation of theatre at Cadbury's cocoa and chocolate factory. It may seem peculiar perhaps that it is only at this point in a consideration of the firm's theatrical history that the group is being positioned centre stage? There is a strong rationale for this. Established in 1912, Bournville's Dramatic Society was a relatively late addition to the factory's recreational groups, trailing behind many others dedicated to literary, artistic, sporting, and musical pastimes. More significantly, its formation was made possible by earlier theatrical activities that had taken place on site: as previous chapters have laid out, a form of theatre that interwove the firm's promotional, recreational, and educational agendas had been realised at Cadbury's by 1912. Yet – the success of these performances notwithstanding – when the proposal for this new recreational dramatic group was formally presented to senior staff for endorsement, it was met with caution. Records of formal discussion and approval of the item connected to a dramatic society at Bournville can be found in a minute from April 1912's Committee of Management meeting which reads, 'the Board agree with the proposal to form a dramatic society in the Works provided it is taken up on the right lines' (CAHS/CMM/282). In this chapter, I explore Bournville Dramatic Society's activity, focusing on their response to this direction that theatre 'on the right lines' must be produced: guidance that governed the group's output, created distinct entertainment models, and forged and strengthened close, productive connections between the group, the firm's educational agenda and recreational provision, and Birmingham's wider cultural activity.

Making Theatre on the Right Lines

Large- and small-scale staged performances were familiar events for Cadbury's factory audiences from the early years of the twentieth century, and this series of theatrical entertainments did not cease when the dramatic society was created; the group was not to be the most significant producer of in-house theatre and entertainment at Bournville until over a decade after its first performances. Dramatic society activities were deliberately designed to be distinct from these other productions – despite regular crossovers of factory staff in their performance, design, and technical roles. In 1923, the British Drama League journal, *Drama,* recorded that the 'policy' that guided the first decade of Bournville's recreational theatre group was the aim to 'provide something different' from what was already on offer at the factory; 'to study plays' rather than 'give entertainments'. With a few exceptions, the account went on to note, its productions to date 'have consisted of staged readings' (2:27: 122). Early dramatic society events were small-scale, focused on learning and self-development, and were characterised by the absence of full production elements (Williams, 1931: 181). The exception was costume, society members taking part in staged readings were regularly part-costumed, but this was presented as means to gain increased understanding of the play, rather than a concession to theatrical spectacle – a device to increase understanding of the play for its performers and spectators – who were, for the most part, also society members.

Dramatic society activity was firmly aligned with the educational potentials of participation and spectatorship. Interactive engagement with plays was sought by the group. As William Cossons – editor of *Bournville Works Magazine,* author of 1928's *Visions,* and founding member of the dramatic society – recalled in a chronicle published to celebrate the group's twenty-first anniversary, their very 'best work' was 'jolly', 'haphazard', 'sincere and stimulating', where the 'audience were the actors and the actors the audience' who 'clapped and criticised and argued' as they continued their discussions of what they had seen and heard as they left the meeting and made their ways home (Cossons, 1933: 6). The society's audiences and productions increased in scale from the early 1920s, but semi-staged plays and readings remained key to their repertoire, and their activities continued to centre, and be defined by, their educational agenda, a remit designed to benefit both members and Cadbury's wider industrial community. To return to William Cossons, while society 'members make no claim to great histrionic ability or technical skill, to originality or more than average good taste in presentation', they did 'believe they have done *something*, if only in putting before an audience – largely one of people who probably seldom visit a professional theatre – a range of plays' that represented a survey of 'dramatic effort of the past and present (1933: 3). By 1933, Bournville's dramatic society members attracted fortnightly audiences of around 800 to their staged readings, and around 2,000 for each of the three fully staged, two-day production runs that they offered each year (3). Across two decades of activity, the group had created and sustained a form of theatre that aligned with the firm's values, a quickly established and relatively simple model of putting plays before an audience that had a wide reach. This was 'theatre on the right lines', materialised by a group of familiar, respected Bournville performers who came together to present a strategic, carefully communicated plan for regular recreational theatrical activity that would build on the recent history of successful factory productions many of them had been involved in. To understand this success, it is necessary to understand how the society came to be.

In June 1912, the works magazine reported on a small meeting that had taken place following a suggestion that a dramatic society could be formed at Bournville. Noting that there has been 'for some time past' an evident 'active interest in the drama' at the factory, albeit one that 'as far can be seen is confined to a dozen or more people', the account concluded that a strong resolution had been passed in favour of developing the idea further (June 1912: 175). November 1912's edition of *The Bournville Works Magazine* reported that:

> During the last few months two or three meetings have taken place to discuss the possibility of forming a dramatic society at the Works.
> Summer Parties of recent years and the performance of Molière's *Mock Doctor* last winter have brought together a group of lovers of the drama who, it was felt, might form the nucleus of a permanent society. (323)

The statement, and this entire issue of the works magazine, was edited by Cadbury's in-house journalist Thomas Badger Rogers (1875–1956). Alongside his professional writing career at the firm, Rogers was a playwright, and his work was later staged by the factory's dramatic society and in other spaces. His talent as a wordsmith was recognised and valued at Cadbury's. As an editor of the works magazine from 1905 to 1936, and author of other key in-house publications including *Bournville: A Century of Progress* (1911) and *Welfare Management: Social Institutions at Bournville Works* (1906) Rogers was responsible for publicising and developing the firm's image and his reputation, experience, and influence was vital to the setting up of the dramatic society. Rogers's craft as a writer is evident in the two sentences cited above; a short statement that brought together a complex set of vested professional interests, behaviours, and practices, with his authorial presence as the appointed keeper of the Bournville Spirit through the magazine, and his role as a high-profile, personally invested advocate for regular recreational theatrical activity at the firm. The tone of this article on the possibility of a new dramatic society is suggestive, rather than documentary. It is carefully played. Rogers presents a gentle, discursive approach to the possible formation of the group, a pitch that set the tone for the process of securing approval from Cadbury's management committees and that continued through to William Cossons's skilfully constructed memories of the group published in 1933. Noting that meetings had already taken place, Rogers outlined ongoing conversations around the proposal that foregrounded vocabulary such as 'felt' and 'might', word choices that indicated a dialogue was in process and that any dramatic society would be the result of shared agreements and understandings. Taking into account the step-change represented by admitting open-air drama at Bournville's Quaker-guided firm (outlined in Chapter 4), it is likely that the path to approval was more difficult for the dramatic society than for other, earlier groups dedicated to cultural activities. It is in this context that earlier theatrical activities – particularly the 1911 and 1912 John Drinkwater masques, *An English Medley* and *The Pied Piper*, and a performance of Molière's eighteenth-century farce *The Mock Doctor* staged at 1912's New Year Party in February – played a significant role.

1912's New Year Gathering featured an entertainment programme organised by a 'select and influential committee', chaired by Clarkson Booth. The summer parties had freed up these smaller annual occasions for more limited audiences; guest lists drawn from senior staff that reflected much earlier events at Bull Street and Bournville. The band played, and songs were sung, before 'rather boisterous' skits on marriage were performed by a 'professional humourist' who was – in the reviewer's eyes – 'a strange intrusion to Bournville, and not quite in its element'. An eclectic range of magic lantern pictures was followed by Edward Cadbury's speech on the business, its staff growth and developing international trade. After a break for refreshments, and a speech of thanks to the hosts, the point of the evening was reached when it would ordinarily come to a close. But not on this occasion. For 'at this friendly party convention was again upset', the curtain was 'drawn aside' and it soon became evident that 'we were in for excellent comedy' in the production of Molière's *The Mock Doctor*. Enjoyment was largely down to the audience quickly seeing how the 'wit of woman' rapidly 'outwitted the dull, slow reasonings of man' the works magazine reported. Production photographs, several of which were published to accompany the article on 1912's party, were taken outside; likely a practical decision, but nonetheless one that re-staged the action that had taken place on a temporary indoor factory stage in a way that aligned the play and players with summer works party entertainments (March 1912: 67–70). *The Mock Doctor* added another layer to dramatic activity's usefulness at Bournville. Cadbury's management struggled to resolve the need for ongoing staff social occasions with the growing size of the business and its increasing employee numbers during the first decades of the twentieth century, as we have seen. 1912's New Year Party performance demonstrated that staff theatre could benefit smaller scale company occasions, providing entertainment that was simultaneously enjoyable, respectable, and logistically viable, as well as serving the larger participatory summer events. Repeat performances of plays at the firm's parties were to become standard practice for the group. In this case, *The Mock Doctor*'s timing was ideal for those planning the factory's first dramatic society.

The staff members who drove the creation of Bournville's dramatic society would have followed clear factory guidance and a set approval process. 'Control' of the factory's societies was 'not run on paternal but on democratic lines' by elected group members overseen by the firm's works committees. To create a new group a convincing case that set out the contributions the proposed society would make to employees' wellbeing, industrial productivity, and the wider image of the firm was required (Cadbury, 1925: 6–7). The persuasive approach captured in Roger's prose in the works magazine indicates the benefits of gentle, strategic engagement with the firm's cultural politics and business operations, which were administered and sustained through the committee structure. Before discussion at the Committee of Management, the proposition for the new society had been tabled at the Men's Works Committee, the group that governed and made decisions on approving and funding recreation at the factory. The minutes from their deliberations on this item are interesting. They note that the question was discussed 'at some length', with members reaching the consensus that the Board should be asked 'whether they would favour such a Society being formed'. Reflecting *Drama*'s account of the style of production staged by the group, these minutes record that it was suggested that the society might be run along the lines of the local amateur Pilgrim Players (founded by Barry Jackson and including John Drinkwater in its membership) with 'scenery of the simplest possible description' and that, if this model was adopted,' it is thought it would prove to be of educational value'. The phrase 'on the right lines' originated with this committee and was fed up, with the escalation of the proposal, to the Management Committee. The final reference in the minutes is to those who had proposed the Society, with direct reference to Spencer Pumphrey, Thomas Badger Rogers, Lottie Allen etc' (CAHS/ MWCM/April 1912: 2854). Positive reception of *The Mock Doctor* and the summer works party outdoor plays, coupled with the established favouring of recreational societies that showcased Cadbury's to external audiences, had laid strong groundwork for the expansion of dramatic activity at the cocoa and chocolate factory, but the standing and reputation of the employees who pursued its creation were as critical to its approval, endurance, and legacy.

At its inaugural meeting on the eighth of November 1912, the officers who would serve on the first dramatic society executive committee were announced to its forty-eight founding members (Cossons, 1933: 5). George Cadbury Junior was named as president. This was an honorary, rather than active, role that adhered to routine practice at the firm; each society was allocated a president from among the Cadbury family, but was run by a body of elected officers. As the minutes of the Men's Works Committee indicate, those who were voted into these dramatic society officer roles were already very familiar from their professional roles, Bournville's cultural scene, and earlier theatrical activity and works party entertainments. During its earliest years, the society was governed by two vice presidents, Clarkson Booth, the first editor of *Bournville Works Magazine* and popular reciter and reader at factory entertainments, and Walter Pedley Hunt. We have encountered both of these personalities earlier in this study. Clarkson Booth was a familiar figure from the factory stage, best known for his recitations, lectures, and readings at parties and other events. On his retirement in 1913, just one year after the dramatic society was established, he was remembered as a 'raconteur' and 'poet', for his 'wide reading', 'fresh humour', and for the 'hearty reception' he received on all the occasions he entertained Cadbury's audiences (*B.W.M.*, December 1913: 397). Walter Pedley Hunt was a tall, striking-looking factory foreman who was in his mid-fifties in 1912. His day job involved responsibility for the engineers' stores, but he was better known for his regular performances in many of Bournville's pre-dramatic society theatrical events. By the time he stepped into this co-presidency, he was already a factory celebrity, known for his roles as Little John in 1909's summer play, the Pied Piper in Drinkwater's 1912 masque, and James, servant to Sir Jasper, in *The Mock Doctor* – that instrumental 1912 New Year Party performance. Outside of Bournville life, Pedley Hunt also performed on the amateur vocalist circuit, participating in fundraising performances across the city and throughout the West Midlands.

Clarkson Booth and Walter Pedley Hunt were supported by an executive committee of seven: accountant and forewoman Lottie Allen;

forewoman Florence Showell; clerk Sidney Davies (1886–1958); the factory's timekeeper Thomas Davies (1867–1945); in-house journalist and editor Thomas Badger Rogers, and Cadbury's dentist Thomas Watt (1875–1962) (Cossons, 1933: 5). Together this group embodied innovative recreational and welfare provision, with several directly involved in its wider delivery at Bournville, as well as actively running its newest society. Most of them remained influential players in Cadbury's theatre well into the 1920s. Lottie Allen had joined the firm in 1902, and she was to remain with Cadbury's until her retirement in 1926 (CAHS/312/001884/ *Girls' Registers, 1854–1905*). We encountered Allen – the 'Ellen Terry' of the Bournville stage – in Chapter 3, but it is worth taking a moment to be reacquainted (*B.W.M.*, April 1946: 87). Reflecting the firm's forward-looking approach to gender equality for unmarried women, Allen was regularly promoted. As Forewoman, Chief Clerk in the Wages Audit Department, and Chair and member of key recreation and staff welfare committees, she was a familiar and well-respected member of Cadbury's management team. Her involvements with factory dramatics actively contributed to her professional status (*B.W.M.*, January 1926: 29). In 1912, as the dramatic society came into being, she had recently played the leading role of the Mother in Drinkwater's *Pied Piper* masque and served on the pageant sub-committee for the same event. Like Pedley Hunt, she also performed outside of Bournville's factory theatre. During the previous year, Allen had been cast in Thomas Foden Flint's amateur dramatic company production of Haddon Chamber's play *The Idler* (*Birmingham Mail*, 10 March 1911: 4). Flint was a Pilgrim Player and he was to be the first stage manager of Birmingham Repertory Theatre, created in the same year as Bournville's Dramatic Society. The link between Allen and Flint was one of many connections between the dramatic society and the city's newest theatre that would prove central to the early years of recreational performance at Bournville, and that I will return later in this chapter. Thomas Davies had played Robin Hood in *Robin Hood and the Pedlar* (1914), the Mayor in 1912's *Pied Piper* masque, and served on the entertainment sub-committee of the 1912 summer works party. Sidney Davies had similar experience of entertainment committee membership. Florence Showell became a member of the 1912 pageant entertainments committee during her first year with the firm. Hired as a forewoman, she was a trained teacher in her early thirties and brought first-hand experience of working in local civic education to the factory; her previous job was as an assistant mistress for Birmingham council schools. Like Allen she was regularly promoted and an active member of the leadership of factory recreation and welfare schemes for female staff members. She was to go on to be a 'prominent actor' in the society's productions, and to serve on its committee for thirteen years, two of them as Chair (*B.W.M.*, June 1926: 183).

The professional roles and status of the nine individual founding officers elected to the dramatic society committee signal that involvement in previous, successful theatrical performances, and knowledge and experience of recreational governance and delivery at the firm were central to the creation of Bournville's first formal theatrical group. It was the entwined individual and collective, professional and recreational reputations of these members of staff that secured regular dramatic activity onsite at the factory. Further support came from the ongoing, active presence of John Drinkwater. The local writer, actor and producer took centre stage at the dramatic society launch and was involved with the first, and many following, seasons of society activity; his assistance repaid to some extent by use of the group and the factory as a work in progress space to try out new plays and ideas, including *Cophetua* (1913), a reading of *The Tigers of Wrath* (later produced under the title *Rebellion*, 1913), stagings of *The Storm* in the 1915–1916 and 1917–1918 seasons, readings of *Lincoln, the work that was to become his most successful piece for the theatre, in 1918*, and *The God of Quiet* in 1922, a restaging of *Cophetua* in the 1924–1925 season and of *X=O* in 1930–1931. It appears that the support of the dramatic society was significant to the playwright. In recording *The Tigers of Wrath* reading for the works magazine, one in-house journalist (who, with the crossovers between the dramatic society and the publication is likely to have been present at the event) recalled that Drinkwater's words were met with an hour and a half of 'intense silence'; members offered an attentive, engaged audience and development space (*B.W.M.*, December 1913: 404). Drinkwater's speech at the society's inaugural meeting cemented the group's model of theatre 'on the right lines', stressing the creative, educational, and health – or wellbeing – benefits of drama, and authorising them from his external, professional, trusted perspective. 'Remember that you are the servants of a great art' he encouraged the new members, an 'art that will give you a quickened understanding of life, new joy in your days'. 'Embark on your service humbly. Learn to love good plays, cherish the beauty of them, exert all your energy to understand their significance, and open yourselves to their inspiration' (cited in Drinkwater's obituary, *B.W.M.*, May 1937: 168). This was, to all intents and purposes, a society mission statement for the new group, and one that aligned them with Cadbury's priorities as an employer. Framed in this way, theatre offered a way to learn, and a way to serve the industrial community. A transcript of John Drinkwater's

Figure 22 *'Cophetua'*
Bournville Works Magazine, February 1913. Cadbury Archives and Heritage Services.

address was published across a series of works magazine articles, and large sections reprinted in the firm's obituary for their house-playwright and producer. They document a persuasive and fluent argument. Like Thomas Badger Rogers, his skill as a writer is clear. Simultaneously, it is important to bear in mind that Drinkwater was a performer, and his delivery can only have added to the impact of his words. The magazine's coverage of the society's inaugural event focused heavily on the cultural affirmation Drinkwater's presence signified: his 'name is now associated with the vital dramatic movement of to-day' and its 'interest in the drama that is true and healthy' the article explained, and in this he stands alongside writers and producers including 'John Galsworthy, Granville Barker, W. B. Yeats and Miss Horniman' (November 1912: 323). Similar cultural status was accorded to the dramatic society's leading figures, with their remit of bringing theatre to an 'audience – largely one of people who probably seldom visit a professional theatre' featuring as a key part of their local authority, and the public service their theatrical activity was presented as encapsulating (Cossons, 1933: 3).

John Drinkwater's speech sanctioned dramatic society activity at Cadbury's and presented it as a transformative force with roots in social reform and progressive intellectual and spiritual education. Grounded in the same ethos as earlier theatrical activity at the factory, it was distinct from the predominate use of performances to create community, identity, and place within an increasingly large firm, and the closer connections to the wider commercial entertainment industry that defined them. With the dramatic society came a larger social agenda for theatre. The cast were familiar from other theatrical events, but in society mode, they shifted Cadbury's drama onto a different landscape, one that was more aligned with the educational initiatives discussed in the next chapter and deliberately affiliated with the early phase of the new provincial repertory movement. These connections with education, self-improvement, and cultural activities resulted in an adapted house theatrical style that complemented other local initiatives, and that are reminiscent to some extent of the origins of the academic study of drama through the lens of English Literature. It is perhaps unsurprising, with this in mind, that there was a clear crossover in memberships of the factory's literary and dramatic societies, with key figures including Clarkson Booth, Sophia Pumphrey, Beatrice Price, and (John) Robert Quinton being active members of both (*B.W.M.,* November 1908: 3).

There are no records of discussion of Bournville's new Dramatic Society in 1913's Committee of Management minutes, an important absence that suggests that the new factory group did not cause operational, social, or reputational concerns significant enough to be formally raised or debated during their critical first year of operation. Other sources support this conclusion. February 1913's edition of the works magazine noted that the society had hired a collection of dramatic works from the men's library and distributed them at their meetings, with thirty copies issued at the first get together. 'This looks like business', the account concluded (62). High praise indeed in the context of Cadbury's, although – admittedly – also an act of promotion in a works publication edited by a key player in the group. The same edition of the works magazine included a review of the firm's New Year Gathering which had taken place in late January. The entertainment programme was extensive, featuring song, impersonations, character sketches, drama, and comedy, but the two largest items were theatrical. First was *Fantasia* written for the occasion by the firm's superintendent of commercial travellers, Harry Keen (1873–1933). This gentle comedy about Bournville life set in Z Block, Top (a fictionalised factory zone that mirrored the language used to identify real spaces onsite) at 'four thirty yesterday afternoon' was an extended skit written for an audience who lived it. The firm's staff swimming lessons and the idealised 'Bournville Maiden' featured, alongside 'bantering [gently mocking] references' to personalities and activities from the firm's many welfare and recreational committees (35). The evening finished with a staging of John Drinkwater's one-act verse drama *Cophetua* (Figure 22), a production praised for its 'exquisitely portrayed' 'haunting beauty', and one that featured most of the key players from Cadbury's very new dramatic society – many of whom were representatives of those committees and activities that had been parodied in the previous skit on Bournville life (37). Likened by James Moran to the poetic, mythological dramas of William Butler Yeats, *Cophetua* was staged in the Girls' Dining Room (2013: 93). As with *The Mock Doctor* a year earlier, a proscenium arch stage had been constructed for the gathering, with curtains that could be closed between scenes. Photographs show that the play was fully staged, with set and costume, and there is no sign of, or reference to, actors holding scripts. This was a full production, and it was staged by the dramatic society, although there is no direct reference to them as a group in the works magazine review of the event. Walter Pedley-Hunt took the lead role as the King, with Thomas Watt and Lottie Allen also in the cast. As for many other theatrical events at the factory, the costumes had been designed by artist and advertising team member Harry Bradbear. The skill and quality of the production praised here are notably different from the rough and ready qualities stressed by Cossons in his memories of dramatic society activity from the same period.

From the dramatic society's earliest years, the group's members demonstrated they could produce small- and large-scale performances. Alongside this, they skilfully negotiated staging theatre that suited the chocolate factory; foregrounding different elements of their performance activity to suit different contexts and aligning the group's activity with the firm's agendas and priorities. The dramatic society's inaugural public event took place five months after *Cophetua*, in June 1913. It was ambitious. First on the two-part programme came a series of scenes from *Twelfth Night* entitled *The Tricking of Malvolio*. Preparations for this performance had started six months earlier, beginning with an un-staged group reading at which parts were allocated to those who volunteered, in the order they put themselves forward. This absence of audition process is significant, representing a clear, practical application of the society's aim to focus on participation, engagement, and learning, rather than virtuosity or talent. *The Tricking of Malvolio* was followed by a re-staging of the New Year Party's production of *Cophetua*, clearly connected with the dramatic society on this occasion. Originally scheduled for April performances inside the factory, the productions were delayed 'due to circumstances beyond their control' to both a later date and an open-air staging on the pergola in the Girls' Recreation Grounds (*B.W.M.*, May 1913: 152). Space and rehearsal time are likely factors in this delay: outside space at the factory had fewer competing demands and was easier to book (through the Girls' Works Committee on which members of the Dramatic Society's executive committee sat). As the first plays chosen by the society *The Tricking of Malvolio* and *Cophetua* interlaced educational drivers (through Shakespeare), and local connections with the Birmingham Repertory Theatre and the affirming, culturally reassuring presence of John Drinkwater (through *Cophetua*). This was carefully chosen drama on the right lines, selected by a group of senior managers who were alert and responsive to the contexts their theatre making took place within.

The works magazine review of 1913's New Year Gathering entertainments was written by Edward Organ, a confectionary buyer at Cadbury's who was to go on to perform at the works, including at the T Block party explored in Chapter 2. He opened:

> I marvelled that Bournville had produced so brilliant an entertainment; and yet I realised that nowhere else in the wide world could one have been produced at all comparable to it. It was not merely in the versatility and artistic excellence of the programme, but in the spirit which it embodied and the tradition which it represented [...] If one of the fallen warriors of Bridge Street days could have looked in upon us, he would have been amazed at the enormous progress in the history of the Firm which the gathering epitomised, but he would not have felt a stranger in our midst. (34)

Hyperbole was typical in reviews of well-received staff socials and their entertainments but, alongside the hype, what Organ captures here is the skill with which the early society was presented and with which key members navigated the cultural politics of Bournville through careful presentation, attentive choice of plays, and a range of production scales. These dynamics should not be underestimated when considering the approbation the group received. Dramatic society members operated in a carefully constructed space located between entertainment and education. Guided and endorsed by John Drinkwater's tested model of factory drama and the educational potential of theatre, the group's repertoire articulated a rejection of audience desire for sensation's 'retreat from life' in favour of a model that prioritised qualities or skills for confronting and contending with life's stresses, and that could offer full theatrical production when it was considered desirable (Drinkwater's speech, *B.W.M.*, December 1912: 357). Simultaneously, the experience and skills the group brought to the Cadbury's social calendar, and their work to secure a place for theatre at the factory, contributed to the ongoing development and presence of the Bournville Spirit; a motif and guiding force that was purposefully located at the core of Cadbury's internal and external identities, became increasingly important to the firm as the business expanded and changed, and captured and sustained that 'spirit' and 'tradition' that employees' Bridge Street industrial ancestors would have recognised.

Repertoire

After its first season, Bournville's dramatic society settled into a pattern of regular fortnightly meetings on weekday evenings that included readings, semi-staged readings, occasional lectures, recitations and monologues, and socials, with additional rehearsal times scheduled in the lead up to staged readings and productions. From early on in the group's meetings members could request time and space to share work that they had been developing outside of the meetings, either individually or in groups. April 1913's meeting saw the first instance of this: after the group had finished their reading of *She Stoops to Conquer* a small group of members offered a work in progress performance of the Trial Scene from *The Merchant of Venice*. Produced by a factory typist Marguerite Thomas (1888–1980) who played Portia, it also featured Clarkson Booth as Shylock. For the group 'the success of this performance illustrated the desirability of members themselves showing initiative in dramatic production' and encouraged the committee to welcome other 'suggestions for the presentation of such items privately rehearsed by members' (*B.W.M.*, May 1913: 152). The dramatic society's early repertoire is relatively easy to trace. William Cossons included a comprehensive list of the plays presented by the society between 1912 and 1933 as part of his published memories of the group, stressing the significance of what they staged to their identity. The works magazine routinely reviewed the plays the society read and staged, offering another important source of information. Play choices were relatively wide-ranging, with most selected and pitched by staff producers who sought to stage them. Repertoire was collectively created within clear parameters; play selection must always stay within the right lines.

As the theatre activity that pre-dated the dramatic society, the ongoing work of factory entertainment committees, and wartime entertainments indicate, Bournville's theatre group never had the monopoly on factory theatre. The Operatic division of the Works Musical Society staged regular operettas, and performances were staged and created amongst other recreational groups, driven by a need for fun, entertainment, and community building. From small leaving events of around thirty employees, to large annual socials that entertained 1,000 or more staff members, events regularly featured factory and external performers, in jokes, skits, songs, and scenes. A clear early example can be found in 1911's season opening concert for the factory's musical society, which included a concert-style party – 'The Bohemians' – who presented songs, recitations and C. H. Parnell and Edith Manders 'Dickens Impressionists' who toured the West Midlands with their act *Pages from Dickens,* on this occasion offering a scene from 'The Cricket on the Hearth' – as well as a sketch, 'Those Clever Tragedies'

(*B.W.M.*, November 1911: 329; *Birmingham Mail*, 23 December 1911: 1). Parnell and Manders were external performers hired in for the occasion. March 1916's social gathering of around 350 evening class attendees from the factory included songs and a dramatic sketch written and performed by the students (*B.W.M.*, April 1916: 123). In 1928 the Works Councils organised and hosted a dramatic recital by Lillah McCarthy (1875–1960) in the still new Concert Hall. The well-known actress and theatre manager was associated with the new writing that often featured on the dramatic society's programme, but on this occasion, she recited poetry by John Masefield, John Keats, Thomas Hardy, William Blake, and William Shakespeare. McCarthy's performance and other entertainments were organised by others but they did not occur in isolation from the dramatic society, nor did the dramatic society's activities take place in a separate, 'air-locked' theatrical space. Each performance, summer party masque, leaving dinner sketch, or New Year or Suggestion party programme drew on a similar set of dynamics around theatre, performance, self-development, creativity, and team work established and honed across the entire factory repertoire, with emphasis placed on different areas depending on the context and participants. Theatre was connected to the identity of employees individually and collectively and the firm as a whole, guiding us to understand Cadbury's both as one large culture with organisational strategies and drivers and a set of complex micro-cultures, each made up by departmental work practices, personalities, humour, and activities – in which theatre played a key part. As the most closely observed and 'regulated' area of activity, what the dramatic society offers is insight into the firm's view on what theatre should be, and how it should operate within the business and its industrial community. These dynamics can be partially traced through repertoire.

Bournville Dramatic Society's first three seasons drew from a familiar canon of established playwrights and popular West End writers, coupled with less well-known new writing and works from modernist avant garde theatrical movements. Playwrights included Pedro Calderón de la Barca (1600–1681), Harold Brighouse (1882–1958), Gilbert Cannan (1884–1955), Richard Claude Carton (1853–1928), Harold Chapin (1865–1915), Anton Chekhov (1860–1904), Oliphant Down (1885–1917), Frederick Fenn (1868–1924), John Galsworthy (1867–1933), Harley Granville-Barker (1877–1946), Isabella, Lady Gregory (1852–1932), St John Hankin (1808–1857), Gertrude Jennings (1877–1958), Jerome K Jerome (1859–1927), Maurice Maeterlinck (1862–1949), Eden Phillpotts (1862–1960), Edmund Phipps (1808–1857), Edmund Rostand (1868–1918), Richard Brinsley Sheridan (1751–1816), Lily Tinsley (1865–1921), Oscar Wilde (1854–1900), Emile Verhaeren

(1855–1916), and William Butler Yeats (1865–1939). Most regularly represented on the society's programmes were James Matthew (J. M.) Barrie (1860–1937), John Drinkwater, Alan Alexander (A. A.) Milne (1882–1956), and George Bernard Shaw (1856–1950). Alongside these readings and productions of published five and one act plays, the society offered space for in-house dramatists to try out their own work in front of audiences, with one or two spaces each season offered to Cadbury-based writers including (John) Robert Quinton, Thomas Badger Rogers, Arthur Knapp, and William Cossons. Despite the mix of styles represented, the works magazine made it clear that selecting plays that would appeal to everybody was a challenge. Announcing the 1922–1923 season, the magazine noted that the programme on offer 'is about as representative a selection of plays as could well be crammed into one season. An attempt has been made to hold the scales evenly between tragedy and comedy, between ancient and modern, and between British and foreign' although 'of course, it is quite impossible to satisfy everybody' (*B.W.M.*, September 1922: 259).

The group's focus on readings and on distancing theatre from spectacle increased the overt representation of politics and social issues on the factory's stages. New writing and smaller productions, often within the problem play model, fore-grounded and tackled contentious national questions through theatre. Early in the society's history Cicely Hamilton (1872–1952) and Christopher St John's (1871–1960) *How the Vote was Won* was produced in one of the society's first off-site public performances; staged at the village-based Ruskin Hall – which had been home to the Bournville School of Arts and Crafts since 1911 (*Birmingham Daily Gazette*, 25 April 1914: 5); 'Anticipating History at Bournville', *Evening Despatch* (23 April 1914: 5). Hamilton was an experienced teacher and a well-known actress, suffragette, and member of the Women's Social and Political Union, Women's Freedom League, Actresses' Franchise League, and Women Writers' Suffrage League. The early production history of *How the Vote Was Won* closely links it with activism; the play was staged at numerous suffrage events around the country in the same year as the Bournville performance. This was theatre as resistance, and the wider context of the event the factory group performed at makes the occasion even more notable. The Ruskin Hall evening had been organised by a local Suffragist Society, as part of their campaign for 'social reform' and conviction that it was 'essential for the welfare of the country' that women should have the vote. The main speech was delivered by local Women's Suffrage Society secretary, public speaker, and journalist Florence Caroline Ring (1871–1944) (5). Through the dramatic society's production directed by Florence Showell political theatre produced at Cadbury's was publicised by a lengthy review in the local press and listings in national suffrage publications, drawing a connection between the firm and the very current fight for Votes for Women. *How the Vote Was Won* was a significant moment in Bournville Dramatic Society's programme, a suggestion of a politically-influenced repertoire feeding into external debates and networks interrupted and redirected by the advent of the First World War. A lot could be done within the right lines.

Active support for women's rights was prominent at Bournville, and first wave feminism was to continue to be a key area of activity at the firm after the vote was won, as we shall see in the next chapter's exploration of drama and speeches at the factory's Girls' Day Continuation School events. While, to a large extent, the dramatic society's repertoire mirrored the male-dominated playwriting scene of the day, significant women playwrights featured, and wider consideration of the group's history reveals the cultural prominence of, and leadership opportunities for, women at Cadbury's amongst its members. Women directed at least half of the productions staged in each season during the dramatic society's early years. The first public performance saw *The Tricking of Malvolio* directed by Florence Showell, and Lottie Allen co-direct *Cophetua* alongside John Drinkwater (Cossons, 1933: 5–6). Several women members continued to perform with the dramatic society after their marriages and consequent resignations from the firm, including Elsie Bradbear (nee Bailey, 1887–1960) who also continued to work at Cadbury's until 1919, and Alice Booth (1864–1934). Advertising placements also spoke to the firm's support of women's education and independence. During the 1920s, Cadbury's promoted their Bournville cocoa line in *The Women Teacher*, the National Union of Women Teachers' magazine, with one exemplar advertisement reading: 'If you have the strain of evening studies a cup of delicious Bournville Cocoa comforts the nerves and often prevents fatigue' (4 November 1927: 1). The National Union of Women Teachers aims were professional esteem, equal pay, pensions, and career opportunities in senior leadership roles for women. Cicely Hamilton was a regular contributor to their journal. Pamela Lunn interrogates the reputation of the Friends for progressiveness on the question of equality for women, arguing that their contribution to action around suffrage and equality was limited and restricted to a few members, nonetheless at Bournville's Quaker-guided operation, the dramatic society, its members, repertoire, and women's rights were entangled and given space, publicity, and implicit endorsement (1997: 30–31). Production histories from the dramatic society offer a different view on the ways that gender was at play in Cadbury's theatrical activity, highlighting the opportunities they offered for women both in the leadership and creative direction of the factory's theatre and welfare and recreation governance.

Dramatic society activity offered staff members opportunities to explore and stage plays that they were interested in and the potential to develop their own characteristic performance and production styles. A report of a dramatic society meeting in early 1923 notes two short plays featured that evening. The second of them was Constance Powell-Anderson's recent Irish comedy *The Courting of Widow Malone* (1922). Powell-Anderson was connected with the Abbey Theatre in Dublin, a crucible for new writing and repertory experimentation. Produced by (John) Robert Quinton, it was identified as being an example of 'the kind of play that appeals to [him] as producer and actor' (*B.W.M.*, February 1923: 50). Involvement with the group offered space to create and explore a creative identity that, in turn, became an accepted part of professional identity. While the names of familiar Bournville personalities repeatedly feature across records of the group's activities, there was also space for new producers and lead performers in roles that could disrupt factory workday hierarchies. The society 'discounted snobbery' celebrated the fifty-year anniversary publication, 'it was the regular thing for members of top and junior management, office and factory workers, foremen and forewomen, University trainees and labourers, mechanics, and secretaries' to form casts and backstage crews (Cadbury Bros, 1962: 9). This approach attracted significant external interest and approval: 'an apprentice in the laboratory had a leading part in a play produced by the head of his own department' on one occasion, on the next their positions were reversed, with the apprentice directing the manager noted the 1926 government report on *The Drama in Adult Education* (117). As a final ingredient, the dramatic society offered a sub community for employees, and particularly, it seems, for women. Or perhaps it is the case that women articulated the value of the society community to them more clearly than men? In 1925, both Florence Showell and Dorothy Wright (1894–?) received farewell gifts to thank them for their service to the executive committee and society. In her thank you speech Showell 'created much amusement by reference to her large "dramatic" family', as an actress – she recalled – 'she had had fifteen children, one grand-daughter, and ten husbands'. In thanking the society for her gift Dorothy Wright, the daughter of a professional actress, 'spoke with feeling of the happy days spent with the Society, and of her sense of loss' and noted that, while moving to London to take up her new job would bring 'many opportunities for seeing drama' she would 'greatly miss' such experiences at Bournville

(*B.W.M.,* May 1926: 164–165). Professional older women at Cadbury's in this period were, by default, single (Florence Showell was leaving the firm to get married, but she was nearly fifty at this time). Census records and electoral registers show many were living alone, a sign of the economic independence created by senior level factory careers, and an indication of how society friendships and community might factor as important elements of day-to-day life. The importance of community for employees without families is further revealed in the case of Maritza Kevorkian (1896–1922), an Armenian refugee who had been supported by the Society of Friends through the Quaker orphanage in Leominster and Sibford boarding school and was then offered a role at the Cadbury's factory. A 'popular actress' 'widely known for her abundant humour and ready wit' and as an 'untiring worker for the society', Kevorkian's early death was met with an outpouring of grief and a large flower tribute from her co-members at her Lodge Hill funeral (*B.W.M.,* June 1922: 172). Involvement with the dramatic society offered companionship, community, and additional leadership opportunities that were of particular significance for women. In the words of Florence Showell, this was a 'dramatic family', and it was one that brought together performers from different backgrounds and staged a wider range of staff backgrounds, identities, and accents than might be assumed.

War Work

Bournville's dramatic society was in the early stages of its existence when Britain declared war on Germany in August 1914, but their already established reputation for entertaining, educational small-scale theatre delivered within a public service model could be adapted to function within the factory's complex blend of national wartime climate, local need and loss, and wider Quaker-guided, pacifist context with relative ease. Cadbury's dramatic personnel could be quickly mobilised, and the extensive role of 'drama as [a wartime] auxiliary service' throughout the ongoing conflict was recognised by William Cadbury in his speech to the New Year Gathering of January 1918, in which he noted that 'at the beginning of the war we had all thought we must live on spartan fare and not have any relaxations, but we had found this was not possible', going on to praise the society for continuing with productions and entertainments for staff, and for regularly entertaining wounded soldiers in nearby hospitals and homes (*B.W.M.,* March 1918: 60). The scale of these 'continuous demands' for external activity is set out in the 1962 publication that commemorated the dramatic society's half century: 'by 1918 something like a hundred programmes had been given outside of Bournville' in 'aid of charity and to entertain patients at military hospitals' including Beaconwood, the Voluntary Aid Detachment hospitals in Harborne and Rubery, and those in Bournville (3). Finding sufficient performers to fill entertainment programmes was challenging, with the increasing need leading to advertisements in the works magazine seeking further support:

> In connection with the Society's work at local hospitals, the secretaries would be much obliged to receive the names of any lady or gentleman who can sing, recite, play any instrument, dance, conjure, ventriloquise, tell a story, or in fact who possess any other accomplishment calculated to interest an audience. (May 1916: 133)

Alongside organising hospital and fundraising entertainments the society continued with its programme of readings and productions for members and factory employees, and organised lectures, socials, and theatre visits to Birmingham's repertory theatre. Reflecting William Cadbury's case for the ongoing – perhaps increased – need for opportunities for relaxation during wartime, the society received an increased number of applications for membership during the first months of the war (*B.W.M.*, November 1914: 338).

Nearly four years into the war, in June 1918 the works magazine reported on the close of the dramatic society's sixth season, one that had been 'notable for its success amid many difficulties. With a much depleted male membership, the difficulties the group had faced last autumn had appeared serious, but the Society had not hesitated'. Supported by veterans and commercial travellers who were returned to Cadbury's headquarters during the war the society had 'not only achieved a good season's work, but have gathered a large following in the Bournville world'. Membership applications and audience sizes had further increased. There are 'always dangers in becoming a vogue', the society member writing for the magazine cautioned, but 'our welcome audiences have appeared satisfied' by the 'earnest work' that went into all activities. After all, the report concluded,' art is always expression from – to'. An audience is essential to dramatic art' (*B.W.M.*, June 1918: 140). By early on in the war, the society had developed a portable repertoire of plays that could be produced at short notice and with minimal labour at hospital entertainments offsite. They faced often challenging production conditions that were likened to those faced by strolling players by a 1915 article in the works magazine. 'Now the Dramatic Society are experiencing some of the delights and some of the difficulties of the old strolling players. Sometimes without scenery, sometimes without even a stage, attempts are being made to interest and amuse the wounded soldiers back from the front' (*B.W.M.,* December 1915: 366). While most hospital entertainments were staged for relatively small audiences, the dramatic society's wartime performances could reach audiences of thousands. The Star and Garter Hospital entertainments, organised by the Lady Mayoress of Birmingham, arranged by a committee of women from Kings Norton (where the factory was located), and hosted on Bournville's recreation grounds attracted a crowd estimated at 1700. Two one-act comedies – *Hyacinth Halvey* (1906) by Lady Gregory and *My Lady Help* (1893) by Arthur Macklin – were performed by the society, both re-stagings of earlier productions that 'brought great credit to the society', and its biggest audience to date (*B.W.M.,* July 1916: 199).

Key figures from the dramatic society and other Cadbury's employees were also involved in a series of entertainments that ran alongside the theatre group's performances, organised by factory entertainment committees and others. Lottie Allen organised concerts at Fircroft and the Beeches, both of which had been turned into hospital and rehabilitation facilities late in 1915. The Youth Club staged theatrical performances at local hospitals, and external performers were invited to contribute to entertainment programmes for soldiers, including the well-known music hall performers Clarice Mayne (1886–1966) and Billy Merson (1879–1947). The 1917 annual report on Fircroft and the Beeches gave particular thanks to the entertainment committee, recording the therapeutic effects of the performances they organised and their ability to 'drive dull care away' from the hospitals' soldier patients with a 'highly tonic effect'. The hospitals' committee was led by Tom Davies, member of the first dramatic society committee and John Drinkwater pageant player (*B.W.M.,* January 1918: 7). In addition to this committee-led activity, teams of staff from factory departments were charged with organising an increasing number of regular entertainments, reflecting both the ongoing war and a need to sustain morale at the firm, and the increase in wounded soldiers housed at local facilities. From the tea, songs, card games, and chocolate that filled an afternoon managed by the Girls' Office at the Stirchley Institute, to the De Luxe chocolate team's entertainment in Bournville School's main hall, with entertainments, dancing and refreshments, these new responsibilities were understood as further endorsement of the Cadbury's factory community's kindness, labour, and social responsibility. 'We are pleased to record how hard each girl worked to make the party a success', noted the works magazine (*B.W.M.,* September 1918: 211; June 1918: 143; July 1918: 170). Patients also became performers, working alongside employees and medical personnel to entertain their fellow soldiers, and hospital and factory staff.

The Clerks' Dining Room hosted 'The Beechnuts' in April 1918, a Pierrot Party troupe founded at the Beeches hospital that performed a programme of songs and duologues and concluded with *The Haunted House*, a dramatic sketch written by one of the patients. Participation remained at the core of the firm's entertainment ideal. Wartime was no exception. 'We have always been of the opinion that the best way of entertaining soldiers, or anyone else, is to provide them with facilities for entertaining themselves, and the Entertainments Committee of the hospitals realise that if more can be done in this direction – that is, in the providing of room and audiences for our visitors – we should be performing an invaluable service' (*B.W.M.*, May 1918: 115). The dramatic society's wartime entertainment service was part of a wider network of events and entertainments delivered by Cadbury's staff for the factory community and local hospitals, and part of a national pattern of activity. It offered the group the most public exposure it had had to date, and prompted a shift to regular productions, as well as unstaged readings; nurturing the 'small but sturdy little plant' of dramatic activity that was flourishing at Bournville by 1915 (*B.W.M.*, November 1915: 159). As entertainment became increasingly important to the factory community, the society focused more on the need to entertain within the clear parameters laid out for their activity. Wartime work cemented the importance of a dramatic society to Bournville, and accelerated its full acceptance and embedding at Cadbury's.

Bournville's post-war dramatic society activity was marked by ongoing attempts to balance the logistics of people, place, and drama 'on the right lines' with the changing, increasing demands and desires of Cadbury's factory audiences. This was not easy. In November 1922, the group staged a triple bill of one-act plays: *The Carrier Pigeon* by Eden Philpott (1862–1920) and *The God of Quiet* by John Drinkwater were fully produced; *The Lost Silk Hat* by Lord Dunsany (Edward Plunkett, 1878–1957) a semi-staged reading. Triple bills offered the society a functional format. Shorter works fitted the model of rehearsed, sometimes semi-produced readings, and each one-act play could be rehearsed and produced separately, evading some of the practical complexities around space and (albeit minimal) props and stage that were incurred by rehearsals and performances of a full-length play. Moreover, the model enabled several productions to be staged in each season. On this occasion in November 1922, the group had staged John Masefield's *Esther*, a four-act version of Racine's seventeenth-century verse tragedy of the same name, just a fortnight earlier. Fully costumed, with set, incidental music, and a cast of ten supplemented by a chorus, the demands of its production scale highlight the need for a logistical, common-sense approach to factory repertoire. It would be simply impossible to stage anything on this scale on a regular basis. Unsurprisingly, then, the triple bill was a popular format for Bournville's theatre-makers, and the history of the dramatic society's repertoire reveals it was used regularly throughout their seasons. Despite this pattern, its familiarity, and the strong reasons behind its frequent use, the works magazine review was critical. It opened with an unambiguously negative statement. 'Frankly we do not care for triple bills'. 'The cinema provides all we desire in the way of varied entertainments and when we go to the play-house we like to get to know the people of the play and share with them their experiences from the beginning to the end of the evening' (*B.W.M.*, December 1922: 346). The tone and content of this review is characteristic of Bournville's in-house dramatic critics; targeted at the factory community and a small external readership, their responses were not softened or cushioned in any way. Dramatic society members may have been co-workers, producing and performing in their free time, but they were regularly subject to stern criticism. Here, the magazine's opinion also reflected the challenges of expectations versus the realities faced by the group, and the pressure on factory theatre makers to produce performances that simultaneously responded to often conflicting agendas and desires that were at odds with the practicalities of production.

Space was the key production challenge faced by the society throughout the years covered here. It was widely recognised as an issue. The critical review of the triple bill format noted that the cast and crew had had no access to the dining hall before their performance took place, and that this was not an unusual situation. Factory societies were offered access to onsite spaces outside of working hours, but the number of recreational activities on offer and the limited number of flexible rooms made access – particularly during rehearsal periods – difficult. Budget and resource allocations from the firm varied across the societies, with committee minutes suggesting that groups with the strongest external profiles typically received a greater share of both. Running costs were met, for the most part, by members' subscription payments, but Bournville's musical and athletics societies, for example, were granted greater amounts of other regular funding and a larger number of ad hoc payments to cover specific needs, including the purchase of musical scores or trophies, engraving costs, or the replacement of musical instruments (CAHS/CMM/November 1912: 918). While sufficient access to space remained a problem, the dramatic society's performances were staged in several, increasingly better equipped rooms in the factory across their history. Earliest productions were staged in the factory's Clerks' Club, a small, social space with an audience capacity of thirty to forty located on the top floor of one of the original staff cottages built onsite (Williams, 1931: 181; Cossons, 1933: 3). In his *Experiments in Industrial Organisation,* published in the same year the society was formed, Edward Cadbury noted that the club had a reading room and billiards table and was used to host regular whist and cribbage tournaments (231). Cossons recalled the smallness of this first 'theatre' space and the fifty or sixty people who squeezed into it for the first play reading of *Twelfth Night* (3). It is clear that the Clerks' Club was not designed to house theatre, and that other larger spaces that were more suitable for performance were available and offered to other societies. While the decision-making process behind this original space allocation is not recorded, the club's smallness and sole-recreational usage seems a good fit with an early 'trial' period for formal theatre provision at Cadbury's, and reflects the careful management of heavily used available space resources that was characteristic at the firm. Access to increased space provision during the early years of the society's activity serves as a symbol of the dramatic society's standing within the firm and marker of the growing centrality of their activity to its industrial community and business operation.

The first decade of the society's history introduces us to two new factory theatre spaces at Bournville. In 1917, amidst the group's wartime theatrical service, their performances were moved to the Clerks' Dining Room, a space provided with an 'improvised' stage and with an increased audience capacity of around 200. In addition to fixed stage curtains suspended from a horizontal frame made of gas piping, the room offered a small amount of stage lighting, consisting of one fixed and two adjustable lights. Dressing room spaces were also available, fashioned from the small dining room and pantry that were located on either side of the stage (1933: 6). Improvements in theatrical space provision for the society continued after the war. From April 1922, the group were given use of the permanent, and relatively 'elaborate', stage installed in the new, purpose-built Men's Dining Room (discussed in detail in Chapter 2). With an audience capacity of 500, the new venue doubled the seats available to spectators (Cossons, 9). Iola Williams's history of the firm and Cossons's dramatic society's twenty-first anniversary publication record that, despite this significant increase, full houses were regularly achieved (181; Cossons, 1933: 9). This third factory space was identified by *Drama* (the magazine of the British Drama League) as enabling a step change in the scale and style of the dramatic society's performances. The opening of the Concert Hall in 1927, fifteen years after the group had been formed, marked their final move in the period covered here. The series of moves and access to larger, better equipped, purpose-built theatrical spaces with increased audience sizes that framed the first decade and a half of dramatic society activity at Bournville tells us more than a story of estate development. Gradually, incrementally, the society was offered access to more spectators, greater publicity, and larger stage spectacle. In these material resources lies an important narrative of approval, one that was rooted in the group's consistent, reliable, strategic production of drama 'on the right lines'.

By 1933, Cossons notes that the dramatic society regularly attracted fortnightly audiences of 800 at play readings, and of over 2,000 for their 3 annual productions; a 40-fold increase in 20 years from those first audiences of around 50 (9). While Iola Williams deemed the dramatic society 'less ambitious' in its early years, a view grounded in the smaller productions that characterised their output during the period, the group's ambition was not connected with scale or spectacle, it was bound to the creation and sustention of a society brand of drama that would be supported by the firm (181). Small performances were the road to fulfilled ambition, and even as the scale of performance spaces and production elements grew a homespun aesthetic remained central to the group's work, albeit one that became more polished over time. Revealing the craft and the labour – the work behind the play – was a key part of the society's identity and of their staged productions. Reviewing a staging of the little-known eighteenth-century ballad opera *No Song, No Supper!* in January 1928 the *Birmingham Post*'s reviewer Raymond Crompton Rhodes (1887–1935) concluded that the 'best' thing about the successful production was 'that everything was home-made – the simplified scenery, the pretty costumes, the properties'. Images clearly reflect Rhodes's description (see Figure 23). There is an artful, theatrically naïve edge to sets such as that shown in the scene between Nelly, played by Violet Bonorino (1907–1984) and Thomas played by Joseph Johnson (?) that reveal – rather than conceal – the nature of factory-made theatre. Rhodes continued that the production was a 'credit' to the society, and by default to the firm, 'because the Society has always fostered a tradition for originality and courage', and 'because it was an all-Bournville production – performers, band, scenery, stage-management, the producer himself, not forgetting the spirit of unity and good team work, without which such a result would have been impossible' (cited in *B.W.M.*, February 1928: 59). The press account carried by the *Birmingham Daily Gazette* was far less complimentary, criticising the poor singing of many cast members, while noting that the audience, nonetheless, 'greatly enjoyed' the show (21 January 1928: 7). Crompton Rhodes's recognition

Figure 23 'No Song, No Supper!'
Bournville Works Magazine, February 1928

of how *No Song, No Supper!* showcased Bournville's creativity identity appears to have held greater sway at the factory, and the production was restaged as part of the programme for the travelling representatives site visit in 1928 (Programme/CAHS/353/001919). What was valued in the factory's theatrical production was clearly identified as an internal affair, regardless of the expansion in the group's activity and the wider external audiences it might be attracting. Valued elements were not consistent – quality of staging and performance were regularly critiqued by the works magazine, as we have seen, but different priorities were applied to suit different contexts and moments in the firm's stage productions.

Summarising 1927–1928's season at the dramatic society's end of season meeting, Arthur Whittaker stated that the committee were aware of recent tensions prompted by the firm's decision to subsidise public performances which were 'largely attended by people from outside of Bournville'. The group's response to this was clear. Subsidy, they argued, came in two forms. First, the use of space without charge for rehearsal and production and second, financial contribution from the firm. The entire season,

Whittaker noted, had been delivered without having to rely on the latter, although it had been offered. The 1927–1928 season included a remarkable twenty-three play readings and sixteen in-house performances that were restricted to society members, their guests and factory employees, a group that now numbered in excess of 10,000 (*B.W.M.*, June 1928: 195; Cadbury, 1925: 5). In addition to this activity, there were five public performances of three plays: *The Cradle Song, No Song, No Supper!* and *Major Barbara*. Perhaps daunted by the high number of tickets it would be necessary to sell to win a reasonable house in the vast new Concert Hall, the decision was made to sell all seats at sixpence. It was a successful strategy, and the annual report for the society notes that more than 5,000 people attended the public shows (*B.W.M.*, June 1928: 195). While the firm appears to have understood the benefits of the society's public-facing activities, the challenges associated with the new factory performance space, and the resulting need to underwrite the financial risk the season incurred, this conclusion was clearly not accepted by all employees. 1929 saw a further adaptation of the dramatic society's model, as they announced their re-formation as a community theatre on the lines modelled by the work of the British Drama League, with all meetings becoming semi-staged performances (*B.W.M.*, September 1929: 282). Full membership remained restricted to Cadbury's employees, with associate memberships available for wives, pensioners, and 'certain' others connected to the works. Voucher books were also produced which members could buy, in order to bring along guests to meetings and performances. External audience numbers continued to increase and by the close of the nineteen twenties the factory's theatrical engagement with the outside world was the source of new debate and some dissatisfaction, but other elements of its relationship with the city were long-standing by this point. Theatre had become increasingly useful to Cadbury's in-house community, but it also offered significant and important access to connections with wider cultural networks.

Bournville and Birmingham's Repertory Theatre: Cadbury's Widening Cultural Connections

While Bournville's dramatic society activity was smaller in theatrical scale during its first decades, the group punched above its weight in relation to the cultural connections between Cadbury's and local theatrical networks and activity that it created and sustained. Bournville had become a part of Birmingham in 1911, but the distinctive presence of the city's Arts and Crafts cultural identity had already been seen in its architecture, and in entertainments including the Girls Baths' staging of paintings held by the city collections by this time (Bournville Publications, 1922: 12). The clearest early examples of increasingly strong connections between the factory's drama society and the city's theatres can be found in the group's first public outdoor productions of *Twelfth Night* and *Cophetua*, and it is evident that John Drinkwater remained the strongest link between Cadbury's and Birmingham's wider culture for many years. Alongside this close connection between the dramatic society and Drinkwater, the group worked with other Birmingham theatrical personalities. Lectures on the art of dramatic criticism were given to the group by local critics and theatre makers, and masterclass-style talks delivered by local stage professionals were programmed in the society's seasons. The factory's theatrical provision, and particularly their Concert Hall venue, provided a valuable resource for other local groups who were offered performance space during the dramatic society seasons, including Birmingham and Oxford University's dramatic societies, and Birmingham's Children's Theatre.

With John Drinkwater came a second important, mutually beneficial connection between the Bournville factory and city drama. Drinkwater offered access to Birmingham Repertory Theatre. The city's new repertory company had developed on a similar timeline to theatre at Cadbury's, they presented a similar repertoire, and shared evolving understandings of how the stage could benefit society. Through their connection with the company and the venue, Bournville's dramatic society claimed a place in what they defined as an early twentieth-century 'renaissance' of theatre. A 'new movement' in which they were 'proud to have been one of the first' (1933: 3). Drinkwater's connection with the Pilgrim Players and with Birmingham Repertory Theatre associated him with a set of central and North Birmingham spaces that would have been familiar to many factory employees. The amateur group had initially met, rehearsed, and performed at Barry Jackson's family home, 'The Grange' in Moseley. In 1907, they moved out of this domestic environment, using two local hired spaces: first St Jude's Mission Hall on Inge Street in central Birmingham; second, and for a much longer, five-year period, Edgbaston Assembly Rooms, a venue that was also used by Cadbury's to house their educational schemes. Twenty-eight productions were staged at the Rooms, with the final years the Players spent there overlapping with those in which Drinkwater was working on the Bournville summer works party plays (Matthews, 1924: 35–36). In 1912, the Pilgrim Players became semi-professionalised, with members receiving a token wage, and in February 1913 they moved into their permanent theatre building on New Street, central Birmingham (now the Old Rep Theatre). The company's purpose-built space was the largest they had performed in to date and offered a new style of theatre design. *Theatre World* recorded that 'the theatre was built and equipped on small but novel and complete lines in every particular', with the auditorium containing two steeply raked tiers of seats, 'a plan new to theatres in this country'. The view of the stage was clear from all seats, ticket prices and seat allocation did not permit, or restrict, better views for some. 'The power of the audience to concentrate on the stage further increased by the quiet colouring and subdued decoration' ('The British Repertory Theatres'. No 1- Birmingham. MM/REF/TH/RE/BRP/1). It is a description of venue design and décor similar to those of Joseph Rowntree's 1935 theatre build for his company employees. Birmingham's new theatre had stage traps, which indicate some commitment to spectacle, but there was no orchestra pit. In the in-house publication produced to mark the company's twenty-first anniversary, Crompton Rhodes recalled that 'in the beginning there was a certain austerity in the theatre that begat austerity in its auditorium', but that the programme made it clear that there was 'room for gaiety in spirit' (Birmingham Repertory Theatre, 1934: 2). Stage spectacle, money, and fame were not the motives behind this theatre build. In his history of the company Thomas C. Kemp stated: 'the theatre of 1913 was crowded with people out to make money or reputation; to take from rather than give to the theatre', but Birmingham's repertory company deliberately resisted and countered this trend (1948: 1). In Barry Jackson's words, they aimed 'to serve an art instead of making that art serve a commercial purpose' (cited in Kemp: 3). Theatre was a form of public and cultural service. Until 1924, the theatre operated a loss-leading model that was dependent on Jackson's personal fortune from his family's dairy business; a redistribution of wealth in social interest that fitted with Bournville's Quaker capitalist ethos.

Birmingham's repertory company offered a practical example and useful cultural activity blueprint for Cadbury's. Opening night for the new theatre was the twentieth of February 1913, four months after Bournville's dramatic society was established. A large group of over fifty dramatic society members accompanied by guests went to see the inaugural production of *Twelfth Night* in its first week; they would have represented around 15 to 20 per cent of the relatively small house. *Bournville Works Magazine* makes it clear that these tickets were not complimentary. The trip was partially subsidised by the dramatic society's budget, but members were expected to pay towards their admission (*B.W.M.,* March 1913: 95). While the theatre had opened its doors five nights earlier to what Bache Matthews recalled as an 'enthusiastic' first night audience, with 'everything look[ing] very promising for the successes of the theatre', 'attendance dropped off considerably during the first week' (1924: 47). Bournville's group booking towards the end of this first week would have been an important group ticket sale for the company, and a likely morale booster. Repertory theatre trips quickly became customary, used as an annual opening event for the dramatic society seasons and forming part of a close and enduring relationship between the factory and Birmingham's theatre group that enveloped people, plays, and places. Company performance styles were held up as benchmarks for society actors. When Bernard Leaver (1888–1960) joined the factory's dramatic society, his first performance received high accolades from the works magazine, the peak of which were that 'he <u>understood</u> the part' and 'almost had the "Repertory" lilt' (*B.W.M.*, January 1916: 15). Bournville and New Street Theatre programmes often mirrored each other. Both groups selected *Twelfth Night* for their inaugural performances, and in the thirty-six plays by twenty-five playwrights produced in the repertory company's first year at their new venue crossovers with dramatic society programming are very clear. Alongside seven William Shakespeare plays, works by George Bernard Shaw, St John Hankin, Barry Jackson, John Drinkwater, John Galsworthy, William Butler Yeats, Henrik Ibsen, Lady Gregory, Maurice Maeterlinck, Harley Granville Barker, Arthur Schnitzler, Oscar Wilde, and John Masefield were staged. Fifteen years later, when the opening programme for the Concert Hall was selected in 1927, all three of the one-act plays chosen had been recently produced at Birmingham Repertory Theatre, where the triple bill was also a common format. To some extent, these similarities in programming were the outcome of practical considerations. Both the New Street theatre and the spaces used by the dramatic society were relatively small (until 1927 and the opening of the Concert Hall), and many repertory company performers had trained through work with the Pilgrim Players, developing smaller-scale aesthetic styles. For both company and society, the play really was the thing; the Rep produced new writing and character-driven theatre that was in synch with dramatic society activity at Cadbury's and when the group watched the opening production of *Twelfth Night* there would have been much that was familiar in the framed stage space and realistic, relatively minimal scenery produced by the theatre's in-house design, scenery, costume and prop workshops (Alan Bland, Birmingham Repertory Theatre Newsletter 1925, M&M/REF/TH/RE/BRP/1).

A network of performers and producers expanded the connections between Cadbury's and Birmingham's new theatre space. When the first group of Bournville society members went to see *Twelfth Night* they would have recognised John Drinkwater as Malvolio, but it is likely they would also have been familiar with Margaret Chatwin, the actress who played Olivia (Drinkwater, 1932: 233). Chatwin was one of the few actresses to hold an annual salaried position within the first repertory company and had been a hired-in performer at Cadbury's events. Born in Edgbaston and trained at the Royal Academy of Music, she began her stage career with the D'Oyly Carte Company (1901–1903), touring in productions of fashionable musical comedies (Parker, 1925: 165). By 1906, she was back in Birmingham and performing at Cadbury's summer works party in a 'dramatic, humorous, musical' recital alongside Willis Crisford; a performance that 'created great amusement' (*B.W.M.*, August 1906: 329; see chapter 3). Between 1907 and 1912 Margaret Chatwin was a member of the Pilgrim Players, remaining with the company as it evolved into Birmingham's Repertory Theatre (Parker: 165). Connections between company and factory people continued to grow. The Rep's production of *The Knight of the Burning Pestle* in August and September 1919 saw five dramatic society members cast as the gentleman who sits and smokes on stage. The factory's staff performed nightly in the same ensemble as a young Noel Coward (1899–1973) (Cossons, 1933: 9). Barry Jackson was in the audience for the dramatic society's production of Clifford Bax and H. F. Rubenstein's *Shakespeare* in 1922 (May 1922: 129). In 1923 Stuart Vinden, a local theatrical personality 'well known to Rep. playgoers', read George Bernard Shaw's 'Androcles and the Lion' at a dramatic society meeting, at a time when he was also offering elocution lessons for society members that were 'proving successful', and serving as both a dramatic competition judge and occasional lecturer at the factory (*B.W.M.*, September: 261). In January 1932, Birmingham's repertory theatre came to Bournville, performing matinee and evening performances of *The Barretts of Wimpole Street* in the Concert Hall under the auspices of the dramatic society. Their visit was prompted by the Rep's current licensee and manager Emilie Littler's (1903–1985) visit to the factory's Concert Hall to see the society's production of *Street Scene,* a play that was also in the current season at the New Street theatre (*Birmingham Daily Gazette,* 4 January 1932: 3). Close connections between Cadbury's theatre and Birmingham's theatrical culture endured throughout the period covered in this study, drawing factory representatives into wider networks of key theatrical figures and cultural stakeholders.

In March 1920, *The Stage* carried a report on the planning of a dinner to honour John Drinkwater. The organising committee was chaired by the Lord Mayor of Birmingham and William Adlington Cadbury, and included the Bishop of Birmingham, the Vice-Chancellor of the University of Birmingham, Neville Chamberlain, M.P., Barry Jackson, Philip Rodway, the Managing Director of 'the Royal', the Chair of Birmingham's Anglo-American Society, Raymond Crompton Rhodes, J. Holman, the editor of the *Birmingham Gazette*, and Sidney Davies, Bournville employee and member of the first dramatic society executive committee (25 March 1920: 4). The cultural and social capital embodied in this organising committee speaks to the additional benefits Bournville's theatrical activity accrued for the firm, and for individual employees. As an aside, it also reveals the progressive environment Cadbury's offered professional women; for the exclusively male representation on this organising committee would not have occurred on Bournville's industrial landscape. What is captured across dramatic activity at the chocolate factory and Birmingham's Repertory Theatre, and particularly at their points of intersection, is an emerging, strengthening model of culture as service subsidised by and within the commercial world. The theatre made in these two spaces spanned intellectual reflection, sociological approaches, and practical action. Key society members were entrusted with managing factory playwriting and running factory-wide monologue and duologue competitions; assessing colleagues' creativity themselves, or liaising with influential external figures who served as judges. As encouragers and facilitators of greater, wider participation in the firm's theatrical creativity, these employees were critical to Cadbury's operation. Regular lectures organised by the dramatic society supply a further clear example of how intellectual and sociological approaches and practical theatre making framed thinking about stage performance within the industrial community and more widely.

What Is Wrong with the Theatre?: Bournville Dramatic Society Lectures

Lectures delivered by local theatrical producers and critics were regular features of the dramatic society's seasons, reflecting the group's wider networks, and materialising, extending, and occasionally blurring the educational remit that was central to their approval: that 'unwritten understanding' that 'the object constantly kept in view' should be 'participation in the drama as an art rather than dramatics as an amusement' (*B.W.M.*, February 1918: 38). The content of lectures organised by the dramatic society typically fell under one or more of three themes: a vision of a better future for theatre, the history of theatre, or effective theatre production. In 1914, Raymond Crompton-Rhodes, the reviewer and writer for *The Birmingham Post* who praised *No Song, No Supper!* fourteen years later, spoke on the 'Past and the Future of Drama'. Advocating for a new form of folk-style, community-created theatre, he covered all three themes, referencing historical production practices, how giving actors greater input increased creative satisfaction, and stage craft and lighting (*B.W.M.*, March 1914: 87). Like John Drinkwater, the association between Crompton-Rhodes and Bournville endured, he regularly returned as a speaker, including the delivery of a further lecture in the 1914–15 season, and an occasion in 1931 when he gave an 'entertaining' lecture entitled 'The Critic', that explored the play and its author, Richard Brinsley Sheridan, based on his ongoing series of publications on the playwright (*B.W.M.*, March 1931: 69). Like Drinkwater the author used Bournville's dramatic society audience as a useful sounding board and promotional space for his ideas. 1915's programme also included a lecture by Henry Astley (1868–1955), a local theatre professional and the owner of a city theatrical costume shop, who gave a masterclass demonstration on stage make up, using dramatic society members as models to illustrate and showcase his work as he spoke (Cossons, 1933: 7). 1918–1919's season included two guest speakers on theatre. The author and Birmingham Repertory Theatre member Gilbert Cannan (1884–1955), whose subject was 'The Future of Theatre', and local amateur dramatics stalwart George Ostins (1870–1942) who spoke on the production of plays.

Gilbert Cannan's lecture was presented at a society event chaired by George Cadbury Jr. Echoing Crompton-Rhodes's focus on new ways of making theatre, Cannan explored the potential for an English theatre style that succeeded in eschewing both commercialism and the 'intellectual decoration' of Russian and German modernist work. Something new was needed, he argued, for while Shaw and Barker had 'thought they could destroy the 'West End' theatre', they 'had not really created anything to take its place'. At the core of Cannan's vision was participation; a production model that would 'develop the artist in everybody' (*B.W.M.*, February 1918: 38). Seven months later Cannan's play, *Everybody's Husband,* was presented by the dramatic society and identified by the works magazine as a wholly unsuitable piece for Bournville. Part dream play, part realistic drama, the work required 'certain conveniences of modern theatre' not available at the factory. Lead performances were to be praised but they could not distract audiences from 'complications' with stage machinery, the 'improvised platform', and 'imperfect lighting' (*B.W.M.*, November 1918: 267). The role of theatre as a recreational tool, or public service, led to a refreshing absence of flattery in works magazine responses to plays and productions, and – as we have seen – the publication was not reticent in expressing its writers' views. On this occasion a chasm between ideas and production conditions is clearly articulated. George Ostins, well-known for his two-decade history of performing and producing with the Commercial Travellers' Association Dramatic Society and his own 'Company of Players', spoke on the practical production of plays (*Birmingham Mail,* 20 December 1915: 4; *Birmingham Daily Gazette,* 27 April 1921: 2). His advice and hints on casting, in a structure framed by Hamlet's advice to his players, 'were extremely useful' the works magazine reported, and would long be remembered by the society (*B.W.M.,* March 1919: 68). Other wartime lecture activity included leading members of the dramatic society speaking to other factory groups. Early in 1918 (John) Robert Quinton gave a lecture on 'The Art of Entertaining' to Bournville Youth Clubs. Covering Music, Painting and the Drama, the talk was 'illustrated' throughout by mini performances by either the lecturer, his daughter Miriam, or the pair together (*B.W.M.,* March 1918: 74).

Lectures appear to have been viewed as a fitting model of wartime activity and also featured as a key part of Port Sunlight's dramatic programme during the conflict (see chapter 1), but their appeal persisted after the end of the conflict. During the winter of 1922 Arthur Esme Filmer (1883–1941), principal director of Birmingham Repertory Theatre from 1919–1922, presented a course of ten lectures that focused on theatre's history, play production, and stage management at the society's request. Topics he addressed included:

> The history of the stage (to show the different theories of production, particularly the cleavage between the representational and presentational methods), the psychological and metaphysical attributes of the producer, the producer as interpretative and as creative artist, and so on to actual stage practice in the keeping of prompt books, of conducting rehearsals, arranging scenery and lighting, make-up and costumes etc.

Filmer also taught through practice. Several of the sessions he led were structured around the application of the group's learning to three production-based models that they worked on outside of his lectures. The first of these was a play that the society had already staged; the second, a play that they hoped to stage in the future; the third a play that they produced under his professional guidance (*B.W.M.,* January 1923: 9). While the number of regular attendees at Filmer's sessions was small, at around a dozen, the practical expertise they gained was understood as directly benefitting and extending the factory's dramatic society. The lecture course was identified as one of the most interesting and successful features of the group's season, with direct impact reported in the production of *Lonesome-Like* in January 1923 – 'a very creditable staging by a member of Mr Filmer's class, who has not hitherto, we think, been seen on the 'regular' Bournville boards either as player or producer' (*B.W.M.*, June 1923: 182; *B.W.M.*, February 1923: 50). Filmer's lectures stressed the value of rehearsal, a key and valued element of Bournville's theatrical model; the work in the play. *Much Ado about Nothing*, staged in the same season, was praised as the 'fruit of long-sustained hard work at rehearsal' (*B.W.M.*, May 1923: 148). Together these lectures and performances focused attention on thinking about theatre and the practical models of preparatory and backstage work that created stage production, processes that have often been missing from our considerations of historical performance.

Opening events programmed to mark the following dramatic season again included a lecture. This time Horace Shipp (1891–1961) took to the platform. Critic, artist, editor of *Theatrecraft*, and well-known figure to 'old Fircrofters', Shipp's lecture was provocatively titled 'What Is Wrong with the Theatre?'. Programmed on a society open night, when all friends and employees could attend, Shipp's 'pessimistic view of the state of the theatre to-day' 'ruined not only by commercialism, but by ostentatious productions' was targeted at the widest possible audience. Quoting the modern dancer and international celebrity Isadora Duncan (1877–1927), Shipp reminded his audience that 'we get the theatre we deserve, and there is not much hope until the public cease to regard the theatre merely as a place of amusement. So long as people attended plays indiscriminately and unintelligently … so long would managers foist on them the vulgar and the inane' (*B.W.M.*, November 1923: 346). Shipp was the co-author of *Community Playing: A Little Guide Book of Production* with John Drinkwater, a text published by the National Adult School Union in 1920. His ideas about theatre for performers and spectators were a neat fit with those espoused by the firm's dramatic society. Lectures and lecturing became an increasingly significant and well-received part of the dramatic society's activity during the nineteen twenties, culminating in a full works council organised weekend theatre lecture school in 1928. Consisting of four lectures on 'The Theatre and Its History', the small course was delivered by Bache Matthews (1876–1948), a member of the Pilgrim Players, Assistant Director at Birmingham's Repertory Theatre, author of the first history of the theatre company (published in 1924), and adapter of multiple plays for production. Like John Drinkwater, Bache Matthews engaged with and worked across many areas of theatrical production and writing. His lecture material was organised thematically under the title 'Rogues and

Vagabonds', a label used for all actors aside those under noble patronage in the Elizabethan period. He covered Medieval, Elizabethan, and nineteenth-century performance – including toy theatres, theatrical prints, lighting, and spectacle – before concluding with a consideration of the modern stage, particularly new playwrighting coming out of Russia and Ireland. The entire course was illustrated with lantern slides and prints from his private collection (150). In his thanks to the firm at the end of the weekend school, Bache Matthews focused his attention on the factory's dramatic society, praising it as a model for activity that made 'people consciously interested in the theatre'; a model on which, he believed, the future of theatre depended (*B.W.M.,* May 1928: 150). The coalescence of theatre, thinking, and learning, noted by Bache Matthews, highlighted in a lecture series organised by the factory's Works Council, and situated at the core of the dramatic society's 'drama on the right lines' infused educational approaches and delivery at Bournville, and it is this area of theatre's influence and impact that the final chapter explores.

CHAPTER 6

Dramatic Methods of Teaching
Theatre and Education at Bournville

In 1912, Cadbury's Works Education Committee published *An Outline of the Educational System connected with the Bournville Works*. Written by the firm's education director Reginald Ferguson (1872–1953) and printed in house, the pamphlet opened with clear statements on the interdependence of education, industrial success, and employee welfare at Cadbury's, and how Bournville's model offered wider benefits. Documenting and reflecting on the increasing number of young people employed in working environments that required nothing of their mind and no specialist skills, *An Outline of the Educational System* confidently situated the firm's activity as evidence of an endemic national problem addressed and resolved at a local level, concluding that:

> The growth in the unemployment of large numbers of young persons in uneducative blind-alley occupations, leading inevitably to casual employment, and ultimately to unemployment in later years, has shown that the organisation of industrial training is a matter of no less urgency from the point of view of Society and the State than from the point of view of the industrial manufacturer. (1)

The details of Bournville's local educational provision that followed were framed as a response to these pressing social and industrial challenges, presenting pioneering approaches that promoted and secured Cadbury's leading role in tackling issues that exceeded their own workforce within a company publication that was clearly targeted at a wider readership. Previous chapters have explored the connections between Bournville-based social and cultural innovations and larger debates around industrial progress, social reform, gender equality, public service, and citizenship. They have also identified the educational drivers that lay behind much of the firm's recreational provision, theatre making, and theatre spectating, exemplifying the challenge Iola Williams noted in his 1931 history of the business that any attempt to draw a 'distinction between what is educational and what is recreative' within this model of Work and Play, leads to a separation that is 'is, perhaps, not very real' (1931: 179). Revising Williams slightly, I would argue any such disentangling would be entirely false. In this final chapter, I weave together recreational theatrical dynamics and forms that have been explored throughout *Theatre in the Chocolate Factory* with a range of Cadbury's educational programmes and spaces. Particular attention is given to the emphasis on creativity that was embedded in educational spaces and the curricula they delivered; activity that peaked during the 1920s in synergy with wider discussions on the use of drama within education, and that identify the firm's leading role in the development and acceptance of theatre in, and as, education.

Cadbury's had an established history of investment in staff education by the time Ferguson wrote his 1912 *Outline of the Educational System*. From 1852, women employed at the Bridge Street factory were allowed to stop work an hour early two days a week to attend evening classes, and voluntary day and evening classes had been available to staff at the Bournville factory from 1899. Under Edward Cadbury's leadership, the firm expanded its educational activity significantly, introducing and financing a range of compulsory and non-compulsory educational organisations and programmes open to factory employees and (in some cases) others that exceeded the series of government requirements enacted during the period. In 1906, the Works Education Committee was founded and attendance at evening school became a precondition of employment at the factory for workers aged between fourteen and sixteen (Williams, 1931: 166). The age at which this additional education ceased to be compulsory was raised to seventeen in 1909, and then again to eighteen during the following year. More senior groups of staff – apprentices and male clerks – stayed in education longer still, with leaving ages of twenty-one and nineteen respectively (167). As the twentieth century progressed, apprenticeship schemes, continuing professional development opportunities, and day-release schooling were included in Cadbury's educational offer, with school and college buildings, teaching staff, and funding for non-vocational higher education scholarships, bursaries, and prizes resourced by the firm. The location of these schemes as integral elements of Cadbury's long-term business strategy is further underpinned by John Kimberley's conclusion that the prioritisation of education and the work it incurred is visible in the committee having two directors, an anomaly within Bournville's organisational structure (2016: 169). Designed to create community, responsibility, and loyalty and to develop creative, civic-minded employees, Cadbury's investment in education was understood to bring short-, mid-, and long-term benefits for business and staff, and was recognised as particularly important for entry-level workers. When 'boys and girls start at the Bournville Works [they] have, as a rule, at least four years of study ahead of them' explained Ferguson in *An Outline of the Educational System*, and with this in mind 'it is essential that they be selected with care'. The longer-term perspective – how applicants would develop within the firm's educational and recreational frameworks – formed part of the recruitment process. 'Appointments at this factory are looked upon as permanencies', he continued, for 'there is no discarding of junior employees when they begin to look for the wages of adults' (4). Teaching and learning were at the core of Bournville's staff development and as a qualified teacher and former school inspector hired by Cadbury's in 1911 to direct the firm's educational programmes, Ferguson was well placed to assess and adjust these activities. One of his first roles at the firm was to lead Cadbury's involvement in the setting up of Bournville's Day Continuation School, a space in which education and theatre were tightly interwoven.

Cadbury's Girls' Day Continuation School: The Pageant of Plays and Playgoers, 1922

In July 1922, Bournville's Girls' Recreation Grounds again served as the performance site for an outdoor pageant. On this occasion, the theatrical production was the main feature of the Girls' Day Continuation School end-of-year celebrations, a large-scale, annual event that typically included a play staged and performed by pupils and staff. The *Pageant of Plays and Playgoers* consisted of five scenes that brought to life biblical, dramatic, and literary narratives, opening with a staged excerpt from the old English epic poem *Beowulf*, followed by the 'Pageant of the Deluge', a short miracle play version of the tale of Noah's Ark acted by students who were also pretending to be members of the medieval Shipwright's Guild. The next episode in the pageant staged scenes from William Shakespeare's *Much Ado about Nothing* with student performers playing both the comedy's characters and a group of Elizabethan strolling players, against the recreation ground's backdrop of trees and grassy banks reframed as sixteenth-century parkland. Excerpts from an unidentified play by the eighteenth-century playwright Richard Brinsley Sheridan and a 'modern phantasy' concluded the afternoon's entertainment.

In addition to offering a whistle-stop tour through a history of British writing and performance, the school pageant sought to present the historical contexts and material conditions of production associated with each

Figure 24 'The Pageant of Plays and Playgoers'
Bournville Works Magazine, September 1922. Cadbury Archives and Heritage Services.

scene. This was a pageant of plays *and* of playgoers. Each piece included an audience of performers, with the actors 'watched' by others who were playing the roles of audience members from the same historical moment as the dramatic excerpt; as an example, the group of 'country folk and pilgrims' attending the fourteenth-century fair that the scene simultaneously staged can be seen around the edges of the pastoral performance space in Figure 24 (*B.W.M.*, September 1922: 263). This acting out of history, combined with the costume and prop research and making, reflected an increasingly popular way of teaching history and literature through dramatic performance at early twentieth-century Bournville; one that would also feature as a key topic in Arthur Filmer's lecture series for the dramatic society later in the same year. The publication of play collections for schools signals formal acceptance of theatre as an educational practice more widely during the 1910s and 1920s. While plays for school settings had been in print circulation since the early nineteenth century, volumes including Geoffrey Alington's *Plays for Schools* (1914), Agnes Day's *Historical Plays for Schools* (1924) and Louie Jesse's *Historical Plays for Schools, vol 1 Wales* (1929) indicate a different set of drivers for educational productions – objectives that focused on the process of learning, rather than solely on staging entertainments, or the elocution and public speaking skills that could be developed through performance. As the journal of the British

Drama League, *Drama,* recorded in 1919, 'in continuation schools special stress is laid on the drama as a part of education', noting that Bournville's activity modelled a very strong example of this (153). The presence of theatre in factory education connects to the wider arts and humanities-driven focus of Bournville learning for girls, with its prominent emphasis on creativity, identity, and local and national histories alongside other core subjects including parenthood and domestic skills. This valuing of creativity appears to have increased during the nineteen twenties, with the launch of a new scheme in 1927 that set out the expectation that every Day Continuation School student must 'use her voice in drama, recitation, or reading aloud, to write something original' and 'to make or do something with her hands' (*B.W.M.,* August 1927: 262).

The opening of Bournville Day Continuation School in 1913, nine years before the open-air production of the *Pageant of Plays and Playgoers,* had marked a key moment in the expanded practical delivery of Cadbury's educational ethos. Developed in collaboration with the City of Birmingham Local Education Authority, Kalamazoo Works (the Impey and Morland paper factory, based in Northfield), and the Co-Operative Society, the school was the first in the country to offer paid employee education during work-time, providing compulsory, post-elementary education for Cadbury's employees who were under eighteen, and for other young workers, including those employed by the other founding partners (Gardiner, 1923: 153). As with all educational activity supported by the Cadburys, its formation was strongly influenced by the Adult School Movement. With origins in late eighteenth-century Quakerism, adult schooling had gained traction during the mid-eighteen hundreds, and by the first years of the twentieth century was understood as a means to create fellowship, increase literacy, share knowledge of the bible, and foster learning within increasingly non-church attending, urban populations (Rowntree and Binns, 1903: 3–10). The spirit of New Quakerism that emerged in the mid eighteen-nineties and the city of Birmingham were at the heart of this expanding adult school movement, a link that John Kimberley attributes to the practical, largely industry-based members of Birmingham's Society of Friends and the way in which their personalities and professions drove communication of their faith through philanthropic work, and outreach; stepping away from evangelical models to focus attention 'on the endeavour itself, rather than the form of the message' (2016: 155). The Cadburys were ideally placed to contribute to, and develop, the organisation, and a long history of association between the firm and the Adult School movement that was in place by the early decades of the twentieth century pre-dated the business's move to Bournville. Richard, George, George Junior, Barrow, William, and Edward Cadbury, alongside several family members who were not involved in day-to-day business operations, and key senior factory employees including Sophia and Spencer Pumphrey served as teachers, leaders, and patrons of the Adult School movement at local and national levels. Simultaneously, Adult School models offered strong inspiration for the organisation of educational delivery at Cadbury's industrial operation. When Barrow Cadbury marked the firm's centenary in a 1931 speech, he focused almost exclusively on its five decades of production at Bournville and on the role of the Adult School Movement in the firm and its principles. Equating the two he argued that the Adult School Movement could be understood as representing the business's core values, for both, he stated, have 'much to do with the creation of what we call the Bournville Spirit'. Barrow Cadbury's words, and the moment and place in which they were delivered, presented a historical narrative for the firm that framed both its present activity and its legacy. Like most of the speeches given at closed events, an account with large sections of transcript was offered in the works magazine. Its message was for all, and the words were designed to be kept, memorialised as a moment in, and a vision of, the firm's history. 'In the Adult School Movement', Barrow Cadbury continued, 'we learn to work harmoniously with those who may entirely differ from us in their politics, in their views of truth, and in their outlooks on life' (*B.W.M.*, April 1931: 98). Practical application of New Quakerism's principles and ethics shaped the mould of Bournville's non-denominational spirit, creating an industrial community, a fellowship, fuelled by creativity, collaboration, and education. Life-long learning and development were firmly positioned at its core.

Bournville Day Continuation School was directly funded by the City of Birmingham Education Authority, with Cadbury's picking up indirect costs, including those connected to space: classes were initially delivered at the nearby Stirchley Friends Institute, a building constructed in 1892 by Richard and George Cadbury as part of their material and personal investments in the city's Adult School Movement. The school community grew quickly. On opening in 1913, attendance had been made possible by a half-day release model for younger members of staff. An initial requirement that they should also attend one evening class a week was withdrawn, with an extra, voluntary half day of schooling introduced in its place. This additional time was unpaid, but as Iola Williams notes 'an unexpectedly large number of students [from Cadbury's factory] – about a third of the whole – availed themselves of this chance' (167). These fast-growing student enrolment numbers necessitated a move for the boys' school, to the Friends Hall, Cotteridge in 1914, resulting in separate girls' and boys' sites. From 1917, most students attended for one full day a week (Fortieth Anniversary Programme/CAHS/360/002202). Despite its collaborative, off-site beginnings, the continuation school was most clearly linked with Cadbury's, mainly through the direct affiliation with Bournville contained in its name (Ackers and Reid, 2016: 133). Wider national continuation school activity was accelerated and cemented by 1918's Fisher Act, education legislation that lifted the school leaving age from twelve to fourteen and referenced and affirmed Cadbury's early adoption and experiment with continuing education. To comply with the act's requirements, the school's provision for under sixteens was adjusted to two compulsory half days a week in 1919, again necessitating more space (Wray and Ferguson, 1920: v). From 1920, The Beeches – a large house on the outskirts of Bournville bought by George Cadbury to serve as a holiday, or respite, home for poorly inner-city children and Salvation Army workers, and used as a hospital during World War One – became the school's base. In 1925, purpose-built permanent girls' and boys' continuation school buildings were opened in Bournville, bringing the organisation that had been circling around the perimeter of the factory estate right into its heart.

Drama was particularly present in the life of the Girls' Continuation School. While a dramatic society was formed at the boys' school in 1924, drama had 'always played a great part in the life of the girls' school' (Nicholls, 1946: 20). Plays were staged within the school's first years. December 1914 saw a fundraising performance of scenes from *The Tempest*, and other entertainments, taking place on the stage of the Stirchley Institute, an entertainment that was restaged the following March in aid of another wartime charitable organisation (*B.W.M.*, May 1915: 160). From 1920, the School had a Dramatic Study Circle that met outside of lessons (Wray and Ferguson, 1920: 50). Within a school ethos that sought to 'inculcate habits of mind and character' rather than 'accumulate facts', that recognised and embedded the benefits of a humanities education, and that focused on the development of 'valuable social and cultural activities', drama offered a useful teaching tool, an artistic and creative process, and a publicly visible outcome (*B.W.M.*, September 1921: 210; Nicholls: 4). Locating Bournville's activity within the wider continuation school sector, the works magazine concluded that 'in most schools of a modern type the study of Literature is rendered real and interesting by adopting the dramatic mode of instruction'. The focus, the article makes clear, should be on process: 'the *study* is the main thing; the interesting performances given to parents and friends' and the fundraising potential 'secondary matters' (*B.W.M.*, May 1915: 160). The 1928 edition of the *Amateur Drama Yearbook and Community Theatre Handbook* lists an entry for the Day Continuation School directly above that for the Bournville Dramatic Society, noting that 'specially prepared [school] plays are produced at Cadbury Bros' Theatre, Bournville Lane' (Bishop: 93). School theatre visits also took place as part of learning (*B.W.M.*, August 1922: 224). While this pedagogic approach guided school dramatic activity, examples later in this chapter will make it clear that performances and charity connections were important factors in student productions and in the growing acceptance of theatre as a teaching tool over the next decades.

Inaugural headmistress Annie Elizabeth Cater (1874–1963) led the girls' school for most of its early history and appears to have been a driving force behind its outdoor theatre. After qualifying as a teacher in 1900, Cater began her career as a pupil teacher at the London Orphan Asylum where her father was a dental surgeon. Bournville was her fourth professional post, following periods as an assistant mistress at schools in Lancashire and Devon and her first headship at Havergal on the Hill (1910–1912) – the new junior school wing of Toronto's residential feepaying school Havergal College, known for its progressive approach to the education of girls and women (Teachers Registration Council entry). One of Cater's former Havergal pupils recalled a 'forceful Quaker' who started a group called 'Pukwudgees or "little wild men of the woods"' made up of 'intrepid girls from the top class' who 'made forays to Sunnybrook farm and to the Lash farm in the West End' (Bryers, 1994: 196). Originating in Native American folklore Pukwudgees are magical creatures, akin to fairies, or wood sprites, who move between mischievous and naughty. Cater's ethos offers a clear connection with Cadbury's focus on the outdoors, exercise, and folk and mythic narratives that we have seen throughout examples of the firm's theatre and that aligned with wider thinking about girls' education (Finlay-Johnson, 1911). She was a good fit for Bournville, staying as head of the day continuation school until her retirement in 1929.

School plays staged on the factory's recreation grounds had been introduced to the sessional closing celebrations in 1920, when the event had been relocated from Stirchley Institute's central hall. The move allowed bigger audiences to attend – an estimated 1,000 spectators watched the first play staged in the new space, including students, their friends, Cadbury's staff, and local educational and civic leaders – and showcased the school and its achievements on the factory site (*B.W.M.*, September 1920: 232). This was important. The educational schemes Ferguson and his colleagues delivered were not achieved without tensions. While the role of educational provision in staff retention and development continued to be identified, expanded, and to some extent legally required, the logistical challenges raised by employees being out of the factory for periods of time during the week and the loss of income from children employed to do piece work presented challenges. Amidst these competing pressures, the school's closing celebrations, at which the pageant and other plays were staged over the years, offered a moment when attendees and their families and friends came together, serving as 'a most valuable means of emphasising the importance of school life, not only to the students, but also to their parents'. Simultaneously, they provided an opportunity to remind invited, key members of Birmingham's Local Education Authority of the work being done at the city's innovative continuation school (Nicholls: 19–20; *B.W.M.*, September 1923: 269). The prominence of theatre at these end-of-year celebrations speaks to the familiarity and acceptance of large-scale drama at Bournville, and positive recognition of performance as a way to communicate in-house messages and create communities. Before moving on to further explore continuation school plays, it is worth taking a brief diversion to consider the other high-profile young people's drama they intersected with; the plays staged at the yearly Bournville Children's Festivals.

Bournville Children's Festivals

'Bournville fell under the enchantment of fairies and gnomes on Saturday' recorded the *Daily News* account of Bournville village's thirtieth annual Children's Festival (27 June 1932: 5). Performing in front of a crowd so large and so loud that Elizabeth Cadbury had to borrow a megaphone to make herself heard, village children played out (John) Robert Quinton's *Buried Treasure* on the recreation grounds, casting their spell over press, families, and public alike. Alongside summer works party plays and continuation school performances, the annual children's festival plays were the third type of regular large-scale outdoor production familiar to Bournville's audiences. Each summer throughout the early decades of the twentieth century, hundreds of young performers staged moralistic, fairy-tale narratives, supported by their school teachers and a group of factory employees who served as writers, producers, and occasional cast members. Second in scale only to the works party plays, the children's festival productions were performed to audiences of thousands, attracting a similar mix of friends, families, factory workers, external visitors, and representatives of the Cadbury family to the day continuation school celebrations. The first Bournville Children's Festival took place in 1902. Organised by the village council, it built on the success of the previous year's smaller fete and celebrated the recent coronation of King Edward VII. Motifs and entertainments common from village fetes were to remain strong elements at future festivals: children maypole dancing, taking part in costumed processions around the village and factory sites, Punch and Judy and Pierrot shows, and conjurors were regular features, reminiscent of fetes, fairs, and seaside visits. While Bournville village was operationally independent from the factory and the business, these yearly events were significant moments of external visibility and publicity for the Cadbury family's commitment to social reform, and it is interesting to note that the first of them synched with the firm's increased investments in in-house publicity, the arrival of the visitor's department, and the soon to be launched works magazine. Throughout this book, the village has surfaced as a backdrop for Cadbury's cocoa and chocolate business. These annual festivals were occasional, temporary moments during which the two separate spaces commingled, with the children's plays serving as the most high-profile element of their coalescence. By 1907, the children's play was clearly identified as the main feature of Bournville's village festivals (*The Garden City Magazine*: 410). Its increasing importance at the events is likely to have been facilitated by the opening of the village school in April 1906, a development that offered a new, onsite community that would have been easier to group together and organise. That year's larger festival was delivered on an epic scale, involving 650 children, attracting a crowd of around 3,000, and offering 7 hours of entertainment that included a procession around the grounds, sports, maypole dancing, a lantern maze, action songs, a fancy dress parade, aquatic displays, and the children's play, *The Queen of Storyland* by author Mary Elizabeth Bryan (1861–1930) (*B.W.M.*, August 1906: 354; *Birmingham Daily Gazette*, 16 July 1906: 6).

Later plays were written for the children's festivals by local authors, factory employees, and Bournville personalities Clarkson Booth and (John) Robert Quinton. Familiar from previous chapters, Booth and Quinton were established members of the dramatic society, but writing plays for children was new territory. Booth was a village resident and former Chairman of the village council, as well as a senior factory staff member, and regular representative of George Cadbury at public events. He personified both firm and village. In 1913, he created a pastoral play, *Trouble in Fairyland*, for the village's children to perform. Described as 'a delightful skit on certain present-day events', there is a clear indication that the play's moral message had immediate context and meaning, although the missing playscript and scant recorded descriptions makes this impossible to evidence (*Birmingham Gazette,* 31 June 1907: 6). A repeat charity performance of *Trouble in Fairyland* was staged to raise funds for the Selly Oak branch of the Cripples Union later in the year, alongside a re-performance of the year's summer works party masque *The Only Legend*. Intended for external audiences, the al fresco double-bill was advertised in the day's entertainment listings on the front page of the *Birmingham Mail*, a clear moment of intersection between factory and village, and in-house and external audiences (10 September 1913). The local communities are likely to have seen these productions before, but the fundraising performances still attracted an estimated audience of 800, suggesting some new audience members alongside returning spectators (*B.W.M.,* October: 317). The following year saw Clarkson Booth write a second play for the festivals. 'Full of Mr Booth's whimsicality and fun', *The Terror of Norwustar* was a love story of a Princess whose hand is demanded in marriage by a fearsome ogre. The ogre is defeated by a Prince disguised as a minstrel, and when his true identity is revealed to the Princess, they all live happily ever after (*B.W.M.,* August 1914: 251). The play was again restaged alongside the summer party pageant at a charity performance (*Birmingham Daily Gazette,* 31 August 1914: 6). This recycling of performances for different audiences is key to understanding theatre's placement and importance within the wider cultural economics of recreation at Cadbury's, few other recreational activities offered such opportunity for spectacle, and for highly visible patronage of local charities and networks. Booth's *The Terror of Norwustar* also had a third outing, with a 1927 restaging taking place twelve years after the writer's death, sustaining the memory of the first generation of Bournville's theatre makers, and the golden age of pastoral plays they produced.

By 1921, Quinton was a long-serving Cadbury's employee who – as we have seen – had been a key figure in Bournville's entertainments and wider arts scene since he stepped in to save 1908's *May Day* pageant. On his retirement from the firm in 1932, Bob (as he was known) was remembered as 'a man of many parts', 'an author, an actor, a musician and a painter', an employee who 'has not only given himself a great deal of that pleasure only experienced by the creative artist, but has given entertainment to thousands of people'; a retrospective on a career that captured the blend of self-development and public service characteristic of cultural work at Bournville (*B.W.M.,* September 1932: 287). Like Booth, Quinton lived in the village, and he was to become the second unofficial resident writer for the children's festivals, creating a series of plays between 1921 and 1935 in a parabolic fairy-tale style that echoed the use of narrative and legend in summer party masques, particularly *The Only Legend*. The first of Quinton's plays was *Goodwill, Illwill, and Merrywill, A Bournville Fantasy*, in 1921. Costumes for the lead performers were designed and made by Frances Quinton (1873–1951), a former worker at the chocolate factory, Bob Quinton's wife, and mother of Miriam Quinton, a regular performer and theatrical producer at the firm, and Beatrice Lindsay (1878–1955), who had been an artistic designer at Cadbury's since 1906. Children with smaller roles were dressed in costumes made by their mothers, under guidance issued by Quinton and Lindsay. Factory employees also appeared amongst the cast, with Alec Reginald Taylor (1901–1990) a printing assistant playing the 'Mephistopholean Ill Will' and his sister, Clara Taylor (c.1899–?) appearing as the 'beautiful, benevolent goddess of Good-will'. The play was accompanied by incidental music, performed by Bournville's Brotherhood Orchestra, an offshoot of the Bournville Brotherhood co-founded by Clarkson Booth and Robert Waite in 1913 to provide interdenominational religious meetings and events. Praised as the 'great event of the day', the strength of the play was identified in it being both 'for the children and *by* the children' (*B.W.M.*, August 1921: 204).

Later plays by Quinton included *The Dream: A Pastoral Fantasy for Children* (1928), *The Wizard* (1929) – with dances choreographed by Amy Forbes, who had been responsible for the chocolate advertisement tableaux vivants in *Visions* the year before – and *A Royal Visit to Playtown* (1932), which received particular praise for its 'delightful spectacle', particularly one scene in which 'a number of nursery rhyme characters were introduced as mechanical dancing dolls' (Library of Birmingham Archives and Collections L/./22.41/372365; *B.W.M.*, August 1929: 252; *B.W.M.*, August 1935: 282). Group choreographed movement was as central to a successful children's play as it was to earlier outdoor masques, it appears. Booth and Quinton drew on images of the pastoral for the festival plays they created, shaping narratives grounded in fairy tale images and structures brought to life through healthy children playing and learning in the fresh air, in space supplied by Cadbury's factory grounds. While there were occasional child performers in the works party pageants and entertainments, this entire child cast makes the festival plays distinctive and powerful, and they remained the main feature of the community events until the mid-1930s, when this study finishes, representing an important part of Bournville's visual culture and theatre. Predating and intersecting with the factory's summer works party masques and continuation school performances, these village productions intersected with the firm through people and through place and are an important element of outdoor theatre on the Cadbury's site that connected with the Girls' Continuation School outdoor plays.

Education and Outdoor Plays

While Bournville's children's festival and summer works party plays were typically created by local writers for the events, continuation school plays reveal a repertoire that reflects humanities curricula and set texts. Outdoor plays remained a standard item at school sessional closing celebrations from 1920 until 1930. Mythical and biblical narratives, and Greek theatre were favoured choices. 1920 saw a staging of Sophocles' *Antigone*, 1923 *Alcestis*, 1928 *Demeter*. Unlike John Drinkwater's masques and the 1922 *Pageant of Plays and Playgoers* the school tended to follow the dramatic society's outdoor play model, adopting the pergola on the Girls' Recreation Grounds as their stage for many productions. With its semi-circular raised platform, shallow steps, and plant-draped columns, the pergola supplied a useful evocation of a pastorally inflected neo-classical mood, and offered a different view of the Bournville backdrop that included factory buildings (see Figure 25). The outdoor environment featured in the performances. Mellow summer evening sunlight added to the visual effects of 1920s *Antigone*, softening, and adding tonal range to the white dresses worn by the chorus (*B.W.M.*, September 1920: 232). Such successful creations of visual spectacle were a regular theme of school play reviews: a recognised house speciality that was well received by large audiences – *Bournville Works Magazine* estimated an audience of between 2,000 and 3,000 in 1921 (September: 210). 1929's production, an occasion that marked the retirement of Annie Cater, as well as the end of the school year, was a staging of the biblical tale of Ruth and was praised for its artistic groupings of characters in coloured robes (*B.W.M.*, September 1929: 266). In both of these performance moments, glimpses of the larger, longer histories of design, tableaux, group choreographed movement, and focus on visual storytelling that have featured throughout examples of Bournville productions covered in this study are visible.

The skills of the worker continuation school cast, including those gained in their employment at the factory, the students' relative maturity compared to those at other educational institutions staging plays, and the school's focus on creative arts benefitted their productions. Performance skills were fostered outside of the annual plays. During the 1920s, the school ran dramatic and recitation competitions, extra-curricular

Figure 25 'A Scene from Alcestis'
Bournville Works Magazine, September 1923. Cadbury Archives and Heritage Services.

opportunities which required students to prepare independently. External specialists were invited to judge the events, including Stuart Vinden from the Birmingham Repertory Theatre in 1923, who praised 'the power of invention' displayed by 'the young players, and the way in which they made a little material go a long way' which 'seemed to him quite extraordinary' (*Birmingham Daily Gazette*, 15 March 1923: 4). Cadbury's continuation school student employees brought work ethic, team working, and a wide range of vocational and specialist skills with them to their theatre making; qualities and useful practical specialisms including artistry and craftsmanship. The plays they made and staged echoed the significance of making and creativity to the Cadbury's enterprise, the direct relationship between these core values and the continuation school, and employees' identities as workers, students, and performers.

Each of the Girls' Continuation School plays was part of a wider end-of-year event, and additional meanings surface when these productions are considered within these occasions. 1920's *Antigone* followed a pageant of fashions from the tenth to the twentieth centuries, in which 'all the costumes were accurate in design and typical colouring' and 'graced their lissom wearers as well as if they had been always used to them' (*B.W.M.*, September 1920: 232). Wearing historical costume is quite distinct from moving in historical costume, as many an under-rehearsed in-costume production attests. The magazine's note that the costumed performers seemed comfortable and at home in them emphasises the idea that dramatic performances brought about learning; on this occasion embodied learning from making and wearing the costumes. In 1921, the staging of John Milton's 1634 masque *Comus* was watched by a crowd of 2,000 to 3,000 in a year when Birmingham had closed all continuation schools in the city aside from Bournville's (which survived only as the result of the fear of successful legal challenge). 'In view of what has befallen continuing education', the works magazine recorded, the annual event had 'significance beyond our own borders' (September 1921: 210). In her speech at the 1921 event, Annie Cater celebrated the 1,100 weekly attendances at her school, noting that these 'girls occupied a unique position in that they were students and also bread-winners' and expressing hope for a better future for the generation they represented (210).

1923 saw Gilbert Murray's translation of Euripides *Alcestis* staged – a production that involved nearly all the teaching staff from the Beeches school site. *Bournville Works Magazine* recorded the challenges presented by the single-sex cast and the outdoor environment but concluded that the production was still an improvement on 1920's Greek play (September 1923: 266). *Alcestis* was preceded by a 'very stirring speech' delivered by Miss Margaret Bondfield JP (1873–1953), universal suffrage advocate, Member of Parliament, and Secretary of the National Union of Woman Workers, who told the girls, and their friends and families, that young women of the day should 'realise their luck' and 'take up arms in the campaign against the giants and dragons of the modern industrial world' to find their place within it. Such messages were not out of synch with education at the Girls' Continuation School (267). Supported by Edward Cadbury's advocacy for women workers' rights, the school offered a curriculum, which gave girls access to, and increased understandings of, society, politics, and culture. An address written and delivered by the philanthropist, adult school teacher, League of Nations activist, and further education advocate Elizabeth Cadbury (1858–1951) in 1920 tells us more about studying at the girls' school, recording that alongside lessons in the humanities and sciences, continuation school students studied citizenship and were taken on trips to London, and Birmingham's Law courts, Welfare Centres and Art Gallery (Library of Birmingham/MS 466/1/1/10/4/11). The tension between this content, Bondfield's rallying calls, and the speech given by Annie Cater which noted that this was 'perhaps the only school in the world where' more than 300 girls received 'systematic instruction' in the art and science of motherhood would doubtless have been evident to many gathered on the recreation grounds. Indeed, Cater's founding of a 'Mother's Study Circle' in the same year can be read as a gently resistant way to address such tensions, as well as ensure the support of parents in their daughters' educations (*B.W.M.,* September 1923: 267; Nicholls, 20). Nonetheless, Bondfield's words reflected the career advancement and promotion Cadbury's offered to unmarried women, as we have seen in the case of employees across this book.

1930 saw a step change in continuation school play performances, with W. B. Yeats's one-act verse play *The King's Threshold* staged inside the Cadbury's factory on the firm's large concert hall stage, accompanied by Bournville Dramatic Society's orchestra. A decade earlier, the annual event's move to the recreation grounds had signified the continuation school's growing association with the firm and its estate. Following Annie Cater's retirement, from 1930 yearly Concert Hall performances supported by factory recreational societies cemented it. A second change was introduced in the same year. *The King's Threshold* was the first continuation school production with a mixed-sex cast of performers drawn from the boys' and girls' schools, with this development the cross-casting and cross-dressing that had been common practices in previous productions was removed (Programme/CAHS/353/1001919). The numbers of students, families, and friends in the audience meant that the end-of-year celebrations for the girls and boys schools continued to be run as discrete events on consecutive evenings, but the joint production brought pupils from the girls and boys schools together in rehearsal, and off stage. It is likely that the new venue and mixed casts also prompted the shift away from classical drama and pageant-inspired plays that mark the nineteen thirties; a decade during which the school productions more closely reflected the factory dramatic society's output, varying from experimental drama to light, comic narratives and signalling links between fashionable, regional metropolitan productions and Cadbury's in-house educational repertoire. 1931's continuation school play was J. M. Barrie's turn-of-the-century Napoleonic period comedy *Quality Street,* with its plot centred on two sisters who set up a school for young ladies. The selection was not unfashionable, despite the play's age it remained a popular choice in fashionable theatre programming and its lead roles were closely connected with current theatrical celebrities. In June 1931, the month before the continuation schools' closing celebration, it had been staged at the Alexandra Theatre in central Birmingham (*Birmingham Daily Gazette,* 4 June 1931: 6). Setting a different tone to previous plays, and demanding very different skills of its performers, Barrie's play also spoke to its context, and perhaps to those tensions confronting working women students from the school whose education spanned citizenship and personal development along with housekeeping and marriage (programme/CAHS/353/001919). Barrie's popularity did not wane during the period covered here. 1934 saw the staging of his three-act comedy *The Professor's Love Story* at a school celebration evening that included a speech by Woodbrooke College lecturer and Society of Friends member Herbert G. Wood (1879–1963) on the significance of leisure to education and society, and the 'problem of using increased leisure to the best advantage'. Wood tapped into questions of recreation, creativity, and self-development that lay at the core of Cadbury's Quaker business model at an event that staged one blueprint model of how theatre could enter into and contribute to these debates (*Birmingham Daily Gazette,* 12 July 1934: 3).

Bournville Day Continuation schools turned twenty-one in the year this study concludes, by the time they came of age theatre was firmly entrenched as a teaching and learning, community building, and promotional tool. Members of the Cadbury family had funded other educational organisations inside and outside the Bournville estate, prompted by their interests in adult schooling, early years education, and open-air learning. These included Uffculme Open Air School, Kings Heath (1911), Bournville School of Arts and Crafts at the Ruskin Institute (1911), and Cropwood Open Air Residential School, Moseley (1922). It was, however, the continuation schools that were directly connected with factory employees and culture and where the largest amount of theatrical activity can be discovered. The progressive nature of using drama as a pedagogic tool in early twentieth-century education this activity reveals should not be underestimated. By 1921, Cadbury's were celebrating and publicising the way in which the 'dramatic method of teaching English Literature in schools' had been 'early adopted in the Day Continuation Schools', with the students 'also successfully present[ing] a number of plays' (Cadbury Bros, 1921: 16). Key members of teaching staff including Violet Nixon (1884–1962), Mabel Newnham (1887–1960) and Frederick Nobbs (1884–1965) were at the forefront of this activity (Nicholls: 21). Collectively they brought extensive experience of education. Nixon was an English Literature graduate from the University of London, with postgraduate teaching qualifications from the universities of Cambridge and Exeter and professional experience gained from positions at St Marys Hall, Cheltenham and the Northampton Technical and Day Continuation School before coming to Bournville in 1922 (*Teachers' Registration Council Registers, 1914–1918*). Newnham was one of three Devon-born sisters, all working for Birmingham Council as teachers by 1911 (census). Nobbs had started his career as a tailor, before turning to teaching. The humanities and creative arts focus is again clear through staff recruitment. Together they developed methods for teaching through drama that were in place eight years before Alice B. Wood published *Educational Experiments in England*; a study of radical and innovative educators and teaching methods that makes it clear that – at the time of research and writing – an understanding of the potential uses of drama as a way of teaching, and of improving school communities and behaviour, remained experimental. Reflecting on the emphasis placed on drama, both within the curriculum and as an extra-curricular activity at one of her case study schools, the Boys Grammar School in Newbury, Woods noted the 'excellent' effect that it had had on the boys' 'bearing and manner' and that a 'great earnestness' was now notable in 'all of their work'. The 'responsibility' given to them in 'all arrangements for the performance' has made them 'very reliable and careful about details', she continued, echoing a case for the strong organisation, communication and teamworking skills gained from production management that are a frequent trope of Cadbury's discussions of theatre (Wood, 1920: 94–95). Wood's discussion moved on to cover community mystery plays, particularly those staged at Glastonbury's Chalice Well (the vision of Rutland Boughton, the composer who had created the music for 1911's *English Medley* masque), using them to support a case that theatre can improve communities; 'raising the tone of village life', enabling families to act together, regardless of age and gender and resulting in 'actors and spectators' being 'educated together' (170). Bournville's outdoor performance space, wider events (the summer works party and the end-of-year celebration) and student and employee casts envelop the majority of theatrical activity at firm within this core ethos and definition of drama as a progressive educational tool.

Published in 1921 as part of the *Bournville Review*, 'Drama and the Worker' clearly articulated how Cadbury's positioned itself as a key player in the 'widely noted … quickening …of 'dramatic imagination' across the country; that shift in 'the art of "make believe" from the preserve of what is called the legitimate theatre noted in Chapter 4. Here the access for wider communities to 'find expression' in the 'joy … vitality … and art instinct' of theatre-making is clearly present in factory education (Cadbury, 1921: 14). Theatre, industry, education, and social reform were working hand in hand at the continuation schools. Bournville's educational activities were presented as strong, deliberate actions delivered in direct response to new debates around British educational provision; an area in which Cadbury's identified and asserted itself as a key stakeholder and pioneer, promoting their activities across in-house and external press and within research and political debate. Their view was that the provision they offered and modelled benefitted a wider community than solely employees, impacting national schemes and society. Arts and humanities were at the core of education programmes that foregrounded skills-based learning and self-development, noted Cadbury's 1926 publication *Work and Play*; areas that created 'sharpened faculty and fully capacities' derived from 'experience and activities' and resulted in 'a larger knowledge of men and affairs' (1926: 4). This was a position that also influenced and moulded the firm's external activities. Ideas about education developed from adult schooling experience at Cadbury's were exported into different external spaces, and it is with two such examples that this chapter, and this study, finishes – moving out from the factory to the wider world its theatrical activity influenced and supported.

Children's Play: Education, Industrial Patronage, and Birmingham's Children's Theatre Company

The role of theatre within Cadbury's-supported educational activity was entangled with wider discussions around the relationship between drama and education, many of which continued to pivot on the question of drama's cultural value. In 1921, a High Court case brought these persistent issues and opinions to the surface. Brought to court by the London City Council Finance Committee, the proceedings hinged on whether taking school children on theatre trips was judged to be an educational activity. In 1920, the London Central Shakespeare Committee of Teachers had hired theatre space and contracted Ben Greet's company to produce exclusive school performances. They used an educational grant to meet the costs. During a routine audit, this activity was deemed ineligible use of their funding, which resulted in a surcharge. The Court's judgment is revealing. While they would have agreed that a trip to the Tower of London, or Houses of Parliament would have undoubtedly qualified for the money and represented an educational opportunity, 'they could not see that a theatre was a place of educational interest' within the definitions supplied by the City Council, and as such the visits did not meet the criteria of the grant. Bache Matthews from the Birmingham Repertory Theatre was one of those who spoke out and condemned the verdict, noting that while it was not feasible to include regular theatregoing in educational curricula, it made sense that schoolchildren would gain more from seeing a play than from reading it, and that 'practical schoolteachers' were 'the people who should know the educational value of the theatre' (*Birmingham Gazette*, 4 November 1921: 3). By 1926, the Government had acknowledged the 'bottom up' surge in drama in education that was reshaping humanities teaching, commissioning the report *The Drama in Adult Education* from the Adult Education Committee of the Board of Education. Birmingham was well represented, with Barry Jackson and Allardyce Nicoll serving as expert witnesses. The conclusions were positive, affirming much of the activity that was already taking place and that Cadbury's had been at the vanguard of. It also reported a U-turn in the case of the London City Council, who now offered and funded school theatre trips in partnership with London's Old Vic Theatre, identifying them as 'an integral part of school education' (97). The nineteen twenties were a vital decade for the valuing of creative, and arts and humanities educations. In a decade marked by political upheaval, lurching between Liberal, Labour, and Conservative majorities, progressive educational policies affirmed the significance of drama, as something to be watched, and something to be participated in. In this context, Birmingham Children's Theatre Company, and their performances at Cadbury's Concert Hall, can be aligned with educational priorities and developments that identified the ways in which the experience of live theatre benefitted both children's and adult education.

Cadbury's social commitments regularly reached outside of the factory's perimeter, as we have seen and their new Concert Hall served the firm's wider community activity. It not only provided a performance venue for in-house events; it offered a large-scale entertainment venue for local groups and organisations; a rare commodity in a thriving metropolitan entertainment culture. During the late 1920s, the Concert Hall was used as a performance space by Birmingham's Children's Theatre Company. Programmes and listings of external events staged at the hall suggest the firm was selective in the groups that were granted access to the venue. They supported entertainments that had a wider agenda than commercial success, and that reflected Cadbury's in-house use of recreation and creativity to address wider social and educational needs. The repeated stock statement of thanks that appears across programmes for these entertainments indicate that use of the venue was interpreted and publicised as patronage. Established in 1925 by a group of school teachers in collaboration with the city's Girls' and Boys' Union (founded in 1906), Birmingham's pioneering children's theatre company aimed to bring a 'better class of entertainment than is usually available to poor children' (*B.W.M.*, November 1929: 353). For the next decade, it modelled a pre-cursor to the engagement and outreach work familiar in today's theatre industry, with an inclusive, access-based approach to creativity and culture that echoed the comprehensive curricula of Cadbury's worker and adult educational provision. The group was the first in the country to operate a children's theatre model, with only two international precedents – one in Moscow, and one in New York (*Birmingham Daily Gazette*, 25 November 1925: 7). At this point in the city's history Birmingham was an international leader of, and national centre for, children's theatrical activity; the site of what Gemma Colclough has identified as 'intersecting', 'idiosyncratic' theatre opportunities for young people (2023). The repertory theatre was a key player in these developments. In her 1927 book *Children's Theatre and Plays* – published as part of the Drama League Library of the Theatre Arts in the same year Cadbury's opened the Concert Hall – American author and playwright Constance D'Arcy Mackay (1887–1966) identified Birmingham's repertory theatre as the architect of children and young people's repertoire and programming (36).

The Boys' and Girls' Unions from which Birmingham's Children's Theatre emerged were outcomes of the social reform work of William Hartley Carnegie (1859–1936), a city priest with a central Birmingham parish. Carnegie had identified the multiple impacts of poverty on the city's children. By forming the unions he sought to 'galvanise the city's educated youth from the university and local affluent areas', bringing them together as a 'union of community participants' who would engage 'children from deprived areas of the city with sports, crafts and drama' (Colclough). Connections with Cadbury's recreational and employee wellbeing schemes are clear here. The Children's Theatre was financially independent of the Unions, but based at their home, Kyrle Hall on Sheep Street, using Cadbury's Concert Hall and other city venues to create ad hoc metropolitan circuits that facilitated their outreach model. Their short appearances at Bournville were organised by the factory's Youth Club, a collaboration that indicates a more expansive relationship between group and firm than an occasional venue use arrangement. Youth Club performances were a regular feature of Cadbury's entertainment, with their production of Lord Dunsany's *The Gods of the Mountain* at the opening celebrations of the Concert Hall offering one high-profile example, along other plays staged to raise funds for the Mitre Club and other local groups. Through the Youth Club, Cadbury's and Birmingham's Children's Theatre group interlocked on multiple levels, with the group's Concert

Hall performances consolidating the firm's prioritisation of citizenship, wellbeing, social reform and action, and creative recreation.

Children's Theatre matinee performances were staged for invited large group school audiences from poorer city areas, with reports of block bookings clearly indicating that they offered an early model of subsidised school theatre trips focused on widening cultural access. The group's repertoire blended plays that remain common choices in curriculum-based theatre production and programming with popular entertainments including short comedies and minstrel performances. It was a mixture that encouraged audiences to attend and develop an interest in and enjoyment of performance, fulfilled theatre's recognised educational potential and, critically, was more likely to sustain the interest and engagement of the child performers who were regularly involved, either solely, or (more commonly) as choruses alongside casts of adult actors. Children's Theatre productions included a five-scene fairy-tale burlesque *Fat King Melon and the Princess Caraway* (1927), by Alan Herbert (1890–1971), a prolific playwright and author known for his association with the satirical periodical *Punch*. In the short period since its appearance, his children's play had become hugely popular with school and community groups, including Brownies, Guides, and amateur dramatic societies. Other productions included *A Nursery Rhyme Fantasy, Unto the King*, a dramatic and musical fantasy, pantomimes, and mystery plays. 1929's staging of *A Midsummer Night's Dream* supplies a strong example of how the Children's Theatre practical, mixed ambitions for their work were realised. Shakespeare's text reflected educational curricula, the production involved Birmingham's Juvenile Orchestra who played an adaptation of Henry Purcell's *The Fairie Queene* as incidental music, and large numbers of local Five Ways School of Dance pupils appeared as the fairies. The programme offers greater detail on staging. Three of the five acts were produced. There were three full sets, and a need for scenery, lighting, and costume designers, two scenery makers, two stage managers, and two props supervisors. The lighting was supplied by an external company, Eric Smith and Company (CAHS/353/001919). A focus on theatrical staging, rather than textual completeness, was prioritised: spectacle and the involvement of as many children as possible in the experiences of performing or watching took precedence. These records provide an interesting contrast to a 1927 account of the group's activity that appeared in *The Stage*. Reporting on a production staged at Kyrle Hall, it was the group's 'unostentatious efforts' and the 'labour of love' they represented that received the greatest praise (14 April: 15). While it is possible that the scale of production increased in the two-year period between these performances, and clear that Cadbury's Concert Hall offered a bigger stage and more opportunity for spectacle, there are echoes of language associated with effort being prioritised over praise for large-scale spectacle here that echo reports of works staged by Bournville's dramatic society.

How theatre was described and articulated across and within publications and discourses was significant to early twentieth-century dramatic activity at the factory, and more widely. Cadbury's continuation school provision and patronage of the city's Children's Theatre underpinned non-denominational movements that reflected the tenets of social action and self-development key to New Quakerism and to ongoing thriving Quaker industrialism. The final educational centres considered in this chapter – Woodbrooke and Fircroft Colleges – move us further out of the factory and back into the sphere of adult education; in these two cases to consider theatre as part of adult education provision deliberately designed to create and lead social change.

Educational Settlements: Woodbrooke and Fircroft Colleges

During the first decade of the twentieth century two further innovative educational centres opened at Bournville: the Quaker college Woodbrooke in 1903, and the non-denominational adult education college Fircroft in 1909. Both were outcomes of the Cadbury family's active engagement with education; distinct from, but closely connected to, the factory's business and educational provision for employees. Woodbrooke and Fircroft formed part of a network of pioneering residential educational organisations established in Selly Oak, an area adjacent to Bournville, between 1903 and 1912: a group that also included the Methodist missionary training college Kingsmead (established 1905), the Quaker teacher training college Westhill (established 1907) and Carey Hall Missionary Training College for Women (established 1912). Collectively these further education providers represented a progressive educational 'fellowship', with reciprocal agreements that enabled the sharing of their spaces and lectures, and a collective Monday morning 'devotional' at Woodbrooke College (Pumphrey, 1952: 5; Leighton, 1959: 8). Delivering residential summer schools and longer courses, the Selly Oak colleges attracted home and international students, staff, and visitors. Scholars from Denmark, Iraq, and China temporarily joined the community in and around Bournville, and visitors including Mahatma Gandhi (to Woodbrooke) in 1931 were drawn to the fellowship to further explore their guiding ideas and provision. It would be reasonable to identify Woodbrooke and Fircroft as peripheral to the focus of this chapter and wider study. Previous histories of Cadbury's have excluded the colleges, or reduced discussion to a bare minimum, with good reason; neither settlement was a direct part of the business (Bradley, 2008; Cadbury, 2010; Williams, 1931). Concurrently, activity at Fircroft and Woodbrooke fed into and off of Bournville's ongoing approaches to education and recreation and involved key members of Cadbury's staff. The works magazine covered Fircroft and Woodbrooke, scholarship opportunities were available to factory employees, and there were staff crossovers in teaching and governance. Connections with Fircroft were particularly clear. In his history of the college Wilfrid Leighton noted that 'from early days the association of the firm with Fircroft has been strong', students from the works 'came into residence', attended evening lectures and social occasions, and in 1920 the Works Councils agreed that up to twelve students could attend classes on two days of the week, an initiative distinct from the full-time sabbatical scholarships offered to three employees that guaranteed a secure job to return to (1959: 26; *B.W.M.*, August 1909: 301). Employee students were asked to apply, with the Works Education Committee selecting successful applicants and recommending them to the College (*B.W.M.*, August 1909: 301). A further clear moment of publicised alignment between factory and college can be discovered early on in Fircroft's history when the college was used for a conference on Welfare Work for Women in Factories (*B.W.M.*, October 1909: 384–385). Organised by Edward Cadbury, the event focused particularly on women employees, education, and career opportunities (Kimberley, 2016: 165). A consideration of theatre and education at Cadbury's that excluded these two adult education initiatives would occlude critical ideas and activity around learning, creativity, theatre, and community at Bournville's chocolate factory.

Woodbrooke College was the result of George Cadbury Junior and John Wilhelm Rowntree's shared conviction that Quakerism needed refreshed teaching ministries and a new vision that fitted the early twentieth-century world (Gilman, 2003: 52). Its mission was to foster and teach Quaker study, faith, and ministry. In Joseph Rowntree's words, Woodbrooke was a 'centre for the diffusion of religious knowledge, a training place of social service, a home of study with university men for those who could otherwise hope for no such advantage, and a power house for the spread of spiritual fellowship'. Such study should be transformational, for 'intellectual development ought to lead not to fastidious aloofness, but to the most earnest and powerful advocacy of all that makes for the highest life' (Rowntree, 1905: xxxvi). Recognised as a pioneer, or mother, college for Quaker education, but not restricted to members of the Society of Friends, the college buildings and gardens were largely financed by George Cadbury. The site was his former home, and the industrialist donated its use, ongoing maintenance, and a lecturer's stipend to kickstart and support the initiative (Vining, 1958: 97). Cadbury's ongoing engagement exceeded financial support, students were regularly hosted by the family at their Northfield Manor home, where they were entertained, fed, and introduced to wider community networks (*The Friends' Intelligencer,* 10 December 1904: 2–3). While Fircroft has a greater history of theatre, Woodbrooke's activities included drama by the nineteen twenties, with the end of the academic year marked by celebrations and entertainments. 1922's garden party was rained off and had to be moved inside. That did not stop the 'grand opera' by the 'Woodbrooke Operatic Company' taking place, a 'clever skit' that had the audience in 'roars of laughter from beginning to end' (*Birmingham Daily Gazette,* 3 July 1922: 3). The familiar skit format is of particular significance in the context of Woodbrooke. Audiences had to be familiar with parodied theatrical conventions to make sense of skits, and the laughter indicates that this audience understood very well. Woodbrooke's event, and entertainment, were covered not only by Birmingham's press, but also by the internationally circulated *The Chemist and Druggist.* There is no indication that the Quaker college's theatrical performance was considered unusual, or controversial, in these accounts (15 July 1922: 74).

Fircroft College for Working Men opened in January 1909, offering residential adult education for twelve students. Like Woodbrooke it materialised ongoing debates around learning, in this case, national discussions about expanding and adapting adult education that had surfaced as a key focus of 1908's National Council of Adult Schools conference in Scarborough. Fircroft's mission was to train future adult school movement's teachers and leaders by making further education more widely available (Pumphrey, 1952 1). Modelled on the working example of the Danish People's High School movement, on which George Cadbury and Fircroft's first warden Tom Bryan (1865–1917) had co-authored a chapter, and delivered in collaboration with the Workers' Educational Association, and Trade Union and Co-Operative movements, the college was a progressive step in access to higher education for working class students. Aside from Ruskin College, Oxford, it was the only institution where working men could access full time, non-technical education (Dover Wilson, 1929: 292). Recalling Fircroft's opening, former volunteer English Literature lecturer and housekeeper Mary Pumphrey (1880–1969) (another representative of the local, high-profile Quaker family that also included Sophia and

Spencer) reminded her mid-twentieth century readers that 'it cannot be fully appreciated by the rising generation what Fircroft meant to mine. Then, not one in ten children received any education beyond the age of fourteen; not more than one in a thousand received a higher education. The workers' children were mortgaged to balance the nation's economy' (1952: xi). Fircroft was designed to offer a small, but significant opportunity for rebalancing society by offering the 'best learning at the lowest fees' (*B.W.M.*, January 1909: 67–68). This was gently revolutionary education: in Tom Bryan's words, 'at the universities the pace is set by the rich man's son; at Fircroft it should be set by those who had not a penny to bless themselves with' (cited in Bournville Publications, 1924: 12). While this was a male college, from 1914 summer school, higher-level education weekly courses were offered to women, 'a landmark in the history of education for women' overseen by college staff and Miss L. Jowitt from Bristol University Settlement (*B.W.M.*, May 1914: 155; September 1914: 281).

There are clear synergies between Fircroft and Cadbury's people management, the Bournville Spirit, and educational provision for factory employees. The college was driven by an entwined set of social, religious and political energies: though a non-denominational organisation, its roots were firmly bedded in Christian and Quaker theologies and reform work. Of comparable importance to the material taught at the college was its fostering of an on-site community. The benefits of the social life and atmosphere of a residential college, and the social and interpersonal skills this demanded and fostered, were positioned as critical elements of developing a new network of education leaders. This was a style of live-in, interactive learning designed to develop the range of skills future leaders would need refined and developed under the direction of Tom Bryan and three dedicated members of teaching staff, supplemented by Cadbury's factory staff including Sophia Pumphrey, Ralph Moorhouse, and Spencer Pumphrey. Bryan had arrived in Bournville by invitation in 1903, bringing experience of social settlement and public health management (Wood and Ball, 1922: 29–33; 43). Leading Fircroft followed a period of lecturing at Woodbrooke, co-authorship with George Cadbury, and joining the Society of Friends. As a strong advocate for the new vision of the adult school movement the two colleges represented, Bryan was a well-known public speaker on the subject, appearing around the country, in addition to teaching English Literature (including through play readings), citizenship, and bible study (Leighton: 5). Fircroft's courses were designed to be as close 'as possible to a university standard', with yearly, multi-year, and term length options available (Gardiner, 1923: 208). Capacity was quickly raised to twenty students who had access to a library, classrooms, gymnasium, and workshop. The gardens were used for 'open-air study – of which there was much' at Fircroft; in line with practices at the factory fresh air was prioritised (Foght, 1914: 22). Lessons included 'nothing technical and exclude[d] nothing which would multiply and develop a man's interest in life' (Wood and Ball, 1922: 61). The curriculum reflected subjects covered in Bournville's early twentieth-century factory-based education: Industrial and Political histories, Rural Problems, English History and English Literature, Local Government, and Nature Study were combined with Gymnastics, Singing, and Gardening (Wood and Ball, 1922: 100). Scrutiny of documents related to Fircroft's courses and timetabling draws a blank in relation to drama, but closer consideration makes it clear that while drama was not a named subject, it was used to deliver English Literature from the college's early years.

Arts, Humanities, and creativity were at the core of Fircroft learning. From Tuesdays to Fridays the morning reading took the form of a sharing of prose or poetry selected and performed by students or staff members (Leighton: 8). A multiuse space served as the college's theatre: 'the classroom served as a Common Room, and as a stage and auditorium for the productions that were not infrequently a part of the life of Fircroft'. In this found space, it was 'proved how much could be done' with theatre 'by the few who had so little' (Leighton: 10). 1911 saw John Drinkwater serve as a temporary lecturer at Fircroft, offering an evening lecture course on 'The Effect of the Drama on the People' (10). Later development of the college offered a 200 seat hall equipped with a stage and dressing/coat rooms (Fircroft Prospectus/CAHS, undated: 7). By the nineteen twenties the presence and familiarity of dramatic activity are indicated by the college's status as an affiliated society of the British Drama League (*Drama*, July 1927: 17). A key benefit of this affiliated membership was access to reduced-price sets of play-texts for study and performance, suggesting group study, reading, or performance was an element of life at the college. Writing in the *United States Education Bulletin* in 1914, Harold Foght (1870–1954) concluded that the distinctiveness of Fircroft – and the influential Danish Folk High School model that had shaped the college – was an aim to promote education not as 'an exhaustive pursuit of facts, nor a desultory acquaintance with them, but a broadening of the whole life' (22). Theatre fitted into this educational model, representing a key part of the cultural matrix it was grounded in a way that was not recognised in formal thinking around education until the nineteen twenties. The clearest records of the teaching of theatre at Fircroft are found in a weekend lecture school that focused specifically on theatre.

Developed from a common practice in the Adult School movement, these short, intensive 'schools' took place outside of standard teaching hours and were open to others (Gee, 1922: 722).

Fircroft's Weekend Theatre Lecture School

In August 1926, under the auspices of Fircroft and the local branch of the Workers' Educational Association, the college hosted a weekend summer school on the playwright John Galsworthy. Delivered by the author Robert Hay Coats (1873–1956), the programme was made up of five lectures and a series of play-readings. Born in Scotland and educated at the University of Glasgow, Coats was a well-known figure in Birmingham's early twentieth-century cultural scene. His involvement in the development of Birmingham Repertory Theatre had been documented in a chapter he wrote for Bache Matthews's *History of the Birmingham Repertory Theatre* published two years earlier. But theatre had not been the sole, or even the main, focus of Coats's career. A member of the industrial thread manufacturing family, he had spent two decades as the minister of Birmingham's Hamstead Road Baptist Church (1899–1921). By the mid-nineteen twenties he had already published eleven book length works; one was a collection of traveller's tales about Scotland, the other ten focused on religious themes, including bible stories, children's prayerbooks, and Sunday School lesson plans. Most had been published by specialist religious presses. Coats was the perfect speaker for Fircroft. He embodied drama, spirituality, and learning. At 1926's summer school, his lectures drew on the content of his newest work and his first book on theatre, *John Galsworthy as a Dramatic Artist* published by commercial, mainstream publisher Chatto and Windus in the same year.

The weather was kind to Fircroft's 1926 summer school, and several sessions took place outside in the large 'Lecture Hut', a sideless shelter with seating located in the carefully tended grounds. Lectures and readings were attended by 'a large number of eager students', who would have had no difficulty hearing Coats, for his previous career as a minister was evident in his 'voice and manner of delivery' that were 'designed for the [large space of the church] building' (*B.W.M.*, October 1926: 297; Binfield, 1995: 86). The works magazine concludes its account of the weekend with a note that the encouraged discussions that followed lectures and readings were 'taken good advantage of' but were marked by 'a slightly unfortunate tendency to discuss *moral* points rather than the *art* of the playwright'. Conceding that 'of course, it *is* "life" we are concerned with at Bournville!', the account acknowledges the location of theatre at the factory as a means to explore wider social, political, and moral issues. A further layer was offered by dramatic readings of the plays Coats discussed. This was novel. 'In the history of the Summer schools, this one will be 'notorious' for the innovation of having play-readings after each lecture performed by a company including many familiar faces from amongst Bournville employees … particularly from the factory's dramatic society'. Some 'excellent renderings of scenes from *The Silver Box, The Pigeon, A Bit o' Love, Loyalties* and *Strife*' were performed for the school students (*B.W.M.,* October 1926: 297). Factory staff were involved in Fircroft Weekend School activities, adding further complexity to the multiple uses and understandings of theatre that defined Cadbury's. There was precedent for Fircroft's theatrical lectures. As we have seen in the dramatic society lectures explored in Chapter 5, visiting speakers and lecture events had long been part of Cadbury's recreational offer, with one-off lectures and themed lecture series featuring external speakers organised by several societies. Fircroft extended this pattern of activity creating a new, but overlapping, sphere of engagement between the college, Bournville's chocolate factory, and the stage.

While the colleges were not a direct part of Cadbury's cocoa and chocolate business, there were close links between them and factory life, particularly in the case of Fircroft. Limited scholarship opportunities realised the holistic style of continuing professional and personal development favoured by the firm, demonstrating their commitment to and investment in employees. Fircroft scholarships were not the only higher education opportunity available to Cadbury's employees. Launched in 1924, an in-house scheme at Bournville administered and supported a competitive Works Council Scholarship in Dramatic Art, with the award decided through an open monologue competition at the factory adjudicated by an external specialist. Records do not document what these scholarships offered, the music scholarship awarded the winner tuition at the Birmingham and Midland Institute, and it seems likely a similar model was in place for drama (Cadbury, 1924: 10). There was no entry fee, to make the opportunity as accessible as possible. The most regular judge was Elsie Fogerty (Anne Elizabeth, 1856–1945), who had founded the Central School of Speech and Drama in 1906. Fogerty was a specialist in voice training and an influential advocate for the benefits of a practical dramatic education for all students. In addition to awarding the scholarship, she created and supplied the Fogerty Cup for Group Work as part of the Bournville factory competitions. Her 1928 visit saw six teams compete for the group cup, including those from the Milk Tray Gift Office, the Fruit and Nut

Gift Office, and the Nomads (Programme/CAHS/353/001919). Fogerty noted that she had been 'struck by the improvement in style and finish' of the group performances that she saw, and particularly by the 'pattern and order' of performers on stage, improvements she credited to the new Concert Hall and the improved resources it offered. The individual recitals, she reported, had not shown such a striking improvement (*B.W.M.*, June 1928: 195). This made sense. Cadbury's decision to provide the venue and subsidise its activities rotated around the value of ensemble performance – a version of teamwork – to the business. Individual pursuits were supported, but were the site of less focus; education was designed to serve collective good, theatre to entertain and develop teamwork and creativity. The judge for the men's scholarship in 1928 was Stuart Vinden, a founding member of the Birmingham Repertory Theatre Company. Building on the Dramatic Competitions introduced at the Bournville Festival in 1922, managed by the dramatic society, and adjudicated by the critic and author Raymond Crompton Rhodes (1887–1935) scholarship competitions brought together the world of professional production and the relatively new sphere of professional, education-based training, embodied here by Elsie Fogerty and Stuart Vinden.

The Cadbury's Model: Learning through Play and Plays

When Iola Williams concluded that 'the distinction between what is educational and what is recreative [at Bournville] is not very easy to draw, and, perhaps, not very real when drawn', he captured the spirit of the performances considered in this chapter and throughout this book (1931: 179). Theatrical events at Cadbury's chocolate factory foregrounded employee participation; sometimes as performers, sometimes as spectators, *always* as learners. In his introduction to a collection of essays on continuation schooling co-edited with Reginald Ferguson, William Wray argued that for the 'unfolding mind' a 'dramatic, imaginative approach' to learning was required (1920: 17). At Bournville, minds were expected to be ever-unfolding, positioning theatre as education and an educational tool, as recreation and an organisational tool. While education and recreation might have been separated out at times in the Firm's organisational structures and publications they were closely entwined and regularly viewed through the same lens. Holistic, engaged models of theatre were prioritised by the firm; a model that takes us back to the figure of Daisy Smart, that first Bournville personality we encountered in this exploration of theatre at the chocolate factory. The role of theatre within educational curricula was a logical extension, an additional facet, of a more generalised understanding and acceptance of the potential of theatrical activity within Bournville's industrial community. Creative arts and humanities formed key parts of Cadbury's educational agendas, with theatre and performance securely located within course content and community creation, and at the heart of the firm's wider workplace and people management models.

From historical pageant performances, to Greek plays, homespun productions in Fircroft's classroom, play readings, lectures on theatre, wartime entertainments, and patronage of Birmingham Children's theatre, performance permeated and shaped Cadbury's factory life, spanning and entangling learning, and leisure for thousands of Bournville factory employees.

Conclusion

A Welfare House of Dreams: Theatre at Cadbury's

In 1927, when Cadbury's leading research chemist Arthur Knapp stood on the stage of the Bournville factory's new Concert Hall dressed as Father Time he promised that those who had created the new venue – that 'Welfare House of Dreams' – would be remembered for all eternity (*B.W.M.*, April 1927: 99). That has not been the case. Time has not been kind to stories of Bournville's theatre: they have more or less vanished from histories of the firm and the factory. Through this book, I have sought to reclaim and understand the rich culture of theatre and performance established at Cadbury's in the first decades of the twentieth century, locate key performers, explore a wide range of factory performances, and define and understand the far-reaching recreational, promotional, and educational functions of the firm's theatre. From skits and burlesques, pastoral plays and tableaux vivants, to wartime concert parties, school drama, and performances by visiting companies and celebrities, Bournville's theatrical activity created and shared a visual language and core company values that remain associated with the Cadbury brand today. Creativity sat at the heart of Bournville's working life. At this – the most renowned of progressive Quaker businesses – watching and making theatre played a leading role in creating and promoting the Factory in a Garden's iconic landscape, model employees, and cocoa and chocolate lines. While other industrial sites reveal shared dynamics, similar approaches, and histories of theatrical activity, no other manufactory produced either the scale or the range of performance that took place at Cadbury's.

In many ways, this attempt to tell the stories of theatre and the employees who made it feels just a starting point for understanding the impacts of creativity and performance on the factory and its people; stories that have been lost for nearly one hundred years; approaches that continue to influence innovative leadership and management today.

Playing at Work

Cadbury's Bournville factory and its departments provided an infrastructure that facilitated in-house theatre. On-staff advertisers, artists, writers, carpenters, electricians, engineers, gymnastics instructors, musical directors, and teachers represented and nurtured key areas of theatrical production that were underpinned by welfare and recreational committee structures and funding. Spaces supplied and developed by the firm materialised the value ascribed to onsite performance, and watching, or participating, in theatre became part of the cultural memory of Cadbury's for employees, their families, and others. Recreational theatre fostered and showcased staff creativity, nurturing and performing the Bournville Spirit and establishing and refining new styles of commercial performance particular to the factory. Each performing body, each production, contributed to the firm's story-telling and identity-making and drew on a wider culture of performance that was embedded in day-to-day working life as a Cadbury's employee. Expectations were high for Cadbury's staff; fulfilling the employee blueprint required recreational participation and engagement, sporting or cultural, or – indeed – often a mix of the two. Entertainment culture at the factory depended on out-of-hours work. Employees gave significant amounts of free recreational labour, at the service of both their own personal development and the business. Evidence from employees supports this statement. In an oral history, Bernard Atkins (1906–1997), a clerk at the firm, recalled that 'you could spend all of your spare time at the factory' (Birmingham Museums/Sound Cloud). This labour – the work in the play – distinguishes factory performances from the amateur world, this was a professionalisation of leisure funnelled through Bournville's culture of service and participation. Recreational theatre became a part of professional identity, most clearly in the group of performers and producers who established the factory's dramatic society. Cadbury's theatre requires consideration through a lens that is not focused on binary positionings of amateur and professional, but one that converges them, homing in on the nexus between them, and the new ideas about performance that were created in that space. This was a hybrid sphere of industrial theatrical activity particular to place, people, and organisational structure.

Performance as business terminology is an area that performance studies have long been alert to, but early twentieth-century Bournville performance as business strategy evades and exceeds these understandings. At the Cadbury's factory, histories of theatre and business, people and employees, work and play are entangled. The early twentieth-century Bournville industrial estate, and the theatre made by the employees who worked there, was a complex, distinct space that crossed the boundaries by which we have organised our understandings of theatre history. The firm has attracted criticism. Some have identified the firm's operation as a model of paternalistic governance, and Kevin Dowd has defined their 'activism' as one driven by Liberal political patronage and grounded in 'manipulative capitalism' in place of civic responsibility and public benevolence (Dowd, 2001: 11). A consideration of theatre at the factory offers a complex and nuanced landscape, one that allows us to read between the lines of policy, to consider individual employees, to 'see' through the imagery fostered and staged ideas about gender, race, work, play, and wellbeing. While staff development positioned developing 'citizenship and life values' as its 'first aim' the range of this factory theatre reflects how the firm sought to develop individuals and their creativity within a culture of performance, entertainment, and education that was wider, and more representative, than might be assumed (Wray cited in *B.W.M.*, October 1920: 264). Accounts narrate how theatre offered staff leadership opportunities, created new networks, and crafted community within the factory environment. In histories of Cadbury's theatre we can trace intersections between performance, social reform, educational innovation, political action, and wellbeing.

The Legacies of Bournville's Factory Play(s)

The first decades of the twentieth century saw Cadbury's carve out their place as a leader in a new model of industrial relations in which play, creativity, and performance were key elements. Cadburys' management team were influential figures in national and international business, social reform, and religious networks populated by leading industrialists engaged with intersecting questions of manufacturing, education, employee health, social progress, and productivity. They were also active proponents of the ideologies and principles of aesthetic groups focused on the importance of making, beauty, and creativity in everyday life. The legacy of understanding the value of creativity and play for both people and business remains today in the practices of market-leading companies including Google and Lego. In April 2022, Lego opened its new campus in Billund Denmark. Five years in the making, the build was designed to 'inspire innovation and creativity'. Its name – headquarters as campus – fuses business with learning. Its design merges work and play. Developed to materialise the company's core values of 'Imagination, Fun, Creativity, Caring, Learning, and Quality', Lego's new site includes a 'People House', offering leisure and wellbeing activities including a cinema, communal kitchens, gym, and a health centre, alongside access to open-air relaxation in outside park space. The alignments with Cadbury's planning of Bournville's industrial estate are clear here. Play features in other areas of the Lego business too. Since 2010 Lego Serious Play kits, workshops and facilitator training have been used in businesses across the globe to 'enhance business and performance', 'foster creativity', 'prompt dialogue' and 'create new skills' (Lego.com). A career with Google brings access to medical staff, wellbeing care, funding for further education, and 'Googley Extras', 'spaces and resources to support your growth, productivity, and wellbeing', including 'art programmes' (www.careers.google.com). The spirit of industrial experiment nurtured at Cadbury's leaves traces in organisations we continue to identify as pioneering today. Across the century between them, the professionalising of creative thought and activity, prioritisation of health and wellbeing, and bringing play into work and work into play, connect their shared approaches.

Further traces of the world of early twentieth-century Bournville can be discovered onsite at the factory and in chocolate products sold across the world. The residual impact of the storytelling that shaped early twentieth-century Cadbury's – a project theatre shaped and promoted – remains in the brand's ongoing leading market presence today through a reliance on its industrial heritage. Histories of people and place underpin Cadbury's position in national and global markets. Post-Brexit design has seen a return to vintage-inspired packaging for key lines, including Dairy Milk and Roses. Echoes from industrialism's past are being drawn on, returned to, in attempts to shape and define its future. Heritage and history saturate the Bournville factory site; highlighted and shared through landscape, wayfinding, and the onsite theme park Cadbury World. The stories spotlighted in heritage spaces are outcomes of creative, selective, and political processes: showcased narratives are the work of cultural production (Bendix, 2009: 253). Still working industrial heritage sites like Mondelēz's Bournville possess a greater level of commercial potential. John Bradley who worked in a range of positions for Cadbury between 1980 and 2004, including brand management and the running of Cadbury World and has since written a history of the Cadbury brand, has argued that the ongoing challenge facing the firm is the 'creation of synergy between the history of the past and the history being made today. Brand equity is nothing but history; it is all consumers know of the brand. Any fool can throw out the old; the hard bit is seeing how the old can be updated in a way that is relevant to today and that adds to the brand (2008: 335)'. Visitors to Bournville today, whether to the village, the largely accessible perimeters and gardens of the factory estate, or to Cadbury World are placed in an imagined time period that is located somewhere between the late Victorian era and the 1920s. The power of the location of this semi-fictional historical moment at the core of Bournville's tourist construct is significant. Factory and village architecture and landscaping represent an era of British industrial history and social action that continues to resonate; architecturally and visually familiar narratives present in many of the public buildings and institutions we continue to see and use, in the green outdoor recreational spaces that break up our urban environments, and from school and University curricula. Early generations of the company understood the evolving importance of brand. At this early moment in the history of mass advertising Cadbury's created a story and a set of images that relied on tradition, ethics, the pastoral, and the past: the result of cutting-edge modern business practices that facilitated collaborative activity entwining people and place with well-crafted story making, and the staging of those stories – often through theatre. Then, as now, history making was a commercial strategy at Bournville.

Cadbury's theatre staged stories, employees, and an industrial ethos. The content, staging, and casts of Bournville's factory productions expand our understanding of British industrial histories, women's leadership, and the significance of Cadbury's to Birmingham's cultural and educational landscapes. Simultaneously, they require a relaxation, a rethinking, of theatre's histories, of where, and how, we look for and define the information we need to understand the significance and presence of theatre and creativity to the working population of the early twentieth century.

Bibliography

Ackers, Peter and Alistair J. Reid (2016) *Alternatives to State Socialism in Britain: Other Worlds of Labour in the Twentieth Century*. New York: Springer

Alington, Geoffrey (1914) *Plays for Schools*. London: G Bell & Sons

Angell, Stephen W. and Ben Pink Dandelion (2013) *The Oxford Handbook of Quaker Studies*. Oxford: Oxford University Press

Anon (1926) *The Drama in Adult Education*. London: His Majesty's Stationery Office

Bailey, Adrian Raymond and John R. Bryson (2007) 'A Quaker Experiment in Town Planning: George Cadbury and the Construction of Bournville Model Village', *Quaker Studies* 11, 89–113

Bailey, Peter (1978) *Leisure and Class in Victorian England: Rational Recreation and the Contest for Control, 1830–1885*. London: Routledge

Balgarnie, Robert (1877) *Sir Titus Salt, Baronet, His Life and Lessons*. London: Hodder and Stoughton

Bartie, Angela, Linda Fleming, Mark Freeman, Alexander Hutton, and Paul Readman (2020) *Restaging the Past: Historical Pageants, Culture and Society in Modern Britain*. London: UCL

Beaven, Brad (2005) *Leisure, Citizenship and Working-Class Men in Britain, 1850–1945*. Manchester: Manchester University

Beevers, Robert (1988) *The Garden City Utopia: A Critical Biography of Ebenezer Howard*. Basingstoke: Macmillan

Bell, Colin and Rose Bell (1972) *City Fathers: The Early History of Town Planning in Britain*. Harmondsworth: Penguin

Bendix, Regina (2009) 'Heritage between Economy and Politics: An Assessment from the Perspective of Cultural Anthropology', in Laura Jane Smith and Natsuko Akagawa, eds., *Intangible Heritage*. Abingdon and New York: Routledge

Binfield, Clyde (1995) 'The Coats Family and Paisley Baptists', *The Baptist Quarterly* 36:2, 80–95

Birmingham Repertory Theatre (1934) *The Birmingham Repertory Theatre, 1913–1934*. Birmingham: Moody Bros Ltd

Bishop, George Walter (1928) *The Amateur Dramatic Year Book and Community Theatre Handbook*. London: A & C Black

Boumphrey, Ian and Gavin Hunter (2002) *Port Sunlight: A Pictorial History, 1888–1953*. Prenton: Yesterday's Wirral

Bournville Works Publications (1912) *Bournville Housing: A Description of the Housing Schemes of Cadbury*. Bournville: Bournville Works

(1924) *Fircroft College*. Bournville: Bournville Works

(1933) *The Bournville Dramatic Society 1912–1933: A Chronicle*. Bournville: Bournville Works

(1936) *Bournville Works and Its Institutions: A Concise Account of the Educational, Recreational and Other Schemes*. Bournville: Bournville Works

Brack, Alan (1980) *The Wirral*. London: B. T. Batsford

Bradley, Ian C. (2007) *Enlightened Entrepreneurs: Business Ethics in Victorian Britain*. London: Weidenfeld & Nicholson

Bradley, John (2008) *Cadbury's Purple Reign: The Story behind Chocolate's Best-Loved Brand*. Chichester: John Wiley & Sons

Brazier, Georgina and Simon Gwynn (2017) 'How Cadbury, Robinsons and Taylor of Harrogate Turned Heritage into Success'. Campaign. www.campaignlive.co.uk

Bromhead, J. (2000) 'George Cadbury's Contribution to Sport', *The Sports Historian* 20:1, 97–117

Bryers, Mary (1994) *Havergal Celebrating a Century*. Erin: Boston Mills Press

Bryson, John and Phillipa Lowe (2002) 'Story-telling and History Construction: Rereading George Cadbury's Bournville Model Village', *Journal of Historical Geography* 28:1, 21–41

Burden, Robert and Stephan Kohl, eds. (2006) *Landscape and Englishness*. Amsterdam: Rodopi

Cadbury Bros (1911) *A Visit to Bournville*. Birmingham: Cadbury Bros

(1912) *An Outline of the Education Scheme Connected with the Bournville Works*. Birmingham: Cadbury Bros

(1913a) *A Visit to Sunny Cocoa Land*. Birmingham: Cadbury Bros

(1913b) *Bournville Bunny*. Birmingham: Cadbury Bros

(1921) *Bournville: A Review*. Birmingham: Cadbury Bros

(1924a) *Elsie and the Bunny*. Birmingham: Cadbury Bros

(1924b) *A Works Council in Being*. Birmingham: Cadbury Bros

(1925) *The Factory and Recreation*. Birmingham: Cadbury Bros

(1926a) *Work and Play*. Birmingham: Cadbury Bros

(1926b) *Another Adventure of Elsie and the Bunny*. Birmingham: Cadbury Bros

(1936) *Bournville Works and Its Institutions*. Birmingham: Cadbury Bros

(1938) *Bournville Personalities*. Birmingham: Cadbury Bros

(1962) *Golden Jubilee of Bournville Dramatic Society, 1912–1913 to 1961/1962*. Birmingham: Cadbury Bros

Cadbury, Deborah (2010) *Chocolate Wars*. London: Harper Collins

Cadbury, Edward (1912) *Experiments in Industrial Organisation*. London: Longmans, Green & Co.

Cadbury, George (1926) *Presidential Address to the Eighth Annual Association for Education in Industry and Commerce*. Birmingham: Cadbury Bros

Chance, Helena (2007) 'The Angel in the Garden Suburb: Arcadian Allegory in the ('Girls' Grounds' at the Cadbury Factory, Bournville, England, 1880–1930. Studies in the Histories of Gardens and Designed', *Landscapes* 27:3, 197–216
  (2012) 'Mobilising the Modern Industrial Landscape for Sports and Leisure in the Early Twentieth Century', *The International Journal of the History of Sport* 29:11, 1600–1625
  (2017) *The Factory in a Garden: A History of Corporate Landscapes from the Industrial to the Digital Age*. Manchester: Manchester University Press
Chapman, David L (1994) *Eugen Sandow and the Beginnings of Bodybuilding*. Chicago: University of Illinois
Charnow, Sally Debra (2005) *Theatre, Politics and Markets in Fin-de-siècle Paris*. New York: Palgrave McMillan
Cochrane, Clare (1993) *Shakespeare and the Birmingham Repertory Theatre, 1913–1929*. London: Society for Theatre Research
Colclough, Gemma (2023) 'The Children's Theatre Movement of the 1920s' in Claire Cochrane, Lynette Goddard, Catherine Hindson, and Trish Reid, eds., *The Routledge Companion to Twentieth Century British Theatre*. London: Routledge
Constantine, S. (1981) 'Amateur Gardening and Popular Recreation in the Nineteenth and Twentieth Centuries', *Journal of Social History* 14:3, 387–406
Cooper, Roger (1997) 'Bernard Sleigh, Artist and Craftsman, 1872–1954', *The Journal of the Decorative Arts Society 1850–the Present* 21, 88–102
Cossons, W. E., ed. (1933) *The Bournville Dramatic Society, 1912–1933*. Bournville: Cadbury Bros
Crawford, Margaret (1995) *Building the Workingman's Paradise: The Design of American Company Towns*. New York: Verso
Crewe, Steven (2014) 'What about the Workers? Works-based Sport and Recreation in England c.1918–c.1970', *Sport in History* 34:4, 544–568
Crosfield, John F. (1985) *A History of the Cadbury Family*. London: J. Crosfield
Cross, Gary (2015) *Consumed Nostalgia: Memory in the Age of Fast Capitalism*. New York City: Columbia University Press
Cullen, Alex (1910) *Adventures in Socialism: New Lanark Establishment and Orbiston Community*. London: A. and C. Black
Culpin, Ewart Gladstone (1913) *The Garden City Movement up to Date*. London: Garden Cities and Town Planning Association
Cunningham, Hugh (2016) *Leisure in the Industrial Revolution, c.1780–c.1880*. London: Routledge
Dale (1907) 'Bournville' *The Economic Review*. January 1907, 13–27
Darley, Gillian (2007) *Villages of Vision: A Study of Strange Utopias*. Nottingham: Five Leaves Publications
Davidson, Lorna (2010) 'A Quest for Harmony: The Role of Music in Robert Owen's New Lanark Community', *Utopian Studies* 21:2, 232–251
Davis, Tracy C. (2007) *The Economics of the British Stage*. Cambridge: Cambridge University Press

Davison, T. Raffles (1916) *Port Sunlight: A Record of Its Artistic and Pictorial Aspect*. London: B. T. Batsford

Day, Agnes M. (1924) *Historical Plays for Schools*. Exeter: A. Wheaton and Co.

Dellheim, Charles (1987) 'The Creation of a Company Culture: Cadburys, 1861–1931', *The American Historical Review* 92:1, 13–44

Dover Wilson, J. (1929) *The Schools of England: A Study in Renaissance*. Chapel Hill: University of North Carolina

Dowd, Kevin William (2001) *The Social and Political Activity of the Cadbury Family: A Study in Manipulative Capitalism*. Thesis, Swansea University. http://cronfa.swan.ac.uk/Record/cronfa42781

Drinkwater, J. (1925) *The Collected Plays of John Drinkwater. Volume One*. London: Sidgwick and Jackson

(1932) *Discovery*. London: Ernest Benn

Ferguson, Reginald Williams (1912) *An Outline: The Educational System Connected with the Bournville Works*. Birmingham: Messrs Cadbury Bros Ltd

Finlay-Johnson, Harriet (1911) *The Dramatic Method of Teaching*. London: Nisbets

Fishman, Robert (1982) *Urban Utopias in the Twentieth Century: Ebenezer Howard, Frank Lloyd Wright and Le Corbusier*. Cambridge, MA: MIT Press

Fitzgerald, Robert (2005) 'Products, Firms and Consumption: Cadbury and the Development of Marketing, 1900–1939', *Business History* 47:4, 511–531

Foght, H. W. (1914) 'The Danish Folk High Schools', *United States Bulletin of Education* 22, whole issue

Foulkes, Richard (1997) *Church and Stage in Victorian England*. Cambridge: Cambridge University Press

Gardiner, A. C. (1923) *Life of George Cadbury*. London: Cassell

Gee, Phillip (1922) *The Industrial Year Book*. London: H. B. Hammond

George, W. L. (1907) *Engines of Social Progress*. London: A & C Black

(1909) *Labour and Housing at Port Sunlight*. London: Alston Rivers

Gilman, Frederick John (1916) *The Workers and Education*. London: George Allen and Unwin

Gilman, Harvey (2003) *A Light That Is Shining: An Introduction to the Quakers*. London: Quaker Books

Graham, John (1915) 'Music in a Garden City' *Musical Herald* (April), 156–600

Griffiths, Alison (2002) *Wondrous Difference: Cinema, Anthropology, and Turn-of-the-Century Visual Culture*. New York: Columbia University Press

Grivetti, Louis E. and Howard-Yana Shapiro (2011) *Chocolate: History, Culture and Heritage*. Oxford: John Wiley and Sons

Groves, Rick, Alan Middleton, Alan Murie, and Kevin Broughton (2003) *Neighbourhoods That Work: A Study of the Bournville Estate Birmingham*. Bristol: Policy Press

Hackenesch, Silke (2017) *Chocolate and Blackness: A Cultural History*. Frankfurt-on-Main: Campus Verlag

Hall Grey Architects (2006) *Rowntree Cocoa Works: Historic Building Report*. York: York City Council

Harvey, William Alexander (1906) *The Model Village and Its Cottages*. London: B. T. Batsford

Havergal, Nick J. (2020) Performing Masculinities in South West England at the Turn of the Twentieth Century. PhD Thesis, University of Bristol

Head, Brandon (1903) *The Food of the Gods: A Popular Account of Cocoa*. London: R. Brimley Johnson

Heniger, Alice Minnie Herts (1911) *The Children's Educational Theatre*. New York: Harper and Bros

Hickman, Clare (2018) 'Care in the Countryside: The Theory and Practice of Therapeutic Landscapes in the Early Twentieth Century', in Malcom Dick and Elaine Mitchell, eds., *Gardens and Green Spaces in the West Midlands Since 1700*. Hatfield: University of Hertfordshire Press, 160–185

Hicks, Canon (1903) 'A Visit to Bournville', *The Manchester Guardian*, July 18: 6

Hoban, Sally (2013) The Birmingham Municipal School of Art and Opportunities for Women's Paid Work in the Arts and Crafts Movement. PhD Thesis, University of Birmingham

Hoffman, J. M. (1993) Imaging the Industrial Village: Architecture, Art, and Visual Culture in the Garden Community of Bournville, England. PhD Thesis, Yale Unversity

Holdsworth, Nadine, Jane Milling, and Helen Nicholson, eds. (2017) 'Theatre, Performance and the Amateur Turn', *Special issue of Contemporary Theatre Review* 27:1

—— (2018) *The Ecologies of Amateur Theatre*. New York: Springer

Holroyd, Abraham (1873) *Saltaire and Its Founder, Sir Titus Salt*. Bradford: T. Brear

Holt, Richard (1990) *Sport and the Working Class in Modern Britain*. Manchester: Manchester University

Hoyland, John S. (1947) *They Saw Gandhi*. New York: Fellowship Publications

Jagger, Mary A. (1914) The History of Honley and Its Hamlets from the Earliest Time to the Present Day

Jesse, Louie (1929) *Historical Plays for Schools, Volume 1 – Wales*. Cardiff: Educational Publishing Company

Kargon, Robert H. and Arthur P. Molella (2008) *Invented Edens: Techno Cities of the Twentieth Century*. Boston: MIT Press

Kemp, Thomas C. (1948) *Birmingham Repertory Theatre: The Playhouse and the Man*. Birmingham: Cornish Brothers

Kimberley, John (2016) 'Edward Cadbury: An Egalitarian Employer and Supporter of Working Women's Campaigns' in Peter Ackers and Alistair J. Reid, eds., *Alternatives to State-Socialism in Britain: Other Worlds of Labour in the Twentieth Century*. New York: Springer, 153–178

King, Mike (2014) *Quakernomics: An Ethical Capitalism*. London: Anthem

Lambert, Cornelia (2011) '"Living Machines": Performance and Pedagogy at Robert Owen's Institute for the Formation of Character, New Lanark, 1816–1828', *The Journal of the History of Childhood and Youth* 4:3, 419–433

Leighton, Wilfrid (1959) *Fircroft, 1909–1959*. Birmingham: Fircroft Trust

Lever, William Hulme (1927) *Viscount Leverhulme*. London: G Allen and Unwin

Lunn, Pam (1997) '"You Have Lost Your Opportunity" British Quakers and the Militant Phase of the Women's Suffrage Campaign: 1906–1914', *Quaker Studies* 2:1, Article 2

Mackay, Constance D'Arcy (1927) *Children's Theatre and Plays*. Drama League Library of the Theatre Arts?. New York: D'Appleton and Company

Marsh, Jan (2010) *Back to the Land: The Pastoral Impulse in Victorian England, 1880–1914*. London: Faber and Faber

Masterman, H. B. (1920) *The Story of the English Towns, Birmingham*. London: Society for Promoting Christian Knowledge

Matthews, Bache (1924) *A History of the Birmingham Repertory Theatre*. London: Chatto and Windus

McCrone, Kathleen E. (1991) 'Class, Gender and English Women's Sport, c.1890–1914', *Journal of Sports History* 18:1, 159–182

Mclintock, John and James Strong (1877) *Cyclopaedia of Biblical, Theological and Ecclesiastical Literature*. New York: Harper and Bros

Meakin, Budgett (1905) *Model Factories and Ideal Conditions of Labour and Housing*. London: T. Fisher Unwin

Mees, Bernard (2016) 'Changing Approaches to Business Ethics' in John Wilson, Steven Toms, Abe de Jong, and Emily Buchnes, eds., *The Routledge Companion to Business History*. Abingdon on Thames: Taylor and Francis

Minnery, John (2012) 'Model Industrial Settlements and their Continuing Govenance', *Planning Perspectives* 27:2, 309–321

Moore, Anne Carol (1920) *Roads to Childhood*. New York: G H Doran

Moran, James (2013) 'Pound, Yeats and the Regional Repertory Theatres' in Neil Alexander and James Moran, eds., *Regional Modernisms*. Edinburgh: Edinburgh University Press: 83–103

Nicholls, Douglas M. (1946) *The Story of a Great Experiment, Being a Brief History of Bournville Day Continuation School*. Birmingham: Cadbury Bros

Nicholson, Graham and Jane Fawcett (1988) *The Village in England: History and Tradition*. New York: Rizzoli

Nicholson, Steve (2004) 'A Critical Year in Perspective: 1926' in Jane Milling, Peter Thomson, Baz Kershaw, and Joseph Walter Donohue, eds., *The Cambridge History of British Theatre*, volume 3. Cambridge: Cambridge University Press

Nworah, Kenneth Dike (1971) 'The Liverpool 'Sect' and British West African Policy 1895–1915', *African Affairs* 70:281, 349–364

O'Malley, Evelyn (2020) *Weathering Shakespeare: Audiences and Open-Air Performance*. London: Bloomsbury

Oral Histories. https://soundcloud.com/birminghammuseums/r0361-oral-history-bernard-atkins-bournville

Ormandy, James (2021) 'Hockey's Religious Foundations, Part 3: Quakers Play and Support Hockey's Development' *Playing Pasts Online Magazine for Sport and Leisure History*

Owen, Robert Dale (1824) *An Outline of the System of Education at New Lanark*. Glasgow: Wardlaw and Cunningham

Packer, Ian (2003) 'Religion and the New Liberalism: The Rowntree Family, Quakerism, and Social Reform', *Journal of British Studies* 42:2, 236–257

Parker, John (1925) *Who's Who in the Theatre: A Biographical Record of the Contemporary Stage*. Boston: Small, Maynard and Company

Parratt, Catriona (2001) *More than Mere Amusement: Working-Class Women's Leisure in England, 1750–1914*. Boston: Northeastern University

Pearson, Lynn F. and Patricia White (1988) *Architectural and Social History of Cooperative Living*. Basingstoke: Palgrave Macmillan

Phillips, Simon (2003) *Industrial Welfare and Recreation at Boots Pure Drug Company*. PhD Thesis. Nottingham Trent University

Pickering, Michael (1982) *Village Song and Culture: A Study Based on the Blunt Collection of Song from Adderbury North Oxfordshire*. London: Routledge

(2008) *Blackface Minstrelsy in Britain*. Ashgate

Pumphrey, Mary E. (1952) *Recollections of Fircroft: An Experiment in Adult Education*. Birmingham: Fircroft College Trust

Purdom, C. P. (1913) *The Garden City: A Study in the Development of a Modern Town*. London: J. M. Dent and Sons

Purkayastha, Prarthana (2019) 'Decolonising Human Exhibits: Dance, Re-enactment and Historical Fiction', *South Asian Diaspora* 11:2, 223–238

Radcliffe, Christopher (1997) 'Mutual Improvement Societies and the Forging of Working-Class Political Consciousness in Nineteenth-Century England', *International Journal of Lifelong Education* 16:2, 141–155

Ramamurthhy, Anandi (2003) *Imperial Persuaders: Images of Africa and Asia in British Advertising*. Manchester: Manchester University

Readman, Paul (2018) *Storied Ground: Landscape and the Shaping of English National Identity*. Cambridge University Press

Rees, Amanda (2012) 'Nineteenth-Century Planned Industrial Communities and the Role of Aesthetics in Spatial Practices: The Visual Ideologies of Pullman and Port Sunlight', *Journal of Cultural Geography* 29:2, 185–214

Richardson, Angelique and Chris Willis, eds. (2019) *The New Woman in Fiction and Fact: Fin-de-Siècle Feminisms*. New York: Springer

Ridge, C. Harold (1928) *Stage Lighting for Little Theatres*. Cambridge: W. Heffer and Sons

Robertson, Emma (2016) '"Belles from Bristol and Bournville in New Surroundings": Female Confectionary Workers as Transnational Agents', *Women's History Review* 25:4, 563–583

Rogers, T. B. (1931) *A Century of Progress, 1831–1931: Cadbury, Bournville*. Bournville: Cadbury

Rose, Sonya L. (1993) *Limited Livelihoods: Gender and Class in Nineteenth-Century England*. Oakland: University of California Press

Rowley, Trevor (2006) *The English Landscape in the Twentieth Century*. Oxford: A & C Black

Rowlinson, Michael (2002) 'Public History Review Essay: Cadbury World', *Labour History Review* 67:1, 101–119

Rowntree, Benjamin Seebohm (1901) *Poverty: A Study of Town Life*. London: Macmillan & Co.

Rowntree, John Wilhelm and Henry Bryan Binns (1903) *A History of the Adult School Movement*. London: Headley Bros

Rowntree, Joshua, ed. (1905) *John Wilhelm Rowntree, Essays and Addresses*. London: Headley Bros

Russell, Dave (1997) *Popular Music in England 1840–1914: A Social History*. Manchester: Manchester University Press

Schulze-Gaevernitz (1900) *Social Peace: A Study of the Trade Union Movement in England*. Translated by Graham Wallas. London: Swan Sonnenschein and Co

Sharpe, John (1855) *Sharpe's Road Book for the Rail*. London: David Bogue

'Sidney Currie', *Mapping the Practice and Profession of Sculpture in Britain and Ireland 1851–1951*, University of Glasgow History of Art and HATII, online database 2011 http://sculpture.gla.ac.uk/view/person.php?id=msib4_1207321560 [accessed 15 Jul 2021]

Silver, Daniel Aaron and Terry Nichols Clark (2016) *Scenescapes: How Qualities of Place Shape Social Life*. Chicago: University of Chicago Press

Siméon, Ophélie (2017) *Robert Owen's Experiment at New Lanark: From Paternalism to Socialism*. New York: Springer, Palgrave Studies in Utopianism

Siraut, M. C., A. T. Thacker, and Elizabeth Williamson (2006) 'Parishes: Street' in R W Dunning, London, eds., *A History of the County of Somerset: Volume 9, Glastonbury and Street*. British History Online, 165–198. www.british-history.ac.uk/vch/som/vol9/pp165-198 [accessed 6 October 2021]

Smith, Chris, John Child, and Michael Rowlinson (1990) *Reshaping Work: The Cadbury Experience*. Cambridge: Cambridge University Press

Spirn, Anne Whiston (1998) *The Language of Landscape*. New Haven and London: Yale University

Stead, F. H. (1902) 'George Cadbury', *The Review of Reviews* (April): 350–357

Strong, Josiah, William Howe Tolman, and Dwight Porter Bliss, eds. (1906) *Social Progress: A Year Book and Encyclopaedia of Economic, Industrial, Social and Religious Statistics, 1904–1906*. New York City: Baker and Taylor Co

Surdam, David (2020) *Business Ethics from Antiquity to the 19th Century: An Economist's View*. London: Palgrave Macmillan

Tarn, J. N. (1965) 'The Model Village at Bromborough Pool', *The Town Planning Review* 35: 4, 329–336

The Rowntree Society (2016) *The Rowntree Legacy: Capitalism, Compassion, Change*. York: The Rowntree Society

Tolman, William Howe (1901) 'A Trust for Social Betterment' in Walter Page Hines, ed., *The World's Work: A History of Our Time*. New York: Doubleday

Towle, G. M. (1872) 'Saltaire and Its Founder', *Harper's New Monthly Magazine* 44, 827–835

Turnbull, Richard (2014) *Quaker Capitalism: Lessons for Today – Enterprise and Faith*. Oxford: The Centre for Enterprise, Markets and Ethics

Vamplew, W. (2015) 'Sport, Industry and Industrial Sport in Britain before 1914', *Sport in Society* 19:3, 340–355

(2016) 'Workers' Playtime: Developing an Explanatory Typology of Work-Associated Sport in Britain' in Richard Pomfret and John K. Wilson, eds.,

Sports through the Lens of Economic History. Cheltenham: Edward Elgar Publishing

Vining, Elizabeth Gray (1958) *Friend of Life: The Biography of Rufus M Jones.* Philadelphia: Lippincott

Wagner, Gillian (1987) *The Chocolate Conscience.* London: Chatto and Windus

Wiener, Martin J. (2004) *English Culture and the Decline of the Industrial Spirit.* Cambridge: Cambridge University Press

Williams, Iola A. (1931) *The Firm of Cadbury, 1831–1931.* London: Constable and Co.

Wilson, William E. (1984) *The Angel and the Serpent: The Story of New Harmony.* Bloomington: Indiana University Press

Wood, H. G. and Arthur E. Ball (1922) *Tom Bryan, First Warden of Fircroft: A Memoir.* London: G. Allen and Unwin

Woods, Alice. B. (1920) *Educational Experiments in England.* London: Methuen

Wray, William and Reginald Ferguson, eds. (1920) *A Day Continuation School at Work.* London and New York: Longmans, Green, and Co.

Yallop, Jacqueline (2015) *Dreamstreets.* London: Jonathan Cape

Yoshino, Ayako (2011) *Pageant Fever: Local History and Consumerism in Edwardian Culture.* Tokyo: Waseda Daigaku Shuppanbu

Index

Adult School Movement, 17, 198, 204–205, 214, 216, 218, 224–227
Allen and Hanbury, 6
Art Nouveau, 132
Arts and Crafts movement, 5, 35, 83, 84, 132, 140–142, 159, 190, 216
Auriol, George, 132

Bantock, Granville, 147
Benson, Frank, 39, 43, 129, 136
Betty in Mayfair, 71
Birkenhead Dramatic Society, 41
Birmingham Children's Theatre, 17, 191, 219–222, 230
Birmingham Girls' and Boys' Union, 219
Birmingham Local Education Authority, 204–206, 208
Birmingham Museum and Art Gallery, 83
Birmingham Repertory Theatre, 17, 136, 137, 171, 176, 191–194, 196, 197, 213, 218, 227, 229
  Performing at the Bournville Factory, 194
Birmingham School of Municipal Art, 84
Bondfield, Margaret, 214–215
Boughton, Rutland, 143, 217
Bournville Children's Festivals
  Performances
    Buried Treasure, 208
    The Dream, a Pastoral Fantasy for Children, 211
    Goodwill, Illwill, and Merrywill, 211
    The Queen of Storyland, 209
    A Royal Visit to Playtown, 211
    The Terror of Norwustar, 210
    Trouble in Fairyland, 210
    The Wizard, 211
Bournville Day Continuation Schools, 17
  Bournville Girls' Day Continuation School, 59
    Cater, Annie, 207, 212, 214–215
    Performances
      Alcestis, 212, 214
      Antigone, 212, 213

Comus, 214
The Pageant of Plays and Playgoers, 202–203, 212
Girls' and Boys' Schools Joint Performances
The King's Threshold, 215
Quality Street, 215
British Drama League, the, 49, 166, 190, 204, 226
Bromborough Pool, 31–34
  dramatic classes, 32
  dramatic society, 32
  Mutual Improvement Society, 32
  The Price Family, 31
Bryan, Tom, 224–225

Cadbury family
  and amateur dramatics, 85
  Dorothy, 99
  Edward, 6, 7, 97, 99, 125, 134, 142, 168, 187, 201, 205, 214, 223
  Elizabeth, 58, 85, 99, 104, 112, 208, 214
  Emma, 103
  George, 3, 11, 12, 58, 98, 99, 126, 205, 206
    and outdoor theatre, 136, 139
  George Jr, 58, 170, 196, 205, 223, 224
  Louis Barrow, 58, 205
  Richard, 3, 58, 98, 132, 205
  William, 58, 112, 114, 132, 133, 182, 183, 194, 205
Cadbury's
  Advertising
    The Bournville Bunny, 69
    Elsie and the Brown Bunny (advertising film), 67–69
  Bournville Dramatic Society, 57, 61, 65, 66, 74, 77–80, 91, 143, 160, 165–199, 207, 215, 222, 228, 229, 232
    Dramatic Lectures, 195–199
    repertoire, 177–180
    wartime work, 182–185
  Bournville Girls' Athletics Club, 66, 78, 100
  Bournville Operatic Society, 65, 177
  the Bournville Spirit, 15, 17, 21–22, 52, 54, 100, 103, 154, 167, 176, 205, 225, 232

245

Index

Bournville – The Factory in the Garden, 16, 95–97
Bournville Works Magazine, 15, 21
Bournville Youth Club, 66, 78, 184, 197, 220–221
Bridge Street Factory, 21, 63, 168, 176, 201
Bull Street Shop, 6, 96
Committee of Management, 55, 64, 109, 146, 150, 165, 174
Dance
    Ballet, 78
    Bournville Centre of the English Folk Dance society, 78
    folk, 1, 3, 5, 106
    maypole, 3, 16, 78, 126, 209
    skirt, 156
employees
    Allen, Lottie (Charlotte), 57, 79, 144, 170–171, 175, 184
    Baldwin, Thomas, 145
    Barrow, Louis, 98
    Barrow, Walter, 67
    Bennett, Gordon, 69
    Bonorino, Violet, 188
    Booth, Clarkson, 52–53, 57, 83, 125–126, 168, 170, 174, 177, 209–211
    Boylin, Maud, 83
    Bradbear (Bailey), Elsie, 180
    Bradbear, Harry, 57, 88, 141, 150–151, 155, 175
    Broome, Frederick, 69
    Coope, Clifford, 79–80, 89–91
    Cossons, William Ernest, 65–67, 80, 81, 166, 168, 175, 177, 179, 187, 188
    Cox, Maggie (Margaret), 156
    Davenport, William, 88
    Davies, Sidney, 171, 195
    Davies, Tom (Thomas), 151, 171, 184
    Duke, Beatrice, 112
    Ferguson, Reginald, 200–202, 207, 229
    Forbes, Amy, 69, 78, 211
    Gallimore, Maud, 112
    Gollings, William, 65
    Goulding, Olive, 69–71
    Greaves, Hilda, 66–67, 74
    Hackett, Arthur, 111–112
    Hudson, Alice, 80
    Hyslop, Annie, 111
    Keen, Harry, 174
    Kevorkian, Maritza, 182
    Knapp, Arthur, 57, 73–74, 77, 88, 115, 179, 231
    Knight, Nellie, 100
    Leaver, Bernard, 193
    Lindsay, Beatrice, 211
    Margetts, George, 74, 119
    Moorhouse, Ralph, 145, 225
    Noon, Kitty (Catherine), 101
    Organ, Edward, 88, 176
    Pedley Hunt, Walter, 57, 79, 145, 151, 170, 175
    Price, Beatrice, 144, 174
    Pumphrey, Sophia, 57, 84–85, 141, 205, 225
    Pumphrey, Spencer, 84, 170, 205, 225
    Quinton, Bob (John Robert), 126–127, 145, 174, 179, 181, 197, 208–212
    Quinton, Miriam, 126, 197, 211
    Rogers, Thomas Badger, 74, 167–168, 170, 171, 173, 179
    Showell, Florence, 57, 88, 171, 179–182
    Sylvester, Frederick, 147, 149
    Thomas, Marguerite, 177
    Thompson, Peggy (Margaret), 69
    Watt, Thomas, 171, 175
    Weeks, Hugh, 79
    Whitehouse, John Henry, 52
    Whittaker, Arthur, 66–67, 79, 190
    Wright, Dorothy, 181–182
Girls' Works Committee, 54, 55, 57, 109, 169, 175
Girls' Works Council, 55, 178, 198, 223, 228
horticulture and gardening, 100, 135
Joint Works Council, 55, 178, 198, 199, 223, 228
Men's Works Committee, 54, 55, 109, 169, 170
Men's Works Council, 55, 178, 198, 223, 228
New Year Parties, 63–72, 87–89, 99, 124, 168–169, 174–176, 182
performance spaces, 175
    the amphitheatre (on the Girls' Recreation Grounds), 98, 133–134, 136, 142
    T Block, 86–89
    the Clerks' Club, 4, 187
    the Clerks' Dining Room, 62, 185, 187
    the Concert Hall, 4, 15, 62, 63, 72–75, 77–82, 86, 114, 120, 178, 187, 190, 191, 194, 215, 219–222, 229, 231
    Opening Week, 77–80
    the Girls' Dining Room, 62, 112, 115, 175
    the Girls' Recreation Grounds, 126, 130, 131, 184, 202
    the Girls' Swimming Baths, 4, 81–86
    the Lecture Room, 4, 72, 89–91
    the Men's Dining Room, 4, 62, 187
    the Men's Recreation Grounds, 101, 104, 105, 107, 110
    the new dining hall, 75–77, 81, 86
    the pergola, the Girls' Recreation Grounds, 212
    the recreation grounds, 1, 208
    the Sports Pavilion, 4, 62, 100

performances
- *The British Empire Tableaux*, 106, 110–116, 138
- *The Burlesque Cricket Match*, 106, 116–120, 139
- *The Burlesque Man-agerie*, 106, 121–123
- *Cophetua*, 172, 174–176, 180, 191
- *The Courting of Widow Malone*, 181
- *An English Medley*, 125, 137–147, 151, 168, 217
- fancy dress parades, 100–101, 104, 106, 209
- *Fantasia*, 174
- fire brigade display, 105
- *football burlesque*, 10, 106, 120
- illustrated songs, 82, 85
- *Madame Fontainebleau and her Performing Dogs*, 101
- magic, 4, 65, 102, 117
- *May Day*, 103, 126–127, 130, 131, 136, 137, 145, 210
- *The Mock Doctor*, 167–170, 175
- *No Song, No Supper!*, 80, 188–190, 196
- *The Only Legend, A Masque of the Scarlet Pierrot*, 125, 153–155, 210, 211
- *Orinoco Assorted*, 1–3, 71
- *The Pied Piper A Tale of Hamelin City*, 125, 129–131, 146–157, 168, 170, 171
- recitations, 82, 84, 88, 170, 177
- *Robin Hood and the Pedlar*, 125, 146, 156–157, 171
- *Sherwood's Queen*, 129–131, 136
- swimming displays, 10, 85
- tableaux vivants, 1–3, 10, 16, 62, 69–72, 82–84, 88, 90–91, 101, 106, 111, 115, 118–119, 126, 144, 150, 212, 231
- *The Tricking of Malvolio*, 175–176, 180
- *Twelfth Night*, 191
- *Visions*, 65–73, 86, 140, 142, 166, 211
- *Votes for Women*, 179–180
- *Water Carnival, the*, 104–106, 110

Quaker morning meetings, 21
Recreation and Welfare Sub Committee, 55
recreation grounds, 68, 98, 127, 137, 151, 159
Sao Thomé and Principe, 114
summer works parties, 1–3, 10, 16, 73, 97–160, 169–171, 191, 194, 208, 211
- budgeting, 109
- swimming, 1
- Visitors Department, 54, 57, 95, 109, 209
- Works Education Committee, 200, 201, 223
Cannan, Gilbert, 178, 196–197
Carnegie, William Hartley, 220
Chamberlain, Neville, 195
Chatwin, Margaret, 102, 193–194
Clarks of Street, 6, 23, 46
Coats, Robert Hay, 227–228

Crisford, Willis, 101, 102, 194
Crompton-Rhodes, Raymond, 188–189, 192, 194–196, 229
Curie, Marie, 155
Currie, Sidney, 150

Drinkwater, John, 16, 85, 109, 110, 123, 125–161, 212, 226
Duxbury, John, 42

Edgbaston Assembly Rooms, 136, 191
Edgbaston Botanical Gardens, 128–129, 137

Filmer, Arthur, 197–198, 203
Fircroft College, 17, 184, 198, 222–228, 230
Fisher Act, the, 206
Flint, Thomas Foden, 171
Fogerty, Elsie, 229

Greet, Ben, 128–129, 218
Grey, Morden (Mary King Griffen), 42

Harvey, William Alexander, 81
Horniman, Annie, 42, 173

Jackson, Barry, 136, 169, 191–195, 219
Joseph Rowntree Trust, the, 45

Lally, Gwen, 48
Letchworth Garden City, 116
- *The Garden of the Leech A Masque of Letchworth*, 158–159
Lever Family
- The Joyville Theatre (Thornton Manor), 38, 40
- The Manor Mummers, 40–41
- Thornton Manor, 40–42
- William Hesketh, 36, 38, 40, 43, 134
- William Hulme, 41
Lloyd George, David, 118

Matthews, Bache, 192, 198–199, 218, 227
McCarthy, Lillah, 178

New Earswick village, 23, 44–48
- dramatic society, 48
- summer school, 48
- performance spaces
  - the Assembly rooms, 45–46
  - the Folk Hall, 46–48
- Sorensen, Bee and Carl, 47
- theatre, 46–48
New Lanark, 24–28
- Institute for the Formation of Character, 25–26
- School for Children, 27
New Quakerism, 136, 204, 205, 222

Open Air Schools, 141, 216
Ostins, George, 196, 197

Page, John Byrd, 102–103
Pageantry, 125–129
Parker, Barry, 45, 159
Parker, Louis Napoleon, 49, 127–128, 138, 149
Pentland Street Robins, 148
Pentland, Joseph, 148–149
Pilgrim Players, the, 136–137, 169, 191–194, 198
Pinchard, Arnold, 137
Pinchard, Betty, 137
Port Sunlight, 34–43
  dramatic society, 36–38
  employees
    Somers, Sophie, 41
  minstrel troupe, 37
  performance spaces
    the Auditorium, 38–40, 134
    Gladstone Hall, 37, 38, 40, 41, 46
    Hulme Hall, 36, 38, 40
    the Lyceum, 42
  Shakespearean Reading Circle, 38
  Staff Training College (Day Continuation School), 41
  The Sunshine Girl (Gaiety Theatre), 34
Pumphrey, Hilda, 84

Quaker Capitalism, 5–6

Rowntree Family
  Benjamin Seebohm, 44–45, 47, 49, 50
  John Wilhelm, 223
  Joseph, 44–46, 48, 223

Joseph Senior, 51
Julian, 47
Rowntree's
  the Cocoa Works Dramatic Society / The Rowntree Players, 48–50
  employees
    Benson, Brynhild, 44
    Harlock, Gulielma, 46
    Mockett, Irene, 48
  the Joseph Rowntree Hall, 50

Salt, Titus, 28, 30
Saltaire, 28–31
  institute, 28–31
  minstrel troupe, 30
  Shipley and Saltaire Elocution and Dramatic Society, 29–30
Sandow, Eugen, 118, 121, 123
Shipp, Horace, 198
Sleigh, Bernard, 140–142
Stirchley Institute, 62, 184, 205–207
suffrage, 63, 120, 179–180, 214

temperance movement, 61
third party, the, 113–115

Unwin, Raymond, 45, 159

Vinden, Stuart, 194, 213, 229

Whitley Report, 55
Woodbrooke College, 15, 18, 216, 222–225

York Citizens' Theatre, 50